Key Thinkers in the Sociology of Religion

Key Thinkers in the Sociology of Religion

Richard K. Fenn

continuum

Continuum International Publishing Group

The Tower Building   80 Maiden Lane
11 York Road   Suite 704
London   New York
SE1 7NX   NY 10038

www.continuumbooks.com

British Library Cataloguing-in-Publication Data
A catalogue record for this book is available from the British Library.

ISBN-10: HB: 0-8264-9941-4
         PB: 0-8264-9942-2
ISBN-13: HB: 978-0-8264-9941-7
         PB: 978-0-8264-9942-4

Library of Congress Cataloging-in-Publication Data
Fenn, Richard K.
Key thinkers in the sociology of religion / Richard K. Fenn.
    p. cm.
Includes bibliographical references.
ISBN-13: 978-0-8264-9941-7 (HB)
ISBN-10: 0-8264-9941-4 (HB)
ISBN-13: 978-0-8264-9942-4 (pbk.)
ISBN-10: 0-8264-9942-2 (pbk.)
1. Religion and sociology. I. Title.
BL60.F455 2009
306.6092'2–dc22   2008035243

Typeset by Newgen Imaging Systems Pvt Ltd, Chennai, India
Printed and bound in Great Britain by The Cromwell Press Group, Trowbridge, Wiltshire

Contents

Acknowledgments

This book would not have been brought to completion without the strong and consistent, as well as patient editorial support of the staff at Continuum, and particularly Tom Crick and P. Muralidharan. Because of their flexibility and determination, the end result is far different, and, I trust, far better than what we initially had imagined. As readers of this book will soon discover, the classical thinkers in the sociology of religion began by using the terms "religion" and "the sacred" more or less interchangeably. Modern thinkers in the field are far less sure of the relationship between religion and the sacred. Indeed, in our time, that relationship has become more obscure, dynamic, and problematical. As a sociologist on a theological faculty, I have had the opportunity to ask a generation of students just what the sacred may be, and what relationship, if any, the sacred may have to religion. Especially for theological students, that is a provocative question. I want to thank all my students over the last 25 years for their creative approaches to searching for the sacred in what are, for them, unlikely places. Whereas some of the earlier, "classical" sociologists of religion were concerned with the origins and foundations of the self, of the individual, and of the psyche, more contemporary writers in the field have been understandably preoccupied with, well, religion, while concerns with the psyche and the unconscious have spun off to other disciplines like psychoanalysis and theology. In talking with others about the psyche, friends have become colleagues and colleagues have become friends. My heartfelt thanks go to Professors Sally Brown, Donald Capps, James Moorhead, Randall Nichols, Iain Torrance, Robert MacLennan, and Dana Fearon, friends and colleagues all. I am indebted beyond words to all those who have sustained me during the writing of this book, in a particularly difficult time of life. I have met the sacred in you.

Introduction

In an undertaking such as this, the author inevitably has to choose between providing relatively complete overviews of the work of several "key thinkers" or focusing on the central tendencies of their work. Given the complexity of each author's work, I have chosen the latter course; I have looked for what is central in the concerns and the arguments of each of these major thinkers. In the case of such "classical" figures as Emile Durkheim, Sigmund Freud, or Max Weber, their entire body of work is extraordinarily complex, varied, and at times difficult to interpret. As the literature on them attests, a single book provides too little scope even for a satisfactory overview of any one of them. The work of more recent writers is only slightly less diverse and complicated.

In choosing to look for what is central to their concerns, and for recurrent tendencies in their work, one question has forced itself on my attention time and time again: "How does Weber (or Durkheim, or Martin, or Bell, or any of the others) understand the relation of religion to the sacred?" At first the question seemed to be unnecessary; after all, many of the earlier writers seemed to use the terms religion and the sacred almost interchangeably. Yet even in their work it became obvious that there is a difference between what is religious and what is sacred, and on their understanding of that difference depends much of their path-breaking work in the sociology of religion.

In the course of becoming familiar with the key thinkers in the sociological study of religion, the reader will find it necessary to come up with his or her definition not only of religion but of the sacred. For the purpose of getting started, I offer the following definition of the sacred: the sacred represents a crisis that has emerged, been confronted, and transcended. What might have happened, chaos, dissent, subversion, disloyalty, even death, has been endured: its worst or most lasting effects averted, new possibilities discovered, and the future initiated. There may have been symbolic deaths, as the person is transformed from a youth to an adult, from a neophyte to an initiate, but the person has survived even in the process of being transformed. A Queen has passed through the city and, having faced a number of symbolic tests, is allowed to return to the Palace, bearing, however, the burden of the expectations of the people that she live up to the qualities that she has been said to embody. The Emperor has passed through a number of provincial cities, where the graffiti have reminded him that he is but a man and therefore mortal: a symbolic death threat, which, once survived, allows the Emperor to return, however burdened by a fresh reminder that he lives through the mercy or sufferance of the people. A President has been shot outside a Book Depository in a Southwestern city, but the nation has endured, the government continued, and the people restored to equanimity even in the midst of apprehension and sadness.

After such a crisis has been experienced and, for the time being, resolved, the memory of the moment endows the time of the crisis with a sense of the momentous. Things are not the same again; in retrospect, it is realized that a tipping point has been reached. Losses have been suffered but in time will have been redeemed through fresh devotions and new sacrifices. The possibility of mayhem and sudden death has been encountered and, for the time being, forestalled or averted. The possibility of a future that is different from the past is filled with hope for transformation. The time and place of the crisis is held sacred in memory and, if possible, embodied in practices such as ritualized forms of commemoration and reenactment.

Not all forms of the sacred are based on so dramatic or decisive a crisis. Some forms of the sacred are objects or texts that over time become loaded with the memory of crisis. They function much in the same way as does a screen memory: a memory, like the crucifixion, on which one later projects the sufferings and resolutions of other times and places. Observers were amazed, when Princess Diana was killed in an automobile accident, at the extent of public devotion and sorrow, and yet it became apparent that her death had become the time and place at which were offered a wide range of often long standing personal tribulations. That it took the sudden death of such a public figure to supply the occasion for unprecedented public demonstrations of private grief and grievance may have been an indication of the extent to which other public rituals had lost their ability to function as the occasions for sanctifying the experience and memory of personal crisis.

Religion, then, is a social institution which unites as many as possible of the manifestations of the sacred into a single system of memory and observance. The memories are united, more or less systematically, into a framework of belief that provides a measure of explanation and justification for the crises. Such a belief system may provide the crises, both public and private, with an appearance of coherence by suggesting that they share a single essence of some sort: a reflection of human error or disobedience, the consequences of prior deficiencies in lives past, the baneful effects of such sources of social pollution as enmity and dissent, or the discipline imposed on a people by a god who seeks to teach the people a lesson or test their devotion. Whereas the sacred commemorates and reenacts crises that have been transcended, religion offers a surrogate way of transcending crisis through vicarious forms of sacrifice, renunciation, obedience, self-offering, and the postponement of demands for the satisfaction of various grievances.

The sacred, like silver or gold, constitutes the hard assets underlying the promises of the currency of religion to pay for old losses and to fulfill old longings. Like silver and gold bullion, the sacred is difficult to transfer or transport to other times and places. It is marked with the sign of its maker or owner, stored in particular places, and it is not easily converted to a wide range of purposes unless hammered into smaller and uniform shapes. Converted, however, into the currency of religion, the sacred can be used to support the sanctity of a high God in a temple, or to provide a treasury of merit on which the holy can draw a measure of social or political as well as religious credit. Representing under the auspices of religion a more abstract form of transcendence over crisis, the sacred may be converted into beliefs in providence, submission to a particular form of sovereignty, assent to ends that are thought to be rooted in Nature or the cosmos, or conviction in the rightness of a particular, however unequal, distribution of worldly goods and services.

A crisis creates a division between the present and the past. Things will never be the same again, precisely because a crisis is by definition and in human experience a point at which decisions must be made. Some possibilities are dismissed for the time being or lost forever; they become the past. Others, formerly part of the future, become part of the present, for better or for worse. As an embodiment of a moment so critical that it became a tipping point between the past and the future, and after that changed what was understood to have gone before, the sacred constitutes a kind of time that is qualitatively different from the mere passage of time, the flow of one moment into another, the end-less succession of *befores* and *afters*. Set apart from such other times, the sacred takes on the aura of the momentous.

Such critical moments are originally deeply personal, particular as to time and place, and as fleeting as they are eventful. The needs that are to be met are very practical as well as pressing. A decision has to be made that will change relationships and foreshadow outcomes for an indefinite period of time, and perhaps forever. The past will never be the same again, once the decision is made. In the celebration of the Last Supper or the Eucharist Christians often hear the words: "On the night in which he was betrayed he took bread." The story of that moment, however, has become assimilated to other moments, such as those in which Jesus ordered his disciple to feed thousands of people who were stranded in the wilderness late in the day and who were therefore about to be dispersed. The feeding prevents them from scattering, just as the last supper could have prevented Jesus's most intimate followers from scattering from the foot of the cross. Custodians of the oral tradition, who told the story of Jesus, later brought the memory of that crisis to bear on later suppers, such as those that characterized the first gather-ings of followers of Jesus after his execution on the cross: the so-called love feasts of the early church. Eventually they transformed the story of the last supper into what became a major sacrament of the Christian community: a reenactment of the time when the death of Jesus was remembered collectively as a critical moment, after which life would be changed for his followers, and if they only knew it, for the world, for-ever. As the community developed, practitioners replaced followers, the oral tradition took written form, and scribal communities took on them-selves the safeguarding and interpretation of the texts. In this process the early forms of the Christian tradition reshaped the sacred moment of the last supper into one episode in a narrative of transcendence over the passage of time.

At first the sacred moment was understood to be intensely personal, ("Is it I Lord?") extremely local (the upper room), a crisis (On the night in which he was betrayed), and it was soon understood to break the tradition of Passover Suppers. Instead of being one more celebration of a unique meal that nonetheless embodies a tradition of meals which look forward to the next year's celebration, the story of the Last Supper essentially disrupted the continuity of the feasts in the Jewish community; it forged a new covenant. Fleeting though it was, this meal and its reenactments created a past in which old promises and old obligations were once and for all fulfilled. Disruptive, critical, fleeting, local, personal, and practical: these are the hallmarks of the sacred, before the sacred becomes part of a set of religious beliefs and practices that place such moments in the context of a longer narrative in which they only foreshadow rather than constitute the end.

If religion offers a derivative and vicarious participation in transcendence over the passage of time by creating a network of such critical moments, some of which foreshadow or fulfill the others, the sacred offers a direct, immediate, highly specific, local and personal immersion in the critical moment.

In deflationary periods, religion may find that it needs fresh consignments or offerings of the sacred to undergird its institutions, enhance devotion to its practices, add credibility to its promises and authority to its beliefs. That is, it may need signs and wonders to ensure its followers that under the auspices of religion, crises can be anticipated, averted, endured, or overcome. A natural disaster, a major war, or a slaughter on the scale of the Holocaust may present religion, however, with evidence of crises that far exceed its capacity to endow them with some sort of credible transcendence. On such occasions nothing may seem sacred, or fresh occurrences and manifestations of the sacred, well outside the provinces of institutionalized religion, may demonstrate a capacity to endure or ritualize crisis. Tattoos may replace tithes.

As you read about these seminal thinkers, then, ask yourself how each one of them understands the sacred, or religion, and the relation between the two. Does religion seem to have a monopoly on the sacred, or does the sacred seem to have a life of its own apart from religion? This is a way of asking about the extent to which the sacred is "differentiated" from religion. The more likely it is that any manifestation of the sacred is likely to occur under the auspices of a religious tradition, the more likely it is also that the sacred is part and parcel of the religious. All the local gods and goddesses, in other words, have been redefined as saints or angels within the dominant religious tradition, even though

earlier they may have done very well on their own without being
included in a church's calendar or a religious pantheon of gods and
demi-gods. When Durkheim spoke of the old gods as being dead and
the new ones as not yet being born, was he speaking only of the deity
understood within the Christian and Jewish traditions of the West, or
was he thinking also of all the manifestations of the sacred that, in the
years since his death, increasingly manifest themselves outside the halls
of traditional religion?

Certainly Christianity has varied greatly in this regard over the centuries. Weber spoke of his colleagues as guarding a shrine from which the
deity had long since absconded. Religion indeed does vary from one
place to another in its ability not only to define, own, and circumscribe
the sacred but to regulate and interpret the sacred. Even when the
sacred has taken wings and flown from the shrines and protection
offered by religion, it may still be subject to the indirect influence and
surveillance of religion. Forms of the sacred that seem to be largely
under the direct control of individuals, small groups, and local communities still flourish in many parts of the West, but these may still be her-
alded by their devotees as manifestations of the Virgin or even Sophia
rather than an earth goddess, Gaia, who has been receiving unauthorized devotion from people and in places that are beyond the interpretive
capacity and control of traditional religion. Thus a second question to
keep in mind is the extent to which religion is able to control and reinte-
grate into its own tradition popular or public devotion to novel, irregu-
lar, or unauthorized forms of the sacred. Especially in societies where
mass enthusiasm is concentrated in sports arenas or concert halls, or in
events that are well beyond the symbolic range of traditional religion,
the sacred itself may be largely outside the normative influence or control of traditional religion. The more anthropologically trained writers
like Maurice Bloch, Clifford Geertz, and Catherine Bell will be of extraordinary assistance in exploring this question.

A third question to ask concerns the extent to which the sacred
retains some of its old potency even when it has escaped the confines
of traditional religion. Bryan Wilson and David Martin, two sociological
colleagues and contemporaries, differ greatly from each other in their
approach to this question: Wilson being impressed by the demoraliza-
tion (in many senses of that word) of the West, and Martin exploring the
resacralization of nature and of the nation, as well as everyday life under

the auspices of a disciplined and yet enthusiastic Christian movement, Pentecostalism. Contrast what an author like Catherine Bells says of the sacred, in reference to drama, the theater, and other public events, with what Freud and Durkheim say of the dangers of allowing too many people direct access to the sacred without controls that not only preserve the sacred from pollution but preserve the public from the dangers of too close a contact with the sacred itself.

A more intractable question has to do with certain possible biases in the way that the sociologist or anthropologist in question is approaching the study of religion and the sacred. As Bell herself points out, religious leaders tend to have a stake in claiming that current practices derive from or are at least consistent with traditional forms of the sacred; they seek to find an essential coherence between the practices of the present and those of the past. Scholars may share this interest in coherence and for locating the past in the present, but they may also have a tendency to search for and to find continuity rather than mere coherence; they may seek to tell a story. Thus sociologists may argue that even modern societies are the outgrowth of a religious tradition with a highly transcendent deity who makes people responsible for their world and accountable for their behavior. Thus the secularity of the modern world is an inevitable legacy of a God who is so transcendent that the cosmos and the world of human endeavor are by theological definition entirely secular.

The bias toward transcendence as a metaphor for the sacred leads to several forms of indifference or neglect toward those manifestations of the sacred that are closest to the mundane, the personal, the particular, and the transient. For instance, the notion that the sacred is inevitably transcendent may influence a scholar to look for ways in which the sacred breaks into everyday life and shatters social conventions or religious traditions. Durkheim focused on collective effervescence, Weber on charisma, Freud on the unconscious: all of which are sources of disruption, novelty, innovation, or even transformation. The assumption underlying these notions of the sacred is that the sacred somehow transcends the mundane and the everyday, the personal and the practical, and so its appearance in the secular world is inherently novel and disruptive. It takes a Luhmann to note that societies, at least complex, modern societies, make themselves up as they go along, make their own rules, form and break their own expectations, justify themselves by their own precedents, and satisfy grievances by reference to their own practices rather than appealing to a transcendent source of authority that defines, legitimates, corrects, and controls the society from a point outside the social system.

On the other hand, some sociologists tend to believe that the sacred inheres in a society's traditions, and that no matter how much apparent change may be taking place, the apparent novelty of a practice is better understood as a reenactment of a traditional pattern or reaffirmation of a traditional value. Every innovation stands self-consciously on the basis of the past even while announcing the beginning of the future. You may see a tendency of this sort in Parsons's approach to the study of religion: a tendency to look not only for continuity and coherence between the past and the present but a certain repetition in the patterns of a society over time. For different reasons, Freud too was interested in why it is that people repeat past experiences. On such a view connecting the past with the present, whether through coherence, consistency, repetition or continuity, the sacred transcends the immediate and the mundane, and its appearance in everyday life is inevitably disruptive or elevating, a source of meaning or of inspiration that lifts the individual out of the context of his or her most immediate, personal practical and mundane concerns.

Sociologists of religion may work within a conceptual framework that elevates the transcendent over the immanent, and indeed they may feel that religion provides the essential services of transcendence to a social system. By offering continuity in the midst of change, transcendence legitimates new practices in terms of traditional values; transcendence also offers a reason to adopt new truths especially if they can be found to be consistent with or an outgrowth of traditional beliefs; and even a set of beliefs and values to provide necessary forms of correction to a social system that has deviated too far from its core convictions and practices. Thus the sociologist in question may feel that a society can be more flexible and adaptable if its beliefs are stated in abstractions rather than in more specific terms: abstractions that can be interpreted to cover a wider range of contingencies than rules for what to do if your neighbor's ox falls into a ditch on the Sabbath. Both Parsons and Luhmann are alert to the systemic advantages of more abstract forms of religious beliefs and values. Similarly, sociologists have been interested in the movements of the Spirit that seem universal, even though they take very particular forms in local contexts: the universal seeming to them to have more validity than the merely parochial, and continuity with the past more validity than the purely situational inventions of people struggling to get by. Martin is aware that the Spirit makes all things new, but that the civilizing patterns created by the Spirit in Central and Latin America strongly resemble the steps toward betterment taken by workers in the English countryside and mines under the influence of evangelists in the eighteenth and nineteenth centuries.

If some sort of transcendence is characteristic of religion, sociologists are understandably concerned with these forms when they investigate religion in a wide range of social contexts and under a variety of often quite different forms. The transcendent may or may not take the form of the deity; high-level abstractions like Reason, Justice, or Truth will do. Nature itself has provided a reference point for transcendence, especially when nature is understood to include universal, perhaps even cosmic forms of reason as well as rectitude. Ends are far more likely to be imbued with transcendence than means, as if the structural require-ments of a society are more likely to represent transcendence effectively than the practical, day-to-day adjustments that people make in order to get on with their business and their lives. However, the abstract is not more conducive to or characteristic of the sacred than the concrete; neither is the general more characteristic of the sacred than the particu-lar. The sacred is no more sacred if it is universal rather than parochial, no more authentic if it is conducive both to continuity and to change rather than being novel, disruptive, ephemeral, and transitory. Indeed, many forms of the sacred are very concrete and particular, parochial and immanent in this world rather than reflective of some other world that transcends the one in which most people live. The sacred is all the more concrete and particular, parochial and immanent when it comes and goes on its own terms rather than according to a schedule set by religious elites and institutions.

To the practitioner even the humblest of everyday tasks may be filled with the sacred. However, there is a tendency among some sociologists to think of the sacred in terms of the supernatural; natural phenomena, therefore, offer no clues to the sacred and are therefore, to that extent, less interesting than phenomena that have an element of mystery to them. Ask yourself whether the sociologist in question is more likely to identify an object or place, a moment or a person as being imbued with the sacred when there is an element of mystery to it rather than of self-revelation, of the numinous rather than the profane. It may well be that the sociologist might be less aware of the sacred when it appeared as relatively ordinary, obvious, or mundane. Whether or not there is an element of the mysterious or the uncanny, the numinous or the supernatural about the sacred is an empirical question, and it always deserves an empirical answer. The quality of the numinous is not, therefore, a defining characteristic of the sacred but simply one among many variables that, well, vary from one context or circumstance to another. The Constitution of the United States may indeed, for most people most of the time, be sacred, as may be a playing field sanctified by the memory of an extraordinary player or extraordinary play. However, the mysteriousness of the place may indeed vary over time, just as the mysteriousness of a particular time, like Halloween, may vary from one place to another even on the day itself. But always, the sacred is embedded in objects as particular and practical as the Constitution or as mundane as a playing field. The residues of a crisis may take many forms, from dreams and myths to rock or a carving.

A sociological interest in transcendence may also appear when the scholar draws a sharp distinction between activities that are practical, utilitarian or even self-serving and practices that are more obviously dedicated to the well-being of the community or larger society and are to that extent self-legitimating, sacrificial, or even ends in themselves. Note that Bloch, for instance, locates the sacred in the activities, many of them symbolic and ritualized, that dramatize and embody the social structure of a community: in its traditions, in hierarchies, and in the symbols of its essential identity. These he distinguishes from the more mundane activities of everyday life in which people work and play, get and spend, argue and embrace, all in the normal course of events. For Bloch, as for many sociologists, it is the secular that characterizes the everyday and the utilitarian, the mundane and the practical, whereas sacred words and deeds confirm, reenact, perpetuate and renew the structure of the society and thus transcend the mundane.

Bloch argues that there are elements of false consciousness in the minds of individuals who are blinded to their own self-interest or unaware of their own priorities and powers interest by the honors conferred on the social system. Transcendence in the sense of innovation and creativity, experimentation and departures from tradition, as well as the capacity to reshape social traditions in the light of the experience of each new generation, are also forms of transcendence that, for Bloch, must not be ignored. Others, however, especially sociologists in the Durkheimian tradition, assume that societies ordinarily and necessarily transcend the person; they regard the individual as a social artifact or product: ontologically derivative from the social order, dependent on it, and morally obligated to it. Various forms of individualism that allow an individual to forget the benefits of social life and the obligations of the individual to the society as a whole are, for these sociologists, forms of a false consciousness that can be damaging to the community. I have closed this book with a discussion of the excellent sociologist Catherine Bell, who cites with great respect, even while disagreeing with them, those who, like Robert Bellah or Mary Douglas, take a more Durkheimian view.

Durkheim argued that there is no act of worship that is not to some extent sacrilegious. Put slightly differently, we could say, for Durkheim, that the sacred is an end in itself, and it is secularized to the extent that it is made into the means to some other end. That end could be purely personal or utilitarian, but that end also could be preserving the wellbeing or enhancing the authority of an elite, an institution, or a whole society. The sacred is momentous, even though it may be evanescent, momentary, and ephemeral. Attempts by religion to protect, repeat, reenact and perpetuate the sacred may reduce the sacred to being a means to the end of preserving some social system or at the very least protecting the advantages and authority of those who most benefit from the existing social order. Thus there is always a certain tension between the sacred and religion; religion may reduce the singularity and momentousness, the novelty and disruptiveness of the sacred by making it appear part of a larger story and forcing it to protect a social system that is of more advantage to some than to others.

Some sociologists may see the tension between the sacred and religion as dialectical. That is, sacred elements of a culture may shape and inform the way a society defines and organizes itself and the ways in which individuals go about their business. On the other hand, the ways in which individuals go about their business, or the ways in which a society defines and organizes itself, may shape, give life to, and transform the sacred aspects of a culture. When the creative tension between religion and the sacred weakens, the sacred may just exist as a government in exile, or as a forgotten segment of the population: a source of potential opposition that makes no difference in the day-to-day conduct of societal or personal affairs. Without being a potential source of opposition, the sacred may weaken to the point that it is simply a source of the social imagination: a way of preserving a sense of possibility that is the focus of nostalgia or utopian longing but not of creative tension with the social order as it stands. Finally, the sacred may become simply a distinction that is no longer a source of significant difference; it stands neither as a source of the social imagination or of social opposition and creative tension.

Your answers to all of these questions will provide you with a relatively firm basis for addressing the perennially vexed question of the extent to which secularization has affected both religion and the sacred in Western civilization, as well as in other times and places that have little if any association with what we now call "modernity." It may well be that the sacred, in largely secular societies, has differentiated itself from religion and emancipated itself from the control, direct or symbolic, of religious institutions and religious culture. In this process, moreover, the sacred may have gained new scope and potency under some conditions, and under other conditions become far more episodic and ephemeral – here today and quite literally gone tomorrow – no less momentous, but far more momentary than when it was scheduled, defined, and controlled under the auspices of religion.

KEY THINKERS

Emile Durkheim

Emile Durkheim (1858–1917) is widely known as one of the founders of modern sociology. The usual summary of his work points to his findings that modern societies depend for their coherence and continuity on quite traditional foundations: a common set of beliefs and values, whether they are called culture or religion. Most summaries of his work point out that he derived these foundations from society itself and leaves unexplained how the social order could be based on something of its own creation. Concerned with the moral education of the French student, he sought to remind individuals that their very being, as well as their aspirations and convictions, were derived from the society toward which they owed a debt of moral obligation. On the other hand he argued that the collective sentiments of any society derive from the imaginations and passions of individuals themselves. Despite the obvious contradictions in his work, his essays have continued to foster a wide range of sociological and social anthropological studies.

For Durkheim the social order begins and continues as a figment of the collective imagination. Originating in moments of extraordinary pressure or excitement, the feelings that are generated on such occasions become symbolized in people and objects, and at certain times and places take on a renewed life of their own. Although the social order is really a collective fiction, it imposes itself on the individual psyche with a weight and intensity that can separate individuals from any sense of their own being or even crush their psyches. As Weber noted, individuals seek to acquire a solid and underived sense of their own being. Durkheim enables us to understand why they would have this need. Because they experience the self as a by-product or derivation of the social order, individuals lack precisely this sense of their own selfhood as a given and thus not as not derived from some other source. Originating in the psyche, sentiments, once they become collective, seem to belong to and come from the group. Initially a mixture of instinctual impulses, these sentiments become objectified and potent in their own right. So obligatory and essential is the moral order of the society, that the duties and routines of everyday life seem to become commonplace or relatively empty of significance. Thus Durkheim, like Weber, is tracking the sacred from the point of its origin in a critical moment or event to its more routine and institutionalized manifestations at some distance from the ordinary, the personal, the immediate, the practical, and the mundane.

For Durkheim, a society or a group takes on a life of its own and becomes a social fact over and above the actions that have brought it into being. Once it is symbolized, whether in a flag or a totem, that symbol or set of symbols helps to perpetuate and recreate the sentiments that at first aroused a sense of the group and literally called it into being. It is now the symbols, standing for the group itself, that are perpetuating feelings and passions initially aroused by acting collectively and in concert. "Thus these systems of emblems, which are necessary if society is to become conscious of itself, are no less indispensable for assuring the continuation of this consciousness" (Durkheim 1965: 263). Without them individuals are quickly left to their own devices, and "individual temperaments easily regain the upper hand" (Durkheim 1965: 263). Societies begin with an intense experience of their own vitality, and it is only from this sense of an extraordinary and ecstatic present that a social order begins to emerge with a past and a future.

To read Durkheim, then, we need to keep in mind that group life emerges from what individuals do when they act collectively, in concert and in harmony: "It is by uttering the same cry, pronouncing the same word, or performing the same gesture in regard to some object that they become and feel themselves to be in unison" (Durkheim 1965: 262). It is individuals standing in a public square, waving flags, bearing torches, and shouting slogans that creates the sense of a social order transcending the individual. The social present comes from the intensity of individuals experiencing their own presence in the company of and in concert with others. The very social fact of their acting in such concert creates not only the sense of a group but its very actuality.

Thus the Durkheimian paradox is that individuals experience their being as derived from, and contingent, on a social order that is in fact derived from their own presence and their own actions. The social order is thus contingent on their continued acceptance of a cultural fiction of their own making: a cultural fiction that deprives them of a sense of themselves as being *sui generis* or ultimate. Thus the religious longings discussed by Weber, in which individuals seek to emulate monarchs or the aristocracy, or in which they seek divine or supernatural endowment and revelations, are generated by the Durkheimian paradox. Individuals are longing to recover a sense of their own being as underived from the very social system that is derived, according to Durkheim, from their being and acting collectively and in harmony with one another. Without their original and continued adherence to the symbols that give the society the appearance of continuity, there will be no reality that seems to transcend and supersede the life of the individual. Hidden in this paradox, however, is a rather stark Durkheimian assessment that "a very intense social life always does a sort of violence to the organism." It is as if Durkheim, like Freud, were tracing the origins of neurosis to trauma, but for Durkheim the neurosis is collective, significant, convincing, and potent in its effects; it can even call for human sacrifice, and it causes trauma to the human psyche. Indeed, rites of initiation can be so intense that they do violence not only to the psyche but to the body, and in some cases are fatal. It is as if in sacralizing a social order by investing it with the potency of their passions and the substance of their own psyches, individuals succeed in making themselves seem to have an entirely derived, temporary, and even expendable existence.

In reading Durkheim, however, it is well to keep in mind his comment that "the old gods are dead and the news ones are not yet born." Since Durkheim, much has been written about the way in which these gods appear in a twilight zone. That is, in more complex societies, it is difficult to distinguish totems, which stand for the collective identity, from tattoos, which are both generic symbols and yet imbued with the individual's own sense of identity. Where is the sacred to be found, sharply demarcated from the secular or the profane, when in fact so many apparently secular values and institutions are simply translations from religious language into the more abstract and general language of the larger society? Thus words like "office" and "ministry" still evoke, in governmental language, the time when the state was tutored by the church in many respects. To read modern societies, we need to be aware of many complex signs in the present that evoke a past in which religion permeated the entire society. However, it may be exceedingly difficult to find the sacred in opposition to the secular or even in creative tension with the secular, when so much of what is sacred is still found in every-day life, in the particular, the practical, and the personal.

Durkheim speaks of the more violent ways in which some societies impress themselves on the individual. Identifying various kinds of asceticism that "do violence to the psyche," Durkheim (1965: 351–52) speaks of a "negative cult" that does "violence to our nature." These rites and austerities, although they traumatize the psyche, are laying the necessary psychological groundwork, Durkheim argues, for what he calls the "positive cult": a set of attachments and loyalties to the larger society not unlike what is sometimes called a civil religion. As Durkheim (1965: 355) puts it, "The positive cult is possible only when a man is trained to renouncement, to abnegation, to detachment from self, and consequently to suffering." If individuals derive a sense of their own being from social life, then, it is a sense of their own being as just that: as derived, and therefore hardly ultimate, but rather condi-tional on and conditioned by a wide range of social forces and obligations.

Social life is not only the cure for a chronic sense of personal defi-ciency; it is also the cause of the sense that one's own being is insub-stantial, precarious, and temporary. A society is therefore like a neurosis: a result of projections from the individual psyche that under certain con-ditions, and with the necessary symbolization, take on a life and reality of their own. The same applies to religion: "Religious force is only the sentiment inspired by the group in its members, but projected outside of the consciousnesses that experience them, and objectified. To be objec-tified, they are fixed upon some object that becomes sacred; but any object might fulfill this function." Thus the group itself consists of indi-viduals who project on each other their inner psychic states in a high degree of excitation. Once formed in this manner, the group becomes the cause and origin of the sentiments that form the sacred. For Durkheim, the sacred appears to derive from religion, whereas for Weber the charismatic individual who embodies the sacred is the cause or carrier of what later develops into institutionalized religion.

In these excited and intense states of mind, individuals are most likely to experience the impulses that Freud regarded as erotic and aggressive. That is especially the case when individuals experience these sentiments in the same place at the same time: hence Durkheim's interest in annual collective orgies. Under these conditions of intense personal and collective excitement, a society is able to impress on individuals the extent to which they are members of a collectivity that embodies extraordinary potency. At such times the conventional boundaries separating individuals from each other are broken down and taboos freely violated, whereas in everyday life the group less forcibly reminds individuals of its permanence in time or causes them to observe the same taboos that are subject to occasional collective violation. For Durkheim, as for Weber, and, as we shall see, for other sociologists of religion, an impoverished everyday life is marked by an absence of the sacred: for Durkheim, because collective sentiments have become less appealing, compelling, or apparent in the round of everyday social life; for Weber, because charisma is being put to the practical test, rules are being followed and precedents established. Thus the group, initially a product of individuals acting with an extraordinary and heightened sense of their own presence, takes on a life of its own that appears to be external, constraining, and superior to the individuals who created it. It is the source of the sacred. Just as the sacred is embodied and perpetuated only in symbols and images, objects and places that give the group an extended but surrogate presence in the lives of individuals, the individual derives from the sacred and from the group only a derived and deficient sense of his or her own being.

The group is thus formed in a time when individuals are given an extraordinary sense of possibility. Because on such occasions the group transcends its own taboos, it is easy to see how the notion of transcendence itself takes on new force and meaning. At those times societies suspend their ordinary regulations and permit people to have access to each other who would normally be kept at a safe distance from their own and other's sexual and aggressive impulses. Just as a god is not bound by his or her own ordinances, so a society must on occasion have the right to suspend its own rules, even those against murder or incest. Otherwise its sovereignty over the individual would be conditional. At the time of these collective orgies, there is no terrible gulf fixed between the ordinary individual and the noble, the virtuoso, the shaman, or the priest.

Although Durkheim's argument leads him to the conclusion that sovereignty consists in the exceptional exercise of collective powers on extraordinary occasions, he tends to see tribal, or primitive societies as having a more "intimate" or accessible relevance to their members, as compared with what he calls the "Leviathans" of the modern age: those huge, complex nation-states whose very being does indeed seem to eclipse that of the individual, even in the normal course of events, and not only on occasions of high collective ceremony. Thus individuals in modern societies have a greater deficit in their sense of their own being and a greater, more intractable existential debt to discharge. The more intense and immediate is the contact between the individual and the community or society gathered together in moments of collective ecstasy, the more directly individuals know their own being to be constituted and also subsumed by the collectivity. The deficit in the sense of one's own being could be overcome if only for the time being.

Reading Durkheim in the light of the wars and holocausts of the later twentieth century, however, it is possible to see that even these Leviathans assume the qualities of intimate and intense collective association that Durkheim associated with the more primitive social orders. Thus they could, and did, suspend their own rules and, especially under fascist leadership, created a "state of exception" in which it was constitutionally legitimate to suspend the constitution. Under these conditions individuals once again know themselves to be derived from and dependent on the larger society.

Durkheim was primarily concerned with the loss of collective representations and of a society-wide moral community. However, he argued that societies are based on and perpetuate self-alienation, and they do so by sacralizing their own order and secularizing the person and presence of the individual. Even though the social order is actually derived from the concerted and harmonious actions of individuals and of the projections of individual psyches, it becomes the individual whose ontological status is subject entirely to the society as a whole. If, for Durkheim, there is anything approaching a false consciousness, it is a lack of the sense of one's own being as morally and ontologically derived from and obligated to the community and larger society. Only the elite is to be aware with Durkheim, that the individual's awareness of that community, his or her sense of its uniqueness, power, and superiority, is the result of projections from the psyches of individuals themselves.

Conversely, primitive societies had their secular times and occasions. Indeed, most of the year was given over to secular pursuits, in which individuals went about their pursuits and became forgetful of or at least indifferent to the identity that they had derived from their participation in the intense, collective rites of the society as a whole. Thus secularity for Durkheim had to do with going about the business of everyday life, hunting and fishing, getting and spending, building and harvesting, making and breaking. The sacred, therefore, defined the social order and the experiences in which individuals impressed on themselves the power and authority of their collective experience. Magic, on the other hand, referred to the experiences of individuals as they became intensely aware of the separateness and fragility of their own beings and of their need to buttress their psyches against disease and ill will.

Durkheim is very clear on several points. Societies are imagined; they consist of imaginary entities that, because they are perceived and experienced collectively, are thought to have a life of their own independently of the individuals who imagine them, and to have an order of being external and superior to that of the individuals themselves. However, that does not mean that social life and imagined social entities are not real, any more than it means that an individual's neurosis is only a figment of his or her imagination without a reality that can assert its presence and have its own effects. It is therefore worth repeating here Durkheim's (1965: 259) argument that "a very intense social life always does a sort of violence to the organism, as well as to the individual consciousness, which interferes with its normal functioning. Therefore it can last only a limited length of time." The sacred, however potent, is always temporary in its manifestations, however long-lasting are its psychological and social effects.

The effect of this societal violence on the psyche appears in a form of split consciousness. As Durkheim (1965: 298) put it regarding "moral ideas": "It is society which forces them upon us, and as the respect inspired by it is naturally extended to all that comes from it, its imperative rules of conduct are invested, by reason of their origin, with an authority and a dignity which is shared by none of our internal states: therefore, we assign them a place apart in our psychical life." Note the elements of violence; society forces moral ideas upon the psyche; note also the splitting of the consciousness, as these ideas are given a "place apart" in the psychic organization of the individual. It is as if the individual psyche is split apart so as to allow part of it, at any rate, to be possessed by an external force. Thus Durkheim (1965: 299) speaks of "a particle of divinity" in the human psyche, which is only "a particle of these great ideas which are the soul of the group." Because an individual's internal states hardly have the power and compelling presence of collective experience, individuals inevitably derive from their social life a highly defective sense of their own being. It is the group which is solid, and the individual who is ephemeral.

Durkheim is in no doubt that the psyche, once exposed to the force or violence of the social order in moments of extraordinary excitation or social pressure, really does become split into two parts. "So we are really made up of two beings facing in different and almost contrary directions, one of whom exercises a real preeminence over the other. Such is the profound meaning of the antithesis which all men more or less clearly have conceived between the body and the soul, the material and spiritual beings who coexist within us" (Durkheim 1965: 298).

In addition to the element of force and the psychic splitting that results, Durkheim moves on to emphasize the extent to which there is a strong element of misunderstanding or misrecognition in the idea of the soul, at least as it is later elaborated among somewhat more advanced societies. While the soul is thought to be that which gives the individual a genuine and highly personal identity, it is more like an impersonal force: a generic power that takes up residence in the psyche for the time being, if only to split the psyche and control it from within. However, a casual reading of Durkheim could lead one to the mistaken conclusion that Durkheim, too, imagined the individual to be merely another incarnation of a generic soul that keeps reproducing itself from one generation to the next: "a sort of generic substance which individualized itself only secondarily and superficially" (Durkheim 1965: 300). Therefore it is well to remember that Durkheim fully understood that society is the effect of individuals acting intensively, in harmony, even in unison, through words and gestures highly expressive of individuals' own passions and imaginations, of their desires and their destructiveness. The most fundamental misunderstanding, then, is for individuals to think of the social order itself as something external, superior, and *sui generis*, when, for Durkheim (1965: 283), "Society exists only in and through individuals."

Granted that the soul is that which gives an individual a certain individuality; it is only at best a highly derived individuality. The soul is a replica or reincarnation of an ancestor, and at the same time it is also a personification of the totem by which the group identifies itself to itself and others. There is a sort of Trinitarian consciousness running in Durkheim's arguments, as though the three, the individual soul, the totem, and the ancestral being, were in fact one in three and three in one. Behind this layer of his analysis, however, is an even more generic notion of the power of the society, as if the society itself were an impersonal, magical force, like mana, which can colonize the soul and take possession of it under the right social conditions. Thus Durkheim is fascinated by the extent to which intense social life, however temporary, can leave lasting effects on the psyche, and with the aid of symbols, can develop the appearance of a permanent, external, superior and constraining entity.

Like Freud, then, Durkheim is concerned with describing a split in the psyche: in Freudian terms, a split between the ego, which keeps an eye on the situation, on present opportunities and dangers and seizes the moment, and the superego, which represents the constraints and pressures of public opinion, the approval and disapproval of parents and other authorities to whom one was most closely and intensely exposed as a child. Like Freud who speaks of the superego as a state internal to the psyche, Durkheim speaks of the soul as embodying the impersonal moral force of the community or society.

However impersonal the superego or psyche may be in rendering its judgments on the individual, it draws heavily from the individual's own passions. As we have seen, Durkheim roots the power of social opinion in the psyche in those moments in which individuals become excited together: moments of collective effervescence. At such times aggressive and sexual impulses unite in breaking down old boundaries, and they establish new connections among individuals across a wide range of social distinctions in the cause of momentarily breaking social taboos. Just as the psyche is the result of violent splitting under intense social pressure, the collectivity is constituted in moments when its own taboos are being broken.

What Freud said of the contagion of magical thinking applies to the origin of social life. Social life consists of collective representations: ways of perceiving the common life of individuals as they act together in concert and harmony. However, "collective representations very frequently attribute to the things to which they are attached qualities which do not exist under any form or to any degree. Out of the commonest object, they can make a most powerful sacred being" (Durkheim 1965: 259–60). Durkheim was concerned with the lasting effects of experiences that he calls ecstatic: ones in which individuals are lifted, by the pressure of social life, outside of themselves. Speaking of religion, as one example of such collective experience, Durkheim (1965: 258) argues that "religious life cannot attain a certain degree of intensity without implying a psychical exaltation not far removed from delirium. . . . The images out of which it is made are not pure illusions like those the naturists and animists put at the basis of religion; they correspond to something in reality." What they correspond to, of course, is simply the "the moral forces" that are created when individuals act collectively with a high degree of intensity and harmony.

So much has been made of the way in which Durkheim reduces religion to an expression of social life, and also of the way Durkheim derives the individual from social life, that it is important to remember how explicitly Durkheim sees social life emerging from the collective actions and imaginations of individuals themselves and from their words and gestures. The more that individuals act in unison, the more their actions seem to take on a life of their own independently of the actors themselves. This life is expressed in symbols that in their turn also endure and take on a life of their own: symbols which become collective representations. Collective representations acquire significance from the states of mind that individuals project into them. Religion is simply one among many such collective representations: a mere projection of the minds of individuals acting collectively. Religion thus becomes the place where the debt to the psyche is remembered and slowly discharged over time. However much religion may seem to come from a source that is external and superior, transcendent and constraining, it therefore emerges from the ecstatic experience of individuals acting in harmony with others. Durkheim (1965: 259) makes it very clear: "if we give the name delirious to every state in which the mind adds to the immediate data given by the senses and projects its own sentiments and feelings into things, then nearly every collective representation is in a sense delirious; religious beliefs are only one particular case of a very general law."

The natural flow of time, as one thing is succeeded by another, yields to a collective sense of how the separate aspects of life are connected. A sense of collective meaning, necessity, or purpose provides a scheme for linking the discrete and temporary aspects of life into an eternal order with its own meaning and purposes. Happenstance yields to a sense of necessity, and mere succession takes on meaning as part of a causal framework. These layers of meaning eventually supersede the flow of life, of one moment or hour, day or week after another. Eventually the mundane and the everyday become relegated to a world that has been subordinated to the collective imagination. The real world of mere coming and going, of living and dying, of sheer, raw succession and happenstance becomes secular; the social order itself takes on the aura of transcendence, and the collective imagination constitutes religion. Similarly, the social order separates life into the sacred and the profane.

The collective imagination thus unites and associates, distinguishes and divides according to its own logic, regardless of any actual distinction or connection among people and things, moments and days. That is, the possibilities that seemed to be superabundant and simultaneous in moments of collective ecstasy become sorted out into possibilities that belong, if not in the present, then in a collective past and future, where they are held in abeyance until another time of collective enthusiasm opens the door to these same possibilities once again. Although the collective imagination links together moments and days, actions and events, things and people into an orderly and meaningful sequence, these elements have no intrinsic or necessary connection with each other.

Not only does the collective imagination define and shape reality according to its own logic and will; as we have seen, it also imposes its scheme on the psyche in a variety of ways, many of them forceful or even violent. After splitting the psyche to make it amenable to the distinctions and connections made by the collective imagination, the society reproduces itself in the psyche of the individual through rigorous, often exceedingly painful rites of initiation, and in doing so deprives individuals of the right to follow their inclinations and to associate mentally or socially with any freedom other than that granted by the social order itself.

The distinction between the sacred and the profane therefore underlies later divisions of the world into the everyday or mundane on the one hand, and of ultimate ends on the other. Whether one is dealing with the distinction between mere utility and, as Durkheim put it, the categorical imperative, or the distinction between the material and the spiritual, one is dealing with a social world divided into binary opposites all of which can be traced to the initial division of the sacred from the profane. That distinction, in turn can be traced to the separation of the social world from the sheer flow and passage of time, and it is realized and reproduced in every generation by the splitting of the individual psyche.

The splitting of the psyche from itself permits the division of the world into a series of binary distinctions, all of which are variations on the initial theme of the separation of the sacred from the profane. Thus feast days are set apart from ordinary days. The time of the society as a whole, public time, becomes separated from merely private time. As Durkheim (1965: 347) put it, "the religious life and the profane life cannot coexist in the same unit of time. It is necessary to assign deter-mined days or periods to the first, from which all profane occupations are excluded. Thus feast days are born. There is no religion, and, conse-quently, no society which has not known or practiced this division of time into two distinct parts, alternating with one another according to a law varying with the peoples and the civilizations; . . . it was probably the necessity of this alternation which led men to introduce into the continuity and homogeneity of duration, certain distinctions and differ-entiations which it does not naturally have."

When a feast day is established, that distinction between sacred and the profane time becomes the mother of a wide range of other differ-ences: between the religious and the secular; between the public and the private; between the societal and the individual; between the extraordinary and the ordinary; between the supernatural and the natu-ral; between the superb and the mundane; between the eternal and the temporal; between the moral and the useful; between the religious and the utilitarian; between ends-in-themselves and mere means.

For Durkheim, secularity emerges when the society in question, having interrupted the passage of time to mark out its identity as distinct from all that is otherwise destined to pass away, creates a category of times that are merely temporal. Thus the secular world is mere "dura-tion," apart from which social life emerges as a rock or island in the otherwise uninterrupted flow of time. The secular still is marked as the merely temporal world that is continuously passing away. One day leads to another, and they all lead to the endless succession of days into the world of those who have gone before. Religion is the cultural guarantee for possibilities that are either relegated to the past or deferred to the future; their day will come, or come again. Religion provides a place, either in the past or in the future, for all the possibilities that cannot be realized in the present. In turn, the continually passing present-time is thus the time-being, and it is merely mundane and useful, everyday and practical. As such, the present is perennially caught up in the process of secularization.

As the repository of all the possibilities that have been relegated to the past or the future, religion is marked by longing, whether for losses or for satisfactions that have been deferred to some time in the future. Religion institutionalized and perpetuates the deficit in the psyche's sense of its own being, and it provides a way of paying off the psyche's debt to those whom the individual imagines to be possessed of a more substantial and valuable being than his or her own. Durkheim (1965: 346) explains why it is necessary on a feast day to abandon every form of worldly activity, particularly work: "for they are sad feasts, consecrated to mourning and repentance, and during which this cessation is no less obligatory. This is because work is an eminent form of profane activity: it has no other apparent end than to provide for the temporal necessities of life; it puts us in relation to ordinary things only. On feast days, on the contrary, the religious life attains an exceptional degree of intensity. So the contrast between the two forms of existence is especially marked at this moment: consequently, they cannot remain near to each other."

The sacred consists of extraordinary moments or sacrifices. It is now threatened by modern tastes or is being reduced to a concert performed to a crowd of devotees in a state of high but temporary emotional excitement. In a more complex society, with a specialized division of labor, the sacred may be the practices of a profession, the secrets given to a doctor or a lawyer by a patient or a client, the promise made by parents to a child, or the right of an individual to dignity or privacy. The boundaries between the sacred and the profane are constantly shifting and are easily eroded, but the sacred is increasingly both personal and practical. Certainly in a society imbued with the Protestant work ethic and the notion of vocation, there may be widespread agreement that there is something sacred about work itself as a way of displaying a person's moral orientation and selfhood.

Durkheim knew that there was nothing natural or inevitable about the distinction between the sacred and the profane. To begin with, the distinction was arbitrary, and inevitably there would be confusion and mistakes in assigning people or places and times, not to mention plants and animals and things, to the category of the sacred or the profane. On a sad feast day given over to mourning, the world that passes away, the profane world of work and politics and play and warfare may all seem to matter very little compared to someone who has been lost and in whose honor the feast of mourning is being given. Similarly, on days of high communal excitement the everyday world of planting and hunting, of working and fighting, may seem to be of little moment compared with the ecstasy of the collective celebration. Nonetheless, it is never obvious or inevitable that the sacred should take one form or another: a stone or a plant, a shrine or a monument. On the contrary, as Durkheim (1965: 271) warned us, "religious thought" is marked by a tendency toward "immoderate confusions as well as sharp contrasts." Those who have tried to define what is secular as apart from what is sacred in modern societies can well attest that modernity is no stranger to the same confusions.

A basic misunderstanding therefore accompanies any attempt to signify some times and places, people or things, as sacred as opposed to profane. As Durkheim noted, this distinction interrupts the natural flow of one thing after another: the simple, sheer flow of temporal succession. In its place comes a succession of things whose relation to each other is by definition accidental, problematical, or arbitrary, until or unless they are imagined to form some meaningful sequence. The sheer fact of succession, of one thing coming after another, may be confused with consequence. What comes after may seem to be a result of what came before: an outcome, or at least an implication; the imagined effect of a possible cause. If the two moments are not causally related to each other, perhaps they are related as an ends is to a means, or as an explicit meaning to what is merely implied.

Durkheim is clear that religious thinking is the school to which human kind first went to try to understand the true relationships among things to each other, even if the relationships it establishes are inherently as arbitrary or as accidental as the distinctions made between what is sacred and lasting, over those that are merely profane and temporal. Nonetheless, Durkheim (1965: 270) argued that "The great service that religions have rendered to thought is that they have constructed a first representation of what these relations of kinship between things may be." It was to religion that people turned to find out what was the relation of A to B, since B regularly came after A. Was one a sign or cause of the other? In giving credit to religion however, Durkheim (1965: 270) was not suspending his own disbelief: "In the circumstances under which it was attempted," he wrote, "the enterprise could obviously entertain only precarious results."

To put it more bluntly, Durkheim is arguing that social life produces a delusional form of collective thinking in order to make sense of life and death, nature and the cosmos, animals and plants, humans and the passage of time. That form of collective make-believe is what Durkheim calls religion, in the generic sense of the term: "It was religion that was the agent of this transfiguration; it is religious beliefs that have substituted for the world, as it is perceived by the senses, another different one" (Durkheim 1965: 268). The essence of this transfiguration is to connect things that are not really connected. Obviously a country is not a flag, any more than a clan is a kangaroo, but in the reality established firmly in the minds of a people, the two may well be identical, and the devotion inspired by the social order becomes conferred on the symbol.

In the same way, Durkheim was arguing, a collective reality principle makes sense of the succession of things one after another by connecting them in some meaningful framework, as though they were part of a sacred history with its own assumptions about meaning, necessity, and purpose. These connections have two basic problems to solve. On the one hand they have to relate the possibilities in the present to those related either to the past or the future. In addition, these connections need to give meaning to the otherwise meaningless residue of temporal events, in the time that is merely passing away. Thus the attempt to regard the past as prefiguring some event in the future places the present in a meaningful relation to lost possibilities and redeems the times from radical insignificance. Such thinking makes it unnecessary to mourn the world that is not eternal: the merely temporal world that is forever passing away. Thus societies resolve the contradiction created by a distinction between sacred and the river of time itself that had been flowing smoothly and without distinction or interruption, before it was interrupted by a solemn day of feasting or fasting celebration or mourning. By creating even a fictitious or imaginary sense of the relation of one thing or moment to another, the sacred assigns meaning to the passage of time and stipulates the relationships of what comes before with what comes after. Conversely, when a meaningful continuity in the passage of time is lost, the sheer succession of one thing after another requires understanding and explanation. However, such comprehension requires highly potent as well as convincing thought, and the project, if it is to be undertaken at all, requires great confidence in the society's collective capacity to think things through. In order to "create a world of ideals through which the world of experienced realities would be transfigured," it was necessary to achieve what Durkheim (1965: 270) called "society."

At the risk of some repetition it is worth pointing out that Durkheim regards social life to be inherently based on delusions of one kind or another: simple delusions. That is not surprising, since Durkheim finds the origins of social life in the collective expression of social feelings, as well as in the very longings and states of mind that Freud considers to be unconscious desires for close connection with or mastery over others. For Durkheim, passionate attachments emerge in moments of imaginary psychological fusion, in which others seem to embody or even cause the sentiments that are rising so powerfully from within the individual's own psyche. In such moments of intense social interaction, Durkheim (1965: 259) argues, individuals are quite literally "outside themselves" in moments of ecstasy; it is they who have transcended their own ordinary state of mind and discovered in themselves wellsprings of emotion that are far outside their normal capacity to conceive or endure. Normally in abeyance, these emotions are so powerful that, when they emerge, they seem to be coming from outside of the individual, and so they are symbolized in objects, like the flag or some other totem, that are similarly external.

It is just at this point that Durkheim could be thought to be saying that it is social life itself that causes and originates these passions, but he in fact makes the quite opposite point that it is individuals themselves who, by acting harmoniously and in concert, create these effects that then become symbolized in some object that stands for the life of the society as a whole. The object or totem becomes imbued with the very capacities of the individuals who imagine themselves to be transformed by its presence in their midst. Durkheim (1965: 263) is very clear that the discovery of the sacred objects depends entirely on the individuals who act in certain ways so as to sacralize whatever an object may be, a tree or an animal, a book or a person.

"Individual minds cannot come in contact and communicate with each other except by coming out of themselves; but they cannot do this except by movements. So it is the homogeneity of these movements that gives the group consciousness of itself *and consequently makes it exist* (emphasis added). When this homogeneity is once established and these movements have once taken a stereotyped form, they come to be symbolized in the corresponding representations. But they symbolize them only because they have aided in forming them." The flag is a piece of cloth until it is marched at the head of a parade, with people in uniform marching in tight ranks and careful harmony, and with the flag being raised aloft and saluted by the masses of people who would otherwise be merely standing by. Once raised and recognized in common devotion, it stands for the nation and elicits the very devotion that created it in the first place. It is the capacity of individuals acting collectively and in concert to create a sense of a larger society superior and external as well as essential to themselves, which gives to individuals a sense of the deficiency or derivation of their own being and of a perennial and unpayable debt.

It is paradoxical and perhaps tragic that individuals become devotees and servants of the objects they have sacralized. Once their intense social emotions are expropriated by the larger society and made to reside in symbols, beliefs, and practices, individuals feel their own beings to be outclassed by the more substantial entity they have in fact created and sustained by their own emotional projections and investments. That sort of delusion could only be achieved, argues Durkheim (1965: 270), by a "super-excitation of the intellectual forces."

Marx was clearly not the only social theorist who thought of religion, then, as signifying the alienation of individuals from a knowledge of their own being. Neither was Freud, who thought that social life was a screen on which individuals projected their own feelings and longings: a screen play in which they themselves become mere character actors and fail to recognize themselves, although they wrote the play. Durkheim concurred with their opinion.

By the consequences of their imaginations and of their own actions, individuals develop a sense of themselves as being derived from a larger, transcendent social entity. Although they themselves create this entity by acting in harmony, and they themselves choose ways of giving that harmony an enduring and evocative symbol, it now seems to them that it is that symbolic entity which is the source and heart of their own being.

Through their membership in a community or society, individuals acquire a double sense of their own being: a temporal self and an identity that will outlast the individual's lifetime and so secure a measure of transcendence; a body and a soul. Religion ties the individual to the ongoing life of the community or society; it endures beyond death and transcends the business of everyday life. A secular identity links the individual to the network of affiliations necessary for catching fish or making investments. These activities and affiliations are necessary, but they do not last, and they provide only a very insecure anchorage for the psyche. Durkheim thus concluded that individuals have a much weaker sentiment of their own being when they are merely going about their own business, hunting or fishing or teaching or leading professional lives than when they are transfigured, if only for a moment, by a deeply personal encounter with the sacred.

As Durkheim argued later in his discussion, society is basically a psychological fact before it becomes a social fact. That is to say, it is all in people's heads. Like Freud, he argued that social life consists of a set of projections from individuals' minds that appear to be real because their effects are real. For Durkheim (1965: 259), "Our whole social environment seems to be filled with forces which really exist only in our own minds." This is a strong statement for a sociologist who some believe gave ontological priority to the society over the individual, but Durkheim is quite clear on this point. Although a flag, as an emblem of the larger society, can inspire admiration, loyalty, courage, submission, or fear, the fact remains, as Durkheim (1965: 259–60) put it, that "We know what the flag is for the soldier; in itself, it is only a piece of cloth. . . . Yet the powers which are thus conferred, though purely ideal, act as though they were real; they determine the conduct of men with the same degree of necessity as physical forces." If societies seem more real than individuals, to have more substance, it is because individuals are looking into an enlarging mirror in which they scarcely recognize themselves, and in that mirror they discover what they imagine to be their true identities, obligations, and destinies. Societies are based on and perpetuate delusions, self-alienation, a split psyche, and a sense of one's own being as ontologically derivative and obliged to pay an existential debt.

Kinds of secularization

At the very heart of the sacred, then, there is a radical uncertainty about being itself. For Durkheim the gods derive their existence, their very being, from the collective efforts and enthusiasm of individuals acting in concert; when acting in concert, it seems to individuals that there is a god amongst them whose being and presence ensure their own. However, in their absence from each other, that god may also seem remote, inaccessible, or unreal, just as, when they are together, they lose a sense of their own individuality and acquire a derivative being from their communion with one another: a communion which they experience as being more solid and enduring than the temporary social cohesion from which it emerges. Durkheim (1965: 389) describes the basic dialectic between the secular and the sacred very clearly when he argues, "We now see the real reason why the gods cannot do without their worshippers any more than these can do without their gods; it is because society, of which the gods are only a symbolic expression, cannot do without individuals any more than these can do without society."

The sacred thus embodies a being that is supposedly underived and ultimate, on whose existence depends the life and being of the individual, and yet it is individuals themselves who bring this double of their own being into existence. Durkheim is at some pains to argue that social life is not merely a collective fiction, even though it emerges only through an exercise of the collective imagination. It is what we might call an emergent property of social interaction, but once it does emerge, social life acquires a being of its own; it is a social fact in its own right, of a different order from that of the individuals who make it, even though, without their consciousness, it would have no life at all. Durkheim (1965: 389) goes on to say, "If we are to see in the efficacy attributed to the rites anything more than the product of a chronic delirium with which humanity has abused itself, we must show that the effect of the cult really is to recreate periodically a moral being upon which we depend as it depends on us. Now this being does exist: it is society."

So long as individuals derive their sense of themselves from their membership in the larger society, they will be unsure of their own being. Similarly, so long as the larger society is effective in impressing or inscribing itself on the psyches of individuals, individuals will have a very split, as well as a derivative, sense of their own being. Unsure of their own being, they will find in their gatherings and common life a guarantee of their existence: a way of transcending the mundane and the passage of time, even death itself.

So long as the sacred depends on occasions of intense and imaginative collective action, it will seem to be at best a cyclical or occasional reality and thus subject to the passage of time. That is, the sacred always is inherently temporal. Durkheim (1965: 387) is quite frank about this temporal aspect even of the gods' existence: "The intermittency of the social life . . . is inevitable; even the most idealistic religions cannot escape it." Outpourings of sacred enthusiasm may come as a surprise, like events that occur suddenly, unpredictably, and in a threatening manner. In the wake of a disaster, a people may come together to affirm their solidarity and loyalty to one another, to their traditions, and to their common destiny, in ways that may surprise even themselves. As Durkheim (1965: 387) puts it, "the emotions aroused by these periodical crises through which external things pass induce the men who witness them to assemble, to see what should be done about it. . . . The common faith becomes reanimated quite naturally in the heart of this reconstituted group; it is born again because it again finds those very conditions in which it was born in the first place." The critical moment is at the heart of the sacred.

There would be no secular or ordinary time if there were no sacred time. As Durkheim (1965: 391) put it, "Society is able to revivify the sentiment it has of itself only by assembling. But it cannot be assembled all the time. The exigencies of life do not allow it to be in congregation indefinitely; so it scatters, to assemble anew when it again feels the need of this. It is to these necessary alternations that the regular alternations of sacred and profane times correspond." However, once religion contains and orchestrates the sacred, workdays and weekdays become secular or even profane, marked not only by the absence of the gods but by activities and sentiments that are repugnant or alien to them. That is why, as Durkheim (1965: 345) reminds us, "all acts characteristic of the ordinary life are forbidden while those of the religious life are taking place. The act of eating is, of itself, profane; for it takes place every day, it satisfies essentially utilitarian and material needs and it is a part of our ordinary existence. That is why it is prohibited in religious times." Whereas the sacred is initially both utilitarian and deeply personal, under the auspices of religion it develops an aversion to the mundane.

In the end, Durkheim seems to have missed the possibility that religion, in its embrace of the sacred, might turn out to be the sacred's undoing. However, as we shall see from our discussion of Max Weber, that is one of the dynamics operating in a variety of religions, notably Christianity: the routinization of charisma, as Weber put it, and the secularization of the routine. To be able to decipher the residues·of the sacred and the secular requires, however, a highly skilled and literate sociological understanding of the patterns, beliefs, values, ways of life, artistic and literary deposits of an entire society. If there is progress in the sociology of religion, then, it will be precisely toward that sort of careful reading of a society's institutions and culture that permits the sociologist to distinguish the sacred from religion.

Reference

(1965) [1915] *The Elementary Forms of the Religious Life*. Translated by Joseph Ward Swain. New York: The Free Press.

Sigmund Freud

Sigmund Freud (1856–1939) started professional life with medical research in the neurosciences, but about his fortieth year turned to the practice of what became psychoanalysis. Living most of his life in Vienna, he developed a theory of unconscious mental processes, the most authoritative and novel description of which appeared in *The Interpretation of Dreams,* published in November, 1899. A close reader of Durkheim who died in 1917, Freud saw enough of authoritarianism and fascism to reinforce his questions about the passions underlying social solidarity. He died, a refugee from Nazism, of cancer in London, in 1939.

To understand what Freud has to say about religion, we need to begin with his discussion of the sacred. After relating the English term to the Roman *sacer,* the Greek *agios*, and the Hebrew *kadesh*, he settles on the term taboo, which, in addition to its colloquial meaning in Western societies, has a wide range of meanings and applications in various cultures around the globe (Freud 1950: 24). At the heart of the notion of the sacred or taboo is the sense of a presence that is both desirable and yet dangerous. Like the person of a ruler or the body of someone long-loved but just deceased, the sacred seems to hold within itself some secret about the nature of our own being: something essential and highly to be desired and yet also feared. Like a ghost or a figure in a dream, it is also evanescent and comes and goes of its own accord. As the personification of the passions that inhabit the unconscious, the sacred carries the potencies associated with erotic longing, but it may also embody the desire to destroy or a wish for death. Endowed with the omnipotence that individuals unconsciously may still attribute to their own thoughts, the very presence of the sacred can be fateful not only for the individual but for the social order, especially when the sacred breaks loose from its proper constraints and becomes all too approach-able. No wonder that Freud then describes the sacred as possessing "a sense of something unapproachable, and it is principally expressed in prohibitions and restrictions. Our collocation 'holy dread' would often coincide in meaning with 'taboo' " (Freud 1950: 24). Unapproachable, autonomous, evanescent, potentially life-giving or life-threatening, the sacred embodies what is both quintessential and yet far beyond human knowledge and control.

The sacred thus may be embodied in a person or a thing, in a moment or situation, that is full of the potential both for great opportunity and satisfaction or for great danger. It is a presence or even the present moment itself that embodies an extraordinary array of possibilities not ordinarily available in everyday life. From the sacred may emerge all sort of practices and routines, beliefs and traditions, that seem to carry on or carry out this initial implosion of possibility into everyday life.

Freud gives another hint about the sacred as being at times demonic: an uncanny, dangerous sort of power. Of course, for Freud demons are merely "creations of the human mind" (Freud 1950: 32). However, for Freud the sacred itself, unlike gods or demons, is not so easily derived from various projections of the psyche's desires and passions or from its many associations with autocratic rulers, tyrants, rapacious animals, and spirits that inhabit the wind and the earth. There is something more primal and original about the sacred; its being is not easily associated with or assimilated to any other. The sacred has a sovereignty and inde-pendence of its own; it is a taken-for-granted necessity, filled with potency as well as passion, and yet the sacred cannot be easily placed into some simple scheme of symbolic opposition, like that separating the sacred from the profane, or the clean from the unclean. As the English psychoanalyst David Winnicott much later observed, the sacred is like the "I am" sounding from the burning bush: too hot to touch, not easily approached, one of its own kind, self-generating, irreducible to something else, not derived from anything else, but the first and last word on its own being. The sacred is quintessential.

For Freud, therefore, the sacred belongs in no category. Long before the sacred is absorbed into systems of religious meaning and practice, and before codes of law and morals seek to circumscribe human behavior, the sacred enjoys a life of its own. As Freud (1950: 24–25) put it, "Taboo restric-tions are distinct from religious or moral prohibitions. They are not based on any divine ordinance, but may be said to impose themselves on their own account. They differ from moral prohibitions in that they fall into no system that declares quite generally that certain abstinences must be observed and gives reasons for that necessity. Taboo prohibitions have no grounds and are of unknown origin. Though they are unintelligible to *us*, to those who are dominated by them they are taken as a matter of course." Thus the sacred carries with it the taken-for-granted sense of necessity and the constraining power of unconscious, potent longings and destructive wishes. In that sense, the sacred is *sui generis*: of ultimate significance and underived from any other source than itself. The sacred is the very embodiment of the sense of one's own being, objectified in some mysterious, potent, desirable and dangerous Other. Whether that Other is a ghost or a demon, an emperor or high priest, its very being is fateful for the society as a whole and even for nature itself, and it is dangerous to anyone who approaches it too closely.

It is not surprising, then, that Freud finds the sacred held in the collective memory of peoples like the ancient Greeks or Israelites. The Greeks, Freud (1955: 88) notes, harbored memories of "a period of outward splendour and highly developed culture which ended in catastrophe – as, indeed, history tells – and of which a faint tradition lived on" in the legends eventually collected in the Homeric epics. Similarly the Jews, Freud (1955: 87) notes, had a "tradition of a great past that continued to work in the background, until it slowly gained more and more power over the mind of the people and at last succeeded in transforming the God Jahve into the Mosaic God and in waking to a new life the religion which Moses had instituted centuries before and which had later been forsaken." This Mosaic tradition was a high monotheistic faith in the Egyptian God, Aton, and carried with it a high ethical sense and a scorn of ceremony. As Freud (1955: 89) puts it, "Probably man still stands under the magic spell of his childhood, which a not unbiased memory presents to him as a time of unalloyed bliss." Thus, especially when the present offers far too little in the way of hope or satisfaction, individuals and entire peoples seek to remember a time when their own lives, their very beings, were upheld in a potent and satisfying social order. Focused on the person of Moses, this tradition remembered a person of extraordinary power, whose presence and power were confirmed in a vision of an underived being, the great "I Am," and whose passions could be both murderous and liberating. If Moses bore the hallmarks of the sacred, it was because he became the repository of the repressed longings of a people not only to recover the potencies and enchanted universe of their childhood but to acquire an undiminished sense of their own being. The sacred, then, is being itself: underived, *sui generis*, quintessential, evanescent, and fateful. Like the soul, it is also an embodied form of self-reflection, an unmitigated sense of "I am."

For individuals to get their hands on the variously objectified forms of the sacred would not only pollute and destroy the sacred itself; it would expose the polluters to the destructive potential of sacred power. Freud (1950: 28) gives accounts of how those who have unwittingly eaten or destroyed the sacred suffer sickness and death: "An innocent wrong-doer, who may, for instance, have eaten a forbidden animal, falls into a deep depression, anticipates death and then dies in bitter earnest." Like the unconscious, the sacred may be taboo because it harbors wishes that are inherently destructive, whether they are turned outward against others or inward against the self. The sacred then, is like an overdose of potent possibility, even though it points beyond itself to a realm of pure potential for life or for death.

Every civilization, Freud (1962: 69) argued, presents "the struggle between Eros and Death, between the instinct of life and the instinct of destruction, as it works itself out in the human species." On the one hand, the instinct of Eros or love seeks to create new unities and to bind people together in an order that will survive the passage of time. On the other hand, that very order is threatened by the instinct toward death. That instinct will either destroy a people from within, when it is directed against themselves as a people or as individuals, or they can save themselves from destruction by turning it outward safely toward others: toward marginal peoples in their own midst who are weak and expendable, or on communities outside their boundaries who represent some abhorrent form of difference. Thus a group may sacralize its own being and secularize the outside world as headed for death and extinction. Once the outside world is sentenced to death, its time is therefore always and everywhere passing away, whereas it is the group itself that has been rescued from death and will continue to live united by, and in bondage to, love.

Erotic desires expand the boundaries of the self to include others, as though the self could be fulfilled only by incorporating into itself the objects of its desire. For Freud (1961: 73; n. 21), Eros is a combination of "narcissistic libido" and the sexual instincts; Eros "seeks to force together and to hold together the portions of living substance. . . . Eros operates from the beginning of life and appears as a 'life instinct' in opposition to the 'death instinct,' which was brought into being by the coming to life of inorganic substance." Just as aggressive tendencies are softened and made amenable to rituals of remorse by their combination with the erotic instincts, so the erotic instincts may provide a disguise for self-destructive tendencies: a thin disguise, whenever the lover is self-immolating or self-sacrificial, or whenever love becomes overly sadistic. Bonding of erotic with aggressive impulses becomes clear in the desire to become "one flesh," or, like Romeo and Juliet, romantically to tear down the boundaries separating lovers of radically different ethnicities or social standing. The same desire to dissolve the boundaries between the self and the other, however, is apparent in what Freud (1961: 66) calls "primitive masochism." Freud finds that original tendency toward self-destruction, the drive to dissolve the boundaries between the self and the other, expressed in a longing for death or for a dissolution of conscious life in some sort of bliss or Nirvana. It is as if the psyche seeks to merge with or incorporate the other in order to supply a deficit in its own being. So dangerous to the self is this primitive form of masochism that individuals turn it outward toward safer targets, and the impulse to self-destruction then becomes homicidal, unless of course it is sublimated to nonhuman targets or to nature itself. Once sublimated, the sense of a defect in one's own being becomes an obligation to pay a debt to some other whose very being is in itself highly desired or feared: imagined to be the repository of a being that is neither derived, subordinate, or destined to pass away.

Along with the unconscious, the sacred is a reservoir of imaginary magical powers, enabling thoughts themselves to assume a kind of omnipotence. Sovereign in its own sphere and domain, the sacred can therefore exercise its sovereignty only at some safe remove from its own immediate sphere of influence. If individuals come too close, they may be destroyed, or they may acquire the very powers of the sacred itself. As Freud (1950: 29) put it, regarding the prohibitions or taboos that surround the sacred, "The strangest fact seems to be that anyone who has transgressed one of the prohibitions himself acquires the characteristic of being prohibited – as though the whole of the dangerous charge had been transferred over to him." Again like the psyche, the sacred works through contagion, through projection and identification, rather than being directly accessible or touchable.

Potent and yet ephemeral, the sacred requires a sanctuary of its own. Just as it cannot easily be compared to or subsumed within anything else, the sacred can be approached only through its likeness. Although the world around the sacred may be divided up between the clean and the unclean, the sacred and the profane, the sacred itself is neither, because it is both. As Freud (1950: 32–33) put it, the notion of taboo preserves the idea of the sacred in close conjunction with the notion of uncleanness; hence "the dread of contact with it. The persistence . . . of this important common characteristic is at the same time evidence that the ground covered by the two was originally one and that it was only as a result of further influences that it became differentiated and eventually developed into opposites." This is an important reminder that the sacred is initially grounded in the ordinary and everyday, the practical and the personal. Only when it is later encapsulated or elaborated in a religious system of beliefs and values, practices and prohibitions, is the sacred taken out of context and made more inaccessible and abstract.

Thus what Durkheim thought was an original distinction between the sacred and the profane was itself a result of an early process of separation. Within the sacred are powers that can destroy and create: forge new bonds and unite with others while separating those who may live from those who must die. It is only when the sacred is differentiated from the profane, that the world is created which is temporal, secular, and existing in a present-time that is always passing away.

Freud analyzes a society as he would a patient. Consider his description of so called "primitive" societies in which the sacred so permeates the many circumstances and routines of everyday life that it is difficult to know where the sacred ends and the profane begins. The more primitive societies are permeated with a sense of taboo: with fear of a demonic power thought to reside in particular people, or in unusual or transitional states of mind or body, or in the "uncanny things, such as sickness or death" (Freud 1950: 29). However, the ancient belief in a demonic power that must be taboo for the sake of all concerned "develops into the rule of custom and tradition and finally of law" (Freud 1950: 31). Therefore, as Freud (1950: 29) points out, we still attribute to "the moral and conventional prohibitions by which we ourselves are governed," including "our own 'categorical imperative,' " some sense of the taboo, so that it is dangerous to break the rules, and those who break the rules become dangerous. Thus tradition creates a present that is linked to the potency of the sacred in the past, even though the present is somewhat less fraught with the possibility that the sacred will erupt into the moment.

Freud thus analyzes social life as though it were a theater of the psyche. In the routine encounters of brothers with sisters, of fathers with daughters and of mothers with sons, of mothers-in-law with sons-in-law, and of godparents with godchildren, he finds situations in which sexual attractions may be so powerful as to tear apart the structure of marriage and the family. That is why patterns of prohibition are needed to enable those who might otherwise be drawn together to avoid proximity and sexual contact. The sense of the untouchable, then, permeates the social order, precisely because the situations of everyday life offer so wide a scope to the expression of desire.

The same highly ritualized patterns of social life also protect people from their own and others' aggressive tendencies. Not only are those with extraordinary powers safely constrained from using them; they in turn are kept at a safe distance from those who might seek forcefully to acquire them by violating prohibited degrees of proximity or contact. The social order is thus a field in which demonic or charismatic forces are at play. Without a maze of social boundaries, formal and informal rites, and without ways of keeping people at a safe distance from each other, the erotic and destructive tendencies of the psyche would have a social field day. The present is as safe as it is from the potencies of the sacred only because some of these possibilities are relegated to the past or deferred to the future through the agency of rituals and the authority of religion.

In *Beyond the Pleasure Principle*, Freud points out that these potent desires or destructive tendencies, when combined with the aggressive or death instincts, would easily dissolve the boundaries between the individual and the other, or between the self and the social or natural world. Freud (1961: 65) speaks of "a death instinct which, under the influence of the narcissistic libido, has been forced away from the ego and has consequently only emerged in relation to the object." Thus the old self-destructive tendency may still be seen in a lover figuratively or literally dying to please the object of his or her desire. That is because masochistic tendencies, initially self-destructive, find their way to their object when they are combined with erotic desire, just as erotic desire may follow a course opened up by aggressive or death instincts (Freud 1961: 65). The erotic instinct is originally dedicated to self-preservation; its job is to deflect self-destructive tendencies away from the self outwardly toward objects. The erotic drive gets help from aggressive impulses in finding an object of desire, and in return the erotic drive keeps the aggressive instinct from destroying the very self. As Freud argued in *Mourning and Melancholy*, without an object for one's desire, grief can turn into melancholy and remorse, and aggression may return to devour the psyche.

Such a self-immolating form of religious devotion did not seem strange to Freud, whose own work led him toward the conclusion that humans are vulnerable, first of all, to a wish for their own destruction. Cautiously, he (1961: 66) concludes that "there *might* be such a thing as primary masochism." The secret that the sacred contains, then, would first of all be an insight not into the object of devotion but into the impulse toward self-sacrifice. Such a self-sacrifice would not only be a way of renouncing life in order to conquer death; it also would be a way to eliminate all the tension created by any difference or distinction between the self and any other being. As Freud (1961: 67) notes, "The dominating tendency of mental life, and perhaps of nervous life in general, is the effort to reduce, to keep constant or to remove internal tension due to stimuli . . . a tendency which finds expression in the plea-sure principle; and our recognition of that fact is one of our strongest reasons for believing in the existence of death instincts."

This interplay of opposed instincts helps Freud to explain how it is that rituals preserve a highly desired object from being destroyed by its admirers, and how adoration becomes placed even at the feet of those who represent a threat to the individual's sense of his or her own being. Freud was fascinated by chiefs who have to be humiliated and beaten before being elevated to the chieftainship or by emperors whose every move is so circumscribed by custom and ritual that their very lives are close to an imprisonment. Whether these constraints are to protect the rulers from the aggressive impulses of their admirers, or the admir-ers from the aggressive impulses of the rulers, is not at all clear. What is clear is that any gods so transcendent that their wills cannot be dis-cerned or judgments affected by any human desire or action, and who have total access to the very people who worship them, are gods of terror. Like a Fuhrer whose subjects, even those who provide him with every outward token of allegiance, may be exterminated at his command, such gods will afford their devotees no protection whatsoever against destruction.

Religion offers a small measure of protection against the terror of such immediate and infinite possibility. By consigning to the future the advent of a God whose word may destroy those who have worshipped him, and to the past the memory of a God whose word was sufficient to create or destroy a world, religion creates a present in which the devotees of such a God have time to conform their will to his, to engage in the sorts of behavior that are conducive to avoiding severe punishment, and to prepare themselves for a final day of judgment, if and when it should ever occur. The present becomes a time of grace, if also of continued and exceedingly heavy responsibility. It also becomes a time that is continually destined to pass away, as it heads into the past and gives way to the future. In that meantime however the believer lives in an extended present, under the protection of Providence, with sufficient memory, embedded in a religious worldview, to provide guidance for the foreseeable future.

The social order thus becomes relatively enchanted, as it comes to represent the very possibilities for merger and self-elimination that are inherent in the sacred itself but are now projected, under the auspices of religion, onto the "world." On the one hand, through identifying themselves with others or through incorporating and consuming the identities of others, individuals may remedy deficiencies in their sense of their own being. The "world" implies a lack of being, a sense of insufficient, partial, defective, incomplete and temporary being, and yet also of possibilities for fulfillment. Thus the social order becomes a scene in which the psyche not only seeks access to others or desires to identify with them and incorporate them into the psyche, but also seeks to destroy all others who signify its own incomplete and deficient being. The combination of these erotic and destructive impulses, played out in various social contexts, infuses them with a high level of ambiguity and ambivalence. As Freud points out, the chief or the ruler was an object not only of longing and veneration but of extraordinarily hostile impulses. Not only were people dangerous to the ruler, but he was dangerous to them. Hence the need for taboos that would simultaneously give people partial access to the chief or king but also keep their contact within strict limits. Thus as Freud (1950: 53) put it, "contact with the king is a remedy and protection against the dangers provoked by contact with the king."

The more societies reflected what Freud thought of as an animistic stage of religious development, the more enchanted was their social universe. That simply meant that every social context was a theater not only for the psyche but for its conflicting impulses, some erotic and others more evidently destructive, but both of them a threat to the very social boundaries that were required for their safe expression. The presence of conflicting desires in a single social context was expressed through ritual and made more routine through custom. Some desires continued to cause intense ambivalence, especially toward people who like ghosts, kings or strangers seemed to embody these twin and highly potent tendencies toward incorporation and destruction. The self does not thrive in the presence of too much possibility, or of far too little. The self, the psyche, emerges with some autonomy and certainty of its own being only when it is in the presence of accessible but controlled possibility. Trauma and terror, as well as emptiness, destroy the psyche.

As kingship and ethnicity become separated from politics and power-seeking, erotic desires may be expressed and contained in different institutions from those that express and contain more aggressive impulses toward control, domination, or destruction. The exercise of power itself may become more rational and less filled with ambiguity and ambivalence. Fewer constraints may be placed on a ruler, and in an entirely rational manner a bureaucratic order may limit or eliminate the livelihoods or the lives of thousands of people. Obsessive and irrational though primitive societies may have been, they contained these contrary and destructive tendencies within ritualized limits. Even savages in the midst of a war would take time out, often to their own detriment or danger, for extensive rituals of mourning for the enemies they had just slain (Freud 1950: 51). As Freud wryly goes on to point out, Americans found such natives insufficiently savage to be good allies in the settlers' own wars against the Apaches (Freud 1950: 51). When Freud came to his conclusions that the only satisfactory constraints against destructive impulses required ways of combining them with sexual desires under relatively high levels of repression, the gas chambers of Nazi Germany had not yet gone into operation, and rational, bureaucratic killing of thousands of people had not yet been perfected.

A secularized world might have a Father God who was far more reasonable, abstract, and therefore disinclined to be irrationally punitive, but
secularity also lacked traditional or primitive constraints on the asexual,
rational expression of destructive impulses.

In relatively primitive societies, then, in which taboos govern virtually
every aspect of everyday life, we would not be surprised to find people
taking extraordinary precautions against any person or situation that
arouses desire or more destructive tendencies. In relatively more secular
societies, religion, law, custom, and moral prohibitions take the place of
taboo, and these in turn are eventually replaced by even more rational
policies and procedures for approaching and gaining access to persons
and situations who may arouse both fear and desire, longing and apprehension. What primitive societies accomplished by taboos, or traditional
societies accomplished by religion, law and custom, modern societies
seek to achieve by the process of differentiation.

Whether a society uses primitive taboos to keep people together but
at a safe distance from each other, depends on how complex it is. More
complex societies use laws and customs: more general, abstract, and in
their application, more flexible than taboos. Still more complex societies
use the process of differentiation which allows particular situations to be
governed by the rules of a specialized division of labor, and which makes
it reasonable and safe for doctors and patients, politicians and business
people to be without supervision in the same room together. It is as if
the implosion of possibilities into the present in a primitive society controlled by rigid taboos, changes into a more extended present in which
some possibilities are relegated safely to the past and await the return of
ancestors, or are deferred to the future, where they await a more auspi-
cious time; the mean time becomes one in which people can temporize
by applying the insights and values of a tradition to a wider range of
circumstances. There are still situations to be avoided, even in a complex, highly differentiated society, but each sub-sector of the society, like
religion, the law, medicine, education, politics, or the economy, has its
own rules for excluding some possibilities and keeping others under
control, and these are constantly in the process of revision as people
temporize in an indefinitely extended present, in which the past offers
little guidance and the future only an uncertain set of possibilities.

As politics becomes increasingly separated from religion, those in
power lose some of their charisma and become objects less of fear and

attraction than embodiments of rational goals and values. They provide policies rather than prophecies, and their capacity either to provide satisfaction or to cause harm is increasingly subjected not only to law but to public opinion and the press. Similarly, those who practice deviant forms of spirituality or sexuality are accorded rights that have the effect of protecting them from the aggressive interests of others while protecting others from unwanted or deviant forms of religious or sexual contact. Thus the process of secularization diminishes the range of possibilities that may inhere in any particular situation; it demystifies the social context and allows one to know more clearly what to expect of any given time or place. On the other hand the same process of differentiation increases the complexity and hence adds to the possibilities that are contained in the environment. For instance, politics becomes related not only to religion but to influences stemming from the family or kinship and from the economy.

To understand Freud's thoughts about the relation of religion to society it has been necessary for us to begin with some of his basic assumptions about the subtle psychological ties that bind individuals to any social order. As Freud made clear in *Civilization and Its Discontents*, every society requires that its members give up some of their basic satisfactions. Neither can they satisfy all of their desires, nor can they attack or destroy whomever stands in the way of satisfying their wishes. Social life requires individuals to repress, or at least to suppress, many of their fondest wishes, and as a result, any social order has to cope with relatively high degrees of dissatisfaction and frustration. Without discontent there would be no civilization. A society in which the sacred is contained within religion creates the "world" filled with possibility. With less enchantment, the society will be less haunted by a sense of attractive or dangerous possibility, unless the sacred frees itself from the confines of religion and becomes once again free to appear, briefly and intensely, in the midst of the mundane.

To summarize: Civilization requires a certain renunciation of desires, and repression works. Indeed, Freud finds in the individual psyche a willingness to give up some satisfaction in the meantime for the sake, in the long term, of satisfying one's most potent desires. That is, repression works by persuading individuals that if they make the right sacrifices in the present, they will triumph in the end. Further, repression works through what Freud calls magical thinking: an "excessive valuation" attached to "psychic acts," or in other terms, "the omnipotence of thought," (1950: 105). Individuals are led, through repression and magical thinking, to believe that if they simply think the right thoughts and say the right words, engage in the right symbolic gestures and perform the right acts, they will gain their satisfactions in the end. Magical thinking buys them time, and simultaneously it saves the social order from running out of time under the pressure for the immediate fulfillment of unsatisfied human longings. Take the magical thinking away from a society's beliefs and practices, and the society will be under extreme pressure to satisfy old grievances and to fulfill ancient longings. Take the magical thinking away from the individual, and some will feel hopeless to the point of giving up life itself, while others will demand the immediate satisfaction of all their desires.

Magical thinking deprives individuals of a sense of their own being. For their own presence they substitute the totem, which in itself stands for the common bond that united individuals with each other in a community transcending the generations. To an observer, if not to the individuals themselves, it is clear that the clan that is being symbolized and enacted by the totem obscures the presence and agency of the individuals themselves, who put on the skin of the animal totem or adorn themselves with the foliage of the totem plant. It is they as individuals who are the totem, just as surely as the totem stands for their collective being and well-being. The social order deprives individuals of a sense of their own being and confers on them a surrogate identity. Individuals lose a sense of their own presence because they do not know who is doing the acting. Is it the totem, the clan itself, who is the primary agent, protecting them from all harm and assuring their survival if they in turn protect it from all harm and accord it proper respect, or is it the individuals themselves who are the agents of their own salvation precisely to the extent that they take the proper precautions to protect the totem and accord it the honors due its name?

Another reason why repression works so well, aided and abetted by the magical assumption that instinctual renunciation is necessary for eventual satisfaction, is that desires, like fears, become displaced from their original object and become focused elsewhere. The larger society thus serves as a stage in which the individual may seek satisfaction. Like a dream, social scripts, plots, and characters may offer little in a way of a clue to the underlying drama. The social play may have only an obscure relationship to the original desire, crisis, and experience of the sacred. Especially when social life becomes serious, and when individuals tend to defeat or hurt themselves, some other fear or desire than the one that is manifestly the subject of the social interaction is at stake.

Repression, then, works very well when, coupled with magical thinking, it blends personal identity with symbols of the larger society or with some totemic figure or leader, provides symbolic satisfactions with objects other than those originally desired, provides individuals with surrogate identities, and requires current renunciation for the sake of an imaginary, eventual triumph. Repression works by making people feel that they have to renounce some satisfactions in order to achieve others that they most long for: a renunciation that is exceedingly convenient for any civilization that can succeed only by inhibiting desire. Repression, combining forces with magical thinking, also works when individuals can be convinced that they are achieving some prohibited satisfactions in the course of preserving the unity and identity of the society itself. They may achieve a nearly erotic satisfaction in defending the society and its symbols against their enemies or by dissolving their identity in self-sacrifice or in death itself. Confused as to whether it is they who are acting or being acted upon, they also find fault with themselves when their own magical thinking inevitably disappoints them; it is some deficiency in their own being that seems to them to explain the failure of their words to become deeds, just as, by magical thinking, they fault themselves for thoughts and wishes that unconsciously have all the force of deeds.

Both Weber and Freud focused on magical thinking and the role of the unconscious in order to get below the surface of social and psychological life. Beneath whatever routines or rational procedures individuals may adopt for coming to terms with their worlds, underlying their adaptive strategies are thoughts and wishes that are clearly magical in origin. In Freud's terms, there is something primitive even about the modern individual who still places an inordinately high value on his own thoughts: what Freud (1950: 112) calls "intellectual narcissism and the omnipotence of thoughts." Initially, as Freud argues, humankind went through an animistic phase in its religious development, in which it really did confuse the world with its own ideas and believed in "the omnipotence of thoughts." This is an illusion, Freud argued, that still can be found among obsessives, who take responsibility for the consequences of a wish or a thought, even though they have done nothing to carry out the prohibited desire. This stage in human development is still most highly visible, however, not only among neurotic adults but also among children who, in their first, auto-erotic stage, take keen pleasure in themselves and their own bodies, as though they could satisfy their wishes and make things happen by operating in some manner upon themselves. Beyond the animistic stage of development comes the religious, in which Freud finds that people transfer their omnipotence "to the gods but do not seriously abandon it themselves, for they reserve the power of influencing the gods in a variety of ways according to their wishes." As Weber noted, at this stage religion allows the individual to take up a position over and against the world, which becomes increasingly a source not only of prohibited satisfaction and unrealized possibilities, but of danger. Only by a proper alignment of the psyche with the divine, of the individual's will with that of the deity, does a person acquire potency over and against the world and the capacity to sustain the psyche against external forces that might seduce or crush it. Under the influence of modern science, Freud argued, individuals have become accustomed to seeing the universe as impersonal, their place in it relatively small and insignificant, and their power over death nil. "None the less," Freud (1950: 110) argued, "some of the primitive belief in omnipotence still survives in men's faith in the power of the human mind, taking account, as it does, of the laws of reality."

Even in modernity, then, there are strong residues of the primitive. No matter how seriously individuals take the laws of reality and nature and see the world around them as relatively indifferent to their presence and their wishes, still there is a tendency to invest the world with the individual's own self-love. As Freud (1950: 111) puts it in his discussion of narcissism, "A human being remains to some extent narcissistic even after he has found external objects for his libido." It is as if the modern individual is an incurable romantic. On the one hand, romantics continue to believe that the world is somehow there to satisfy their desires. The world is aware of them and responsive to their wishes. On the other hand, romantics are enamored of their own thoughts about the world and believe, against all the evidence, that wishing will make them true. Like Weber's charismatic leader, they believe that the deity is with them and will prosper them and give them victory over all their enemies, and they gain followers precisely among those who still harbor a sense of the omnipotence of their own wishes and thoughts. No matter how limited and shrunken is the sense of possibility offered by the larger society, the psyche is a perennial source of a longing for possibilities far beyond the reach of what social reality has to offer.

No one could be more the romantic than the individual who believes that he or she is chosen by God for an extraordinary destiny and will be immune to the dangers and disappointments that afflict more ordinary mortals. Consider these words of Freud, however, as the warning of a Jew who could see the gathering forces of fascism and anti-Semitism in the Europe of his day: a warning to all those who could not believe the evidence before their eyes. Speaking of narcissism as a way of taking erotic pleasure, or of investing self-love, in one's own thoughts, Freud (1950: 112) reminds us of the primitives' belief "in the omnipotence of thoughts, their unshakeable confidence in the possibility of controlling the world and their inaccessibility to the experiences, so easily obtainable, which could teach them man's true position in the universe." Belief in such infinite possibility dies slowly over the course of centuries of secularization.

As with children, so it is with the world of primitive, animistic religion: "In the animistic epoch the reflection of the internal world is bound to blot out the other picture of the world – the one which *we* seem to perceive" (Freud 1950: 106). The world as we imagine it becomes the world as it is, and it is nothing more or less than a reflection of ourselves: our strengths and weaknesses attributed to friends and neighbors, the community and the larger society, to nature and even the cosmos. The world becomes what Weber thought was the object of the prophetic imagination: a world sorely in need of ordering and improvement by the creative action of the individual will. Weber's world of antiquity, in which a self emerges who is drawing on deeply mystical sources of identity and power, and who confronts the world with an ethical imagination that refuses to accept the world as it is and demands that it conform with the individual's sense of ideal or ultimate ends, is a world of animists.

The world is not only a reflection of the self, but a reflection on the self. Weber's ethical prophet, like Freud's magician, takes on responsibility for shaping a world that he or she cannot control. The inevitable result is a sense of doubt about one's own virtues or power: a sense of the deficiency of one's own being. That is because, as Freud (1950: 106) puts it, "A general over-valuation has thus come about of all mental processes," especially of those "psychical acts which are subject to the will." For instance, those who try but fail to achieve their object have only themselves to blame, if, in accordance with their own magical thinking, they initially possessed the power to make the world conform to their desires. The fundamental neurosis then develops as a state of the ethical consciousness, in which individuals feel guilt for conditions of the world over which they have no real control but for which they feel responsible. The notion of sin becomes possible.

Freud (1950: 119), in a passage describing the layers of meaning in a dream, speaks of "the nature and pretensions of a system." Here he has in mind the way a dream may originally have had a logic of its own, with thoughts connected meaningfully in some manner, but these connections become lost as the dream unfolds and is later remembered. What the dream seems to be about may thus have little or nothing to do with its original content, with the essential "dream-thoughts," which have their own "meaning, connection and order." These are superseded by the "manifest content of the dream" in which the original dream-thoughts "are almost invariably arranged in a new order more or less independent of the earlier arrangement" (Freud 1950: 118). Finally, as if a radical editor were at work on the manuscript of the dream, something called "secondary revision" takes place which effectively produces an altogether new system of meaning. It is this system of which Freud was speaking when he referred to "the nature and pretensions of a system." What the manifest context of the dream is to the dream's underlying meaning, religion is to the passions embodied in the sacred.

Compare religion not only to a dream but to a fully developed neurosis or even a phobia, far removed from its original sources in the sacred. These are now available only on the basis of religious assumptions and delusions, and religion's own complex set of associations, most of which owe their origins to magical thinking. The corresponding task of the sociologist of religion is, therefore, to listen carefully to a system such as a society's civil religion and work back through the layers of editing and reinterpretation to the original experience of the sacred, perhaps clustered around a crisis or traumatic event, from which later versions have evolved in the form of religious beliefs. In so doing, the sociologist of religion does well to remember Freud's (1950: 119) comment that "There is an intellectual function in us which demands unity, connection and intelligibility from any material, whether of perception or thought, that comes within its grasp; and if, as a result of special circumstances, it is unable to establish a true connection, it does not hesitate to establish a false one."

Freud's comment applies, of course, to cultural systems in which people may develop a sense of their own uniqueness and superiority, of their entitlement to land or to domination, as a result of earlier sufferings at the hands of unscrupulous overlords and enemies. However, the comment also applies to sociologists of religion who seek to put the pieces of a cultural puzzle together in such a way as to develop a coherent and meaningful picture of a people's history, beliefs, values, and practices. Paranoia shares with cultural analysis a search for connections, patterns, and meaning. Therefore the sociologist must be careful who imagines that, by diagnosing and understanding the religious beliefs of a social system, it is possible to perceive hidden patterns, debunk popular delusions, restore people to a realistic appraisal of their history and condition, and open up a future of reasonable expectation.

When Freud speaks of an "intellectual function" that seeks "unity, connection and intelligibility" in our experience, he is evoking not only the ego, which scans the horizon and keeps watch over the psyche's inner landscape, but also magical thinking. There is in each of us, he suggests, a tendency to make strange sights or people familiar, by projecting into them our own desires and fears, or by identifying with them altogether. In that way we can feel a sense of connection, overcome the feeling of being aliens in an alien territory, and even have the illusion of possessing some control over our surroundings and our future. It is not only the magician or the primitive, then, or even the neurotic, but the intellectual or theoretician who may well be engaged in magical thinking or who trusts in the "omnipotence of thought."

References

(1950) *Totem and Taboo*. The Standard Edition. Translated and edited by James Strachey. With a Biographical Introduction by Peter Gay. New York and London: W. W. Norton and Company.

(1955) *Moses and Monotheism*. Translated by Katherine Jones. New York: Vintage Books,.

(1961) *Beyond the Pleasure Principle*. Translated and edited by James Strachey. Introduction by Gregory Zilboorg. With a Biographical Introduction by Peter Gay. New York and London: W. W. Norton and Company.

(1962) *Civilization and Its Discontents*, Translated and edited by James Strachey. New York: W. W. Norton and Company.

Max Weber

Max Weber (1864–1920), clearly a contemporary of both Freud and Durkheim, seems to have worked independently of them, although Weber's interest in the unconscious may well have owed something to the ideas of the Austrian doctor and his new discipline of psycho-analysis. Weber's systematic treatment of religion and economics in India, China, Rome, and Israel lies beyond the scope of this essay, and yet it is in these studies that we can see him elaborating and testing his provocative thesis on the role of the Protestant Ethic in reinforcing West-ern tendencies to develop a spirit or ethos conducive to capitalist devel-opment: a thesis for which he found additional support in his studies of Protestant sects in the United States of America. Weber used the notion of "disenchantment" to describe a society whose ways and means, whose goals and values were far more rational than either emotional or traditional, and who felt that the world could be studied on its own terms without reference to hidden, mysterious, or supernatural pres-ences, influences, or causes. Neither a German nationalist, a Marxist, nor a convinced Protestant, Weber wanted the politicians and the sociologists alike to study and engage the world through an under-standing of the complex ways in which individuals sought more or less rationally to relate means to goals and objectives, values and ends.

At the heart of Weber's contribution to the sociology of religion is an argument about the extreme, personal and existential loneliness of the individual in Western societies who has come under the influence of ascetic Protestantism. Speaking of the doctrine of predestination, Weber wrote that salvation was impossible to attain, if one had not already been granted it, and impossible to forfeit if one had been granted it, and yet one was responsible for acting with a certainty of one's election that one could not possibly have. "In its extreme inhumanity," wrote Weber (1996: 104), "this doctrine must above all have had one conse-quence for the life of a generation which surrendered to its magnificent consistency. There was a feeling of unprecedented inner loneliness of the single individual. In what was for the man of the age of the Reformation the most important thing in life, his eternal salvation, he was forced to follow his path alone to meet a destiny which had been decreed for him from eternity." No ritual could confer comfort and certainty to the lonely seeker without strong personal attachments, personal friendships (which were to be distrusted), the confessional, or any form of emotional, even ecstatic release, because of what Weber (1996: 105–06) called "the entirely negative attitude of Puritanism to all the sensuous and emotional elements in culture and in religion." Worst of all, perhaps, was the fact that this loneliness was a self-inflicted wound suffered by those who were claiming a grandiose, even an aristocratic sense of entitlement.

The aristocratic element in the Protestant ethic was derived from an imitation of a God whose sovereignty was exercised in the most imper-sonal, rational, purposeful, consistent, systematic and organized fash-ion. Thus those devoted to the monastic way of life had long constituted a spiritual aristocracy of self-disciplined, purposeful, organized behavior for service of the community, devoted only and entirely to the greater glory of God. In the Reformation, Weber (1996: 121–22) argued, this monastic elite gave way to "an aristocracy which, with its *character indelibis*, was divided from the eternally damned remainder of humanity by a more impassable and in its invisibility more terrifying gulf" than any that had "separated the monk of the Middle Ages from the rest of the world about him, a gulf which penetrated all social relations with its sharp brutality."

Being a member of this spiritual nobility, however, entailed a number of serious obligations. To begin with, one was required to put one's cer-tainty of salvation, such as it was, to the test. Calvinism, Weber (1996: 121) noted, asserted "the necessity of proving one's faith in worldly activity." The force of asceticism, then, was no longer to be drained from the world into the monastery but to flow back through all the channels of everyday life. The aristocrats constituting the spiritual elect now, in a posture of supreme noblesse oblige, were "forced to pursue their ascetic ideals within mundane occupations" (Weber 1996: 121).

More was involved however, than the effort of a self-proclaimed spiritual nobility to prove its credentials by applying themselves to the tasks of improving everyday life. What was at stake here was an ethic that intended the total transformation of the individual and of social life. As Weber (1996: 118) put it, what was required was "a fundamental change in the whole meaning of life at every moment and in every action." Only such a transformation could prove that the individual had left the state of nature and entered the state of grace. The paradoxes thus abounded. A religious ethic now left the individual radically alone, without the usual comforts, connections and reassurances of religion and everyday life. A profound religious certainty produced a radical uncertainty that only a transfigured life and a transformed social order could relieve.

For sociologists of religion, Weber's thesis exposes a dynamic relationship between the sacred, represented by the claim to charismatic endowment, and the secular. That relationship may be one of radical opposition, in that there is no way that those who have not been the recipient of divine grace can alter their condition or join the ranks of the elect, just as there is no way that the elect, whatever their behavior, may be reduced to the ranks of those who are destined to eternal damnation. This radical opposition, however, requires that the elect seek an opportunity to demonstrate to others and to themselves the certainty of their election. Everyday life and the mundane then become a theater of the soul, which requires rational, self-disciplined, and purposeful action in every department of social life and in all aspects of the individual psyche and character. In this attempt to put their charismatic claims to the test, the elect opened up a range of possibility for the sacred in the midst of the secular, just as it opened a range of possibility for the secular in the midst of the sacred. That is, religious life could become as potentially mundane as everyday life itself could become potentially sacred. In this creative tension between the sacred and the secular the worship and the life of the church could become utilitarian, disenchanted, and practical, while the world of work could become infused with religious meaning and sacred purpose. Furthermore, in the process of translating religious meanings and sacred purposes into the world of work, much might become lost in translation, and yet the world of getting and spending would also take on the language and the meanings associated with the church, such as mission, ministry, and office.

In this dialectic between the sacred and the secular, what is excluded in one way comes back to haunt the social system in another. The transcendent God, raised far above the mundane and everyday life, comes back as a divine will that requires the impersonal, rational, and purposeful organization of everyday life. Thus Weber argued that, even with the Protestant Ethic, this form of "inner-worldly asceticism" would not have produced modern capitalism in the West if it had not been for the emergence of large scale bureaucracies. As Randall Collins (Weber 1996: xxv) puts it in his introduction to Weber's *The Protestant Ethic and the Spirit of Capitalism*, "Bureaucracy is one of the ingredients leading to rational capitalism, but standing alone it acted more as a negative factor. Hence bureaucracy had to be counterbalanced by yet another factor: there needed to be a certain degree of democracy, an institution of the rights of citizens, and this had to be manifested in a legal system that protected private property. Only through this balance could government bureaucracy be turned into a support for rational capitalism."

The individual, who can do nothing to improve his or her fate in this world, comes back as the autonomous citizen whose decisions become essential to the conduct of government. Thus the very personal considerations excluded from the rule of bureaucracy had to be recovered in the form of individuals acting on their behalf as citizens claiming their rights under the law over and against the rules and requirements of bureaucratic administrations. Those who are not among the elect become, in effect, those who elect their own democratic governments. Even though in the United States the electorate has the popular vote, of course, there is still a residue of the distinction between the elect and the nonelect in the college of the electors who have the final say on who will hold office, regardless of the will of the mass of the people. As Randall Collins (Weber 1996: xxiv) goes on to say in his introduction to Weber's *The Protestant Ethic and the Spirit of Capitalism*, "this is a book about 'the Protestant Ethic and the American way of life.' " By that he (1996: xxv) means that many Protestant groups that interested Weber, the Quakers, the Baptists and the Methodists, for instance, in addition to the Puritans, "left their distinctive marks upon our lifestyle. Weber points out, for instance, that the doctrine of separation of church and state came from these sects, and he refers to the way in which they fostered a decentralized democracy and a distrust of centralized government. Weber comments on the puritan tendency to dislike art but to admire science, as well as the puritan rationale for rejecting charity to the poor as incompatible with predestined salvation or damnation." That there are other tendencies in American social life, and that even a government imbued with evangelical Christian ideas can be expansive or exhibit anti-democratic tendencies would not alter the fact that the sacred, in the form of the Protestant Ethic, has been in creative tension with the secular in modern society and particularly in the United States of America. In that tension it has opened up spaces in which religious predispositions and preferences have an effect on public policy, just as public policy continues to erode the evangelical preference for a sharp separation between church and state.

Before going further into Weber's sociology of religion it is important to see how Randall Collins places Weber's *The Protestant Ethic and the Spirit of Capitalism* in the context of his comparative studies of Western and Eastern religion and social systems. Weber gradually altered his interest in the Protestant Ethic into a concern with "inner-worldly asceticism," a more abstract concept that allowed him to see the same principles at work in the Catholic monasteries that initiated capitalism in the West during the Middle Ages. The same concept also enabled students of Weber to find in the Buddhist monastic orders of Japan comparable tendencies toward disciplined work, saving, technological innovation, and the reinvestment of profits in order to sustain growth over long periods of time. Thus Weber's argument could just as well be stated as finding in monastic disciplines not only the seeds but the first fruits of capitalism in both the East and the West. Indeed, this is precisely Collins's point when he (Weber 1996: xxviii) states that "Weber noted that Calvinistic businessmen, by their hard work and frugality, ploughing back their profits into business, ended up becoming rich. The same thing happened to the Catholic monasteries: their asceticism, with the accumulation of gains ploughed back into monastic property, made them rich. The rest of the dialectic also took place. With richness came laxness and corruption; after a few hundred years, the original spirit of the medieval Catholic ethic was lost. By the early 1500s, the church, as Martin Luther viewed it, was fat and greedy, without redeeming religious merit. It was time to abolish the monasteries. When this happened, a new wave of religious motivation was set off, followed by the expansion of full-scale, mass-production capitalism." Indeed, Collins (Weber 1996: xviii–ix) suggests that the rise of evangelical religion around the world in the late twentieth and early twenty first centuries is possibly the beginning of the third wave of inner-worldly asceticism, which will result in a further capitalist development on a global scale.

Following Collins, then, we may summarize Weber's argument about the Protestant Ethic by saying that the ethic was one component among the factors leading to Western capitalism, and that it depended for its effects on interacting with such other factors as democracy and the rule of law. Capitalism would not have developed so far in the West or so fast had it not been that individuals in the West consider themselves to be the repository of important rights, including those to life, liberty, and the pursuit of happiness. However, the sense that the individual herself has direct access to the ultimate ground of rights is only part of the picture that fascinated Max Weber and continues to absorb the attention of sociologists of religion. Western individuals also tend to carry with them an ethic of responsibility; the individual is supposed to work for the good of others; Emerson's individualists, after all, were people who devoted their lives to building the institutions of the community, and Weber pictured the Western individualist as some-one who could be trusted with other people's money because she was as good as her word and only took carefully planned and disciplined risks. In addition to a responsible voluntarism, the Western individual is also expected to be fairly rational: to figure out the right relationship of means to ends. That is, the right exercise of individuality is known by its fruits, which are to be some form of moral or causal order.

How is it, then, that with such fundamental rights, Westerners bear heavy responsibilities for creating and maintaining a moral and effective society? In the West, the individual is the one in whose name or on whose behalf all political sovereignty is exercised and legitimated. How is it, then, that individuals are called on to surrender their wills and make sacrifices? There is no way really to answer these questions unless we remember Weber's argument that the electorate in the West initially was populated by all those who were not elect, by the vast majority of individuals who knew they were not predestined to salvation, and who could do nothing to improve their fate. This extremely inhuman doc-trine, then, and the loneliness and isolation it imposed on the individual still return to haunt the modern individual who is thought to be the repository of legal rights and democratic responsibilities. It may well be that the individual is, after all, expendable, and that that is the reason why impersonal organizations that confine individuals in a network of rules and responsibilities are the inevitable outgrowth of a belief in a God whose rule was as impersonal and purposive as it was autocratic.

If individuals are entitled to life, liberty, and the pursuit of happiness, why is it that they work so hard for so long, reinvest their savings in houses and stocks whose value will only accumulate slowly over a long period of time, and feel responsible for having something to show for themselves at the end of their lives? Rationality, whether religious or secular, requires even those individuals who believe themselves chosen by god to take responsibility for the consequences of their actions and to know the proper means to achieve ends. There is still plenty of magic, recklessness and gambling in the West, but they are not practiced as such in doctor's offices, classrooms, law courts, and banks. How does it happen that one is able to expect so much accountability from individuals who have the right to claim access to divine revelation and are the carriers of popular sovereignty?

That question has been asked in many ways, not only by Max Weber but by anyone who, like Rousseau, observed that humans were born free but are everywhere in chains. For Weber the question had to do with how it came to be that individuals who had been endowed with so many spiritual gifts or rights, and who carried political sovereignty should end up in what he called "an iron cage." Max Weber was therefore fascinated by those who were inordinately sure of themselves. In describing what he called "the sense of honor or superiority characteristic of the non-priestly classes that claimed the highest social privileges, particularly the nobility" he spoke of their sense of possessing an "underived, ultimate, and qualitatively distinctive being" (1964: 106). These are strong words, and they connote a sense of extraordinary and substantial presence. However Weber was also fascinated by the way in which the Protestant Ethic derived from a belief in the ultimate worthlessness of individuals apart from the grace of God and from a doctrine that consigned the vast mass of humanity to damnation except for the few who were chosen by God from the beginning for ultimate salvation. There is a dialectic in Western civilization, then, between these two notions of the individual: the one as sovereign with a being that is authoritative, substantial, and underived; the other of the individual as being unable to do anything to effect a salvation that is beyond the reach of the vast majority of human beings.

This dialectic had its origins, Weber argues, in classical antiquity. Weber identified tendencies in classical Greek and Roman civilization which, taken together, have shaped both the authoritarian and the democratic developments of Western politics and religion. One of these is the emergence of an individual in the shifting, even chaotic social networks and environments of urban Greece and Rome, where individuals would necessarily confront a world of such complexity and ambiguity that they would require some technique for mental ordering: a rationale, a sense of pattern, an answer to the question of significance, and a transcendent viewpoint from which to place individuals and orient their action. In the West, according to Weber, the individual emerged as an ethical being placed over and against a welter of complex and changing circumstances that required being placed in a moral and causal order.

Consider also what authority was once afforded by the notion of a predestined life. For Weber (1964: 202), the doctrine of predestination "provides the individual who has found religious grace with the highest possible degree of certainty of salvation, once he has attained assurance that he belongs to the very limited aristocracy of salvation who are elect." Note that Weber employs the metaphor of aristocracy here very carefully. Clearly the religious doctrine of election is a way of displacing envy and class consciousness from direct conflict among classes or status groups to a moral battlefield. However, not all forms of predestination result in such a displacement. Weber notes that, in the earliest stages of Islam, the conviction of predestination gave Islamic warriors confidence in their right to conquest and their inevitable triumph over the enemies of God. For them, as for Calvinists, the result of believing in predestination was relief from self-concern and a sense of certainty about their own being. If their being is not entirely an "underived, ultimate, and qualitatively distinctive *being*," at least its legitimacy and endurance are guaranteed. As Weber (1964: 203) puts it, those who believe in their predestination, whether they are Calvinists or Islamic warriors, are marked by "a complete obliviousness to self."

However, Weber also understood that delusions of grandeur, like predestination or election, leave individuals with a chronic sense that they have something to prove. Because religion often carried forward beliefs and values of an undisclosed aristocratic origin, individuals would be burdened with aristocratic obligations to lead an ordered and moral life commensurate with an acquired nobility of soul. Let us return to the doctrine of predestination. In itself an aristocratic ethic, the doctrine assures individuals of an enduring place in the nature of the universe but requires of them a life-long obligation to order their lives in the light of an ethic of responsibility. In return for the guarantee of transcending death, the doctrine requires those predestined to salvation to spend their lives putting their houses in order: a spiritual *noblesse oblige*.

So long as individuals believed in their own predestination, they had a reason to develop what Weber (1964: 206) called "an ethic based on an inner religious mood and oriented to ultimate ends." No wonder that individuals developed what Weber (1964: 114) called "a system-atic, rational, methodical pattern of life (the only possible source of the *certitudo salutis*)," or "the sense of inner-worldly asceticism," and it was far more characteristic, he argued, of the Puritan than of the Jew. For those who have the comfort of rituals, it is possible to know exactly how to do the right things in the right way at the right time: a knowl-edge that Weber (1964: 209) called "stereotypy." For everyone else, there is living in the right way through the methodical conduct of every-day life over a lifetime of moral endeavor. That requires something far more advanced than a set of rituals or even of laws that specify what to do in various contexts. What must evolve is a set of principles abstract enough to cover a wide range of situations, and an independent psyche or character inwardly developed enough to take responsibility for apply-ing those principles creatively and flexibly according to the possibilities and constraints in various contexts (Weber 1964: 209).

In the same context, Weber (1964: 114) speaks compellingly of "a desperate struggle, no longer for the respect of others, but for self-respect and a sense of personal worth," and he knows of a certain "despair at finding any meaning in this world of vanity." He is speaking of the post-exilic Jew, but that same struggle and despair characterize for Weber the modern individual who is still saddled with an ethic of lifelong responsibility but lacks the authorization once provided by being chosen by God and thus being predestined to triumph over death in the end.

For Weber, to achieve that sense of the self without belief in a god requires a certain kind of heroism that is beyond the reach of a modern individual, who knows that he lacks a basis in the order of things. However, the individual is still burdened by the residues of an ethic that requires one to act in a systematic and orderly fashion toward the achievement of ultimate ends. The burden of lifelong obligation remains, although few now have the assurance that their own being is anchored in a cosmic moral order or that they have been chosen to be the instrument for great things within a divine purpose. Whereas the doctrine of predestination gave them confidence to act systematically over a life time toward the achievement of ends that transcended their lifetime and were rooted in the divine will, modern individuals know that their very being is called into question, and their actions may not be oriented toward ultimate ends or even achieve their desired effects. As Weber (1964: 206) puts it, "it is not that he is guilty of having done any particular act, but that by virtue of his unalterable idiosyncrasy he 'is' as he is, so that he is compelled to perform the act in spite of himself, as it were – this is the secret anguish that modern man bears."

The sense of possession of an "underived, ultimate, and qualitatively distinctive" being may also distinguish the noble warrior. Under the influence of "prophetic religion," Weber (1964: 86) notes, warriors could be persuaded to direct their aggressions away from their own people toward outsiders whose being is allegedly deficient or defective. Speaking of Islam, Weber notes a "direct connection between religious promises and war against religious infidelity" (Weber 1964: 86). It was a connection originally based, however, on the transformation of promises to the Jewish people. Instead of merely taking possession of a Promised Land, the "people of Yahweh" would be entitled to the satisfaction of being elevated "above other nations. In the future all nations would be compelled to serve Yahweh and to lie at the feet of Israel" (Weber 1964: 87). Thus the resentment of people who had too long been subordinated to alien landlords or subjected by alien peoples combined with the presumptions of a warrior nobility to a superior form of being. Now it was not only the poor who were entitled, or their betters among the nobility, but an entire "people of Yahweh, as his special community, [who] demonstrated and exemplified their god's prestige against their foes" (Weber 1964: 87). Whether you regard this from a Marxian viewpoint as a way of exporting class conflict between the nobles and the poor, or from a psychoanalytic viewpoint as a way of inflating the narcissism of small differences among neighboring peoples, the effect is the same. A nation imagines itself as the carrier of an extraordinary and superior being. As Weber (1964: 86) points out, such presumption "assumes the existence of a universal god and the moral depravity of unbelievers who are his adversaries and whose untroubled existence arouses his righteous indignation." It is their very being that becomes intolerable.

It was precisely from this sense of being part of a predestined, chosen nation that the West derived a secular sense of its own being as ineradicably deficient: derived, rather than underived, qualitatively not very distinctive, based on a distinction that could be discerned only in the mind of God. According to Weber (1964: 206) "there is no significant possibility of 'forgiveness,' 'contrition,' or 'restitution' – in much the same way that these human qualities were impossible under the religious belief in predestination, with its picture of a mysterious divine plan."

Contrast the road, if we follow Weber, that begins with the assertion of a selfhood, an innermost being, that is beyond the requirements and inducements of everyday life. Weber (1964: 47) notes that what distinguished Jesus was "the magical charisma he felt within himself. It was doubtless this consciousness of power, more than anything else, that enabled him to traverse the road of the prophets." The prophet's being is his work; the message is an end in itself. Therefore the true prophet will not accept any money or other forms of reimbursement, and there is no way to separate the message from the messenger.

Prophecy arose, according to Weber, at a time when individuals were finding their own bases of selfhood in mystery cults, with their mixtures of intense emotional experience and speculation about the nature of life and of the cosmos. In a time when communities were invaded from the outside by a flow of ideas and people, currency and goods, and when large cities placed relative strangers in close proximity to one another, individuals had direct experience of a complex and diverse, ambiguous and uncertain world. Overwhelmed by a surplus of meaning and possibility, individuals were driven more deeply into themselves to find a basis for their own being and a place for themselves in the larger society and the cosmos. Only a god can claim to possess being that does not derive from some other; Christians have long sought to defend the divinity of Jesus Christ by claiming that he was "begotten, not made" and that he was "of one substance with the Father," not a mere emanation.

To put it another way: One of the tasks of any society is to reduce the possibilities that are always and everywhere inherent in any social system to manageable proportions. Individuals as well as societies may be overwhelmed by a sense of possibility and by the knowledge or imagination of a wide range of possible threats and opportunities. The less a society is able to structure a present in which many of these possibilities are relegated to the past or deferred to the future, the more pressure is placed on the individual psyche to govern the self, to respond to dangers and attractions, and to construct his or her own sense of the present. Under extreme conditions, when the social order is unable to limit the sense of the possible, the individual is placed in the situation of one who, like God, can embody possibility and encompass both opportunity and danger. These are the conditions conducive to various kinds of religious movements that promote self-divination.

As Weber (1964: 48) put it, "Emotional cults, emotional prophecy based on 'speaking with tongues,' and highly valued intoxicating ecstasy grew with the evolving theological rationalism (Hesiod). . . . The growth of these emotional cults paralleled both overseas colonization and, above, all, the formation of cities and the transformation of the *polis* which resulted from the development of a citizen army." We will return to precisely such a combination of intense inward religious experience and a complex, highly mobile population of urbanized people when we take up the work of David Martin on modern Pentecostalism later in this book. Here the point is simply that religion in the West was shaped by a world that undermines very conventional or traditional sources of personal identity: a world that therefore produced a search for a radical, irreducible, underived, ultimately authentic basis for one's own being, as well as a God who could easily dispense with the vast majority of individuals.

When individuals are overwhelmed by possibilities, the present itself seems exposed to claims from the past and intrusions from the future, and in such a world their own presence is exceedingly difficult to sense, to create, or maintain. What sort of individual could possibly comprehend and order a world in which crisis was endemic and the sacred in such high demand? It was a complex and challenging world that quite literally brought global influences into one's own immediate neighborhood and family. It was a world so complex that it challenged the religious imagination, and it was so lacking in order that it could only be shaped by the strongest of wills. Weber (1964: 56) in fact traces "a causal connection" between the Near-Eastern notion of a "personal, transcendental and ethical god" and the "all-powerful mundane king with his rational bureaucratic regime." The entire social order, then, emanates from the experience of a monarch whose being permeates every social relationship and indeed the order of nature itself. As Weber (1964: 57) put it, the notion of the world as being created out of nothing comes from the Near East, where out of the desert crops were developed where there had been only sand and arid soil. The difference was made by the monarch, whose control over the flow of water and whose irrigation systems literally made flowers bloom in the desert. As Weber put it, "The monarch even created law by legislation and rationalization, a development the world experienced for the first time in Mesopotamia. It seems quite reasonable, therefore, that as a result of such experiences the ordering of the world should be conceived as the law of a freely acting, transcendental and personal god."

At the heart of the religions that emerged from the Near East then, is the recollection of a being who embodied action, and from whom the entire social order emerged. In his being the nature of things was revealed, and disturbances both in the society and nature could be traced, therefore, to a deficiency in the monarch's being, for, as Weber (1964: 57) put it, "it was always assumed that the reason for the excitation of the spirits and the disturbances of the cosmic order had to be sought either in the personal dereliction of the monarch or in some manifestation of social disorganization." It is a very simple idea, but its implications for the sociology of religion have yet to be fully explored.

Weber therefore noted that in the ancient Near East, the monarchs' presence and will were the primary basis for social order, and they embodied possibility. Their reigns constituted the present era, and their presence alone was entirely authoritative and authentic. No wonder, then, that their very being gave rise to the notion of a transcendent, personal, and ethical god. Western religion therefore emerged in the creative tension between the idea of the individual with direct personal access to divinity and the idea of a sovereign whose very being was the primary basis of all social order. Both individuals and monarchs were to be supremely personal, ethical and to enjoy transcendence, although the individual was to submit to the monarch. The result of this dynamic relationship between sovereignty and personhood was the notion that individuals possess political sovereignty, have direct access to divine inspiration, and are the repository of civil and political rights. Individuals themselves are underived and *sui generis*. These are precisely the characteristics, as we have seen, of the sectarian religious movements that comprised the Reformation, introduced pressure for democratic forms, initiated a rule of law, and fostered the initiatives required for a more expansive and systematic form of capitalism.

How is it, then, that individuals have so many responsibilities and obligations? How is it that good intentions go awry, and means become confused with ends? How is it that the relationship of causes to consequences remains problematical in social life, and that actions often have tragic, unintended consequences? The answer to such questions took Weber to an examination of the sacred in its many forms and appearances. Weber focused on individuals with unique grace or charisma, whose very being seems to be *sui generis* rather than an instance of some more general principle or occurrence. Even if they are not created out of nothing, not begotten, still they seem to have direct access to the sources of life. Underived, they rule either by aristocratic birthright or because they have been chosen by some higher being for a reason that transcends all speculation and calculation, and they serve an end that is always ultimate. They have presence, embody the possibilities open to the social order, and define the times, separating the present from both the future and the past. As embodiments of the sacred, their very presence creates a crisis. Things will not be the same again, and they embody a form of the sacred that is as personal and as practical as it is particular to themselves.

Not to be confused with anything else or reduced to being a mere case of some more general occurrence, the sacred is always unique and irreplaceable. The sacred is not a by-product or offshoot of something else; it is *sui generis*: begotten, not made. Because the sacred embodies a subset of the realm of total possibility, of the transcendent, there is no higher priority than to recognize it and to give the sacred its due. The sacred person thus always represents a moment that is critical and potentially momentous. Because the sources of its uncanny power are not obvious, the sacred is known only through revelation. Transparency belongs to the secular world, where psyches, rational procedures, and business accounts should be open to inspection. The sacred, however, is both a means and an end; any question of how to choose the right means to the ultimate end is resolved by revelation, by message or example. As Weber noted, charismatic leaders are subject to failure when put to the test. Thus the sacred is originally embedded in practical concerns and rational procedure.

There is inevitable tension between the sacred and its opposite. If the individual's psyche, his or her very being, is sacred, then it is "the world" that is by definition secular. Being secular, "the world" is temporary and needs to be ordered by some transcendent purpose that will stand the test of time. In Weber's (1964: 59) view, prophetic religion therefore requires its followers to develop such an orientation toward the transcendental : "a unified view of the world derived from a consciously integrated and meaningful attitude toward life. To the prophet, both the life of man and the world, both social and cosmic events, have a certain systematic and coherent meaning." The sacred needs to be placed in a larger and more enduring context by religion. Thus it is up to the individual to discern that transcendent meaning through the prophet's revelation and to live a disciplined life in accordance with and conducive to the prophetic pattern. As Weber (1964: 59) put it, "The whole conception is dominated, not by logical consistency, but by practical valuations. Yet it always denotes, regardless of any variations in scope and in measure of success, an effort to systematize all the manifestations of life; that is, to organize practical behavior into a direction of life, regardless of the form it may assume in any individual case." The practical yields to the moral, the personal to the collective, the immediate and the local to the more distant, more abstract, and more universal.

To order behavior into a system requires a certain rationality: a set of reasons that may be applied from the general to the particular, and from the abstract to the specific. The more general and abstract religion becomes, however, the more it loses the sacred with its roots in everyday life. As abstract religion is applied on a case to case basis, the focus of attention turns from behavior in general to specific acts, and from an emphasis on inwardness to external circumstances (Weber 1964: 76–77). Religion is not at home in the world of the mundane and practical that gives rise to the sacred.

The attempt to "organize practical behavior into a direction of life" prompts religion to defeat itself by its own successes. The problem begins when the priesthood tries to wean the laity from the prophetic religion that has given them a sense of their place in the world and a moral ground on which to stand in their confrontations with that world, with the powers that be, and with their "superiors." The priesthood needs to deprive the laity of a sense of their own underived and authentic presence in the world, to mediate their access to figures like charismatic leaders or monarchs whose very presence embodies the plenitude of all legitimate possibility, and to redefine the relationship of the present to both the future and the past. Otherwise the laity would have a claim to their own personal and particular sources of sacred inspiration and authority.

In other words, there is a continuing contest for ownership and control of the sacred, for that which is ultimate and cannot be reduced to something else, but which derives its authority from its own being. In the West, Weber argues, that contest has been worked out in the social space created by religious congregations. There, as with the Jews returning to Jerusalem under the auspices of Cyrus, the congregation became a place where a priestly clientele would pacify the Jews enough to exact tribute and loyalty from them over time. "Political associations were annihilated and the population disarmed . . . the religious congregation was regarded as a valuable instrument for pacifying the conquered" (Weber 1964: 63). In the congregation, however, were gathered Jews under the influence of prophets who demanded of them a higher loyalty to a transcendent god, and who placed them under the obligation to order all the aspects of their lives according to that transcendent ethical principle.

In every religious congregation, therefore, the priesthood had to face the forms of the sacred embraced by the laity: "prophecy," "traditionalism," and "lay intellectualism" (Weber 1964: 65). The congregation thus became a place where the sacred was contested, and in that contest the priests laid their own claims to the ownership and control of the sacred: claims dishonored by the laity under the influence of prophets who, "by virtue of their rejection of magic, were necessarily skeptical of the priestly enterprise, though by varying degrees and fashions" (Weber 1964: 66). In many respects congregations in the West are still divided over these competing, conflicting and principled orientations toward the social uses of the sacred in everyday life.

Under the auspices of religion, or, as Weber put it, when the sacred becomes institutionalized in a set of beliefs and practices carried by a community under the leadership of a legitimate authority, the sacred loses its home in the mundane and the practical. The "world" becomes by definition either profane or secular. That "world" is thus both temporal and temporary, ordinary and mundane, expendable and ephemeral, destined above all not to last: precisely what it was before, but now deprived of the sacred. Now, to be relevant to the life of the laity, priestly religion has to become practical. To be authoritative, however, priestly religion has to legitimate the hierarchy of the higher priests over the lower priests and of the priests in general over the laity, (Weber 1964: 73–74). To bridge the gaps created by this hierarchy, and in the pursuit of relevance, priestly religion has to replace the laity's sources of sacred inspiration with canonical literature, but to do so immediately creates a "secular" literature that is a rival to the priestly code (Weber 1964: 69). To convince the laity that they want and need to support the priests, the laity need to be persuaded that in joining the priest's organization they are acquiring a moral or spiritual advantage over nonmembers: a purchase on transcendence and a surer footing in the world that will not pass away (Weber 1964: 70).

Under the auspices of religion, the sacred becomes a relational term that depends for its meaning on the possibility of being negated by either the secular or the profane. For instance, priestly religion has to create a secular world that consists of the external and of the mundane and everyday. Thus the priesthood sought to distinguish themselves from the laity, to create an organization in which the priests have superiority and control over the laity, to suppress the laity's sources of inspiration and authority, to discredit those outside the priestly organization, to persuade the laity that the priestly code is relevant to their everyday life, to devalue the laity's revelations and codes of behavior, to create classes of people and groups who will not stand the test of time, and to devise ritual to simulate the sacred as a critical moment with its own immediacy and relevance to the person, the practical, and the place.

Even priestly religion has built into its own dynamic a tendency toward becoming secular. For instance, to achieve a level of generality capable of encompassing a complex world, priestly religion has to lose its mystery and become rational and abstract, while to achieve relevance to the world, priestly religion also has to become usefully focused on specific acts and circumstances. Religion thus simulates magic in order to be able to recover an aura of mystery and to remain focused on specific circumstances and acts: the very magic that priestly religion has long sought to discredit and exclude, if not entirely to eliminate (Weber 1964: 77–78).

Prophetic religion is no less likely than the priestly to defeat itself by its own successes. Note that prophetic religion is the mirror image of a monarch's own view of the world, in which it is of paramount importance to bring the world's parts into a coherent whole under the direction of the will of the monarch. It is no accident, notes Weber (1964: 58), that prophecy developed in opposition to imperial powers in the Near East. Prophecy was a defense against "the pressure of relatively contiguous great centers of rigid social organization upon less developed neighboring peoples." To counteract one principle, then, for ordering the world, the monarchical or imperial principle, it was necessary to create an equally systematic and rigorous ordering principle by which the individual could retain his or her own access to spiritual sovereignty. The prophetic cure thus mimicked the monarchical disease by requiring the individual to produce "a 'meaningful,' ordered totality" (Weber 1964: 59). *For Weber, Western religion has developed in the tension between the ordering principles of a monarchical central authority and the drive of the individual to order the world into a meaningful whole and to live in accordance with a central ethical tendency throughout all the details of everyday life.* Weber (1964: 59) concluded that "The conflict between empirical reality and this conception of the world as a meaningful totality, which is based on a religious postulate, produces the strongest tensions in man's inner life as well as in his external relationship to the world."

The sacred, on the other hand, whether it is embodied in a person, an institution, a doctrine, or a way of life, is always subject to the test of time; even the aristocrat is subject to public opinion. Thus the presence of the sacred embodies the problem of transience. The sacred is subject to tests of rationality and endurance over time. It is this particular integration of the sacred and the mundane that underlies the dynamism of the Protestant ethic.

The process of secularization

The sacred in its pure state and in its greatest tension with the world, as charisma, embodies and creates a sense of crisis. It subsumes the past and the future into an enduring and indefinitely extended present (Moses said unto you, but now I say unto you) or to an indefinitely delayed future. After all, there was a time when charismatic leaders disdained ordinary employment and could live indefinitely in the present;

like the lilies of the field they did not need to save up for the future. In the same way the charisma of those who made money through windfalls exempted them from long-term planning and investment. Their sense of the present was indefinite and open-ended, and merchants could legitimately enjoy and spend rather than reinvest their windfalls, but they always faced a possibly catastrophic loss. By relegating an increasing number of possibilities either to the past or to the future, religion subordinates charisma to a sacred history that transcends the passage of time and places crises and the moment in a providential or eschatological perspective.

In a world that Weber described as an "iron cage" of bureaucracies, it is exceedingly easy for individuals to experience their own being as extraneous to the social system. Individuals occupy roles, after all, and become professionalized. For Weber, however, this fate was both tragic and unintended, because the origins of the social order are to be found in individuals whose very being embodied the way social relations were to be ordered. They were not only monarchs, but also aristocrats: not only nobles, but prophets. Weber noted that it was forbidden to prophets in the Old Testament to take money or any other form of payment for their prophecies. Indeed, "the apostle, prophet, or teacher of ancient Christianity must not professionalize his religious proclamation . . . the Christian prophet was enjoined to live by the labor of his own hands or, as among the Buddhists, only from alms which he had not specifically solicited." The prophecy, then, must not serve any other purpose than the one for which it was originally intended: the creation of a social order through the message or the example of the prophet himself.

To professionalize a prophet's message or example is to turn it into a role that can be acquired and performed by someone else. To divorce the prophet's message from the being of the prophet is to turn it into a rule that can be followed independently of a relationship to the person of the prophet, or into a commodity that can be bought and sold in the marketplace, or into a performance that can be repeated in a ritual. Institutionalizing charisma therefore reduces personal presence into mere performance.

All these ways of separating the message or example from the very being of the prophet are the beginning of a social order in which the individual *per se* is extraneous to the social system. They transform prophecy from a unique revelation into a commonplace. What was sacred, underived, and original then becomes something that can be reproduced by those with the necessary qualifications and competence. Results replace revelation rather than being revelatory, and legitimacy comes from convention rather than from the shock of the truly novel.

Results or usefulness, satisfaction or custom replace the person of the prophet or the message that she alone has been given to declare. Only the derivations from the prophetic message come to matter: the wrongs righted, the reforms instituted, the grievances satisfied. However, from the outset, "The Israelite prophets were concerned with social and other types of injustice as a violation of the Mosaic code primarily in order to explain god's wrath, and not in order to institute a program of social reform" (Weber 1964: 51). It was the connection between the divine being and the social order that was at stake, not progress or reform. That concern was in keeping with the prophets' sense of their own message as a divine revelation and a gift from the deity: not as a message that could be interpreted and understood, used or misused, applied or ignored apart from a relationship to the prophet and to deity itself.

To put it bluntly, secularization drives a wedge between being and action and opens up a gap between the intentions, the will, and the character of the person and the way things are done. For the monarch, as Weber put it, any social disorder, any disruption of harmony in the society, and any natural disturbance or disaster is an effect of some flaw in the character and performance of the monarch. A modern sense of personal responsibility for the social order derives partly from the residues of an aristocratic ethic. The Stoic aristocrat did have an unqualified sense of the individual's own being: not only one's existence, but also one's ultimate, unquestionable worth, distinction, and endurance precisely because one's being is rooted in the Nature of things and is oriented toward ultimate Ends. For Weber, modernity lacks precisely this assurance, especially in the absence of religious notions like the doctrine of election and predestination. *Nonetheless, there lingers a widespread feeling that somehow the individual must achieve an inner religious conviction capable of sustaining a lifetime of endeavor oriented toward ultimate ends. This is the source of that extraordinary tension that Weber identified as characteristic of the modern world. Even in the absence of absolutes or ultimate principles, individuals were still obligated in the face of an extraordinarily complex society, to achieve a unified worldview that would orient themselves toward that world and guide their action in a diverse and changing set of circumstances.* That is, they somehow had to find a way to live in a present that subsumes the past and the future into a complex set of possibilities with ultimate significance, if without any clearly ultimate meaning.

Without the comforts of religion or the assurances of the aristocrat, however, the modern individual is afflicted either by a chronic sense of guilt or at least by an enduring sense of the deficiency of his or her own being. Weber speaks of a "distinctive type of guilt and, so to speak, godless feeling of sin which characterizes modern man" (Weber 1964: 206). Well versed in ideas current in psychoanalytic circles, Weber would have been very familiar with the notion that individuals experience guilt for crimes they have not committed. Moreover, he is thinking of the individual as still bearing a certain charisma: an obligation to live in the present fully open to possibilities that might otherwise be readily consigned to the past or postponed to the future. *Whether this charisma is a residue of a doctrine of election or a relic of an aristocratic ethic, it leaves the individual with an overweening sense of responsibility for ordering a complex world beyond his knowledge and control.* If residues of the sacred leave individuals sensing their responsibility for a wide range of possibilities over which they have little control, religion will gradually create a present that is bearable because religious beliefs and values have relegated many of these possibilities either to the past or the future.

However, residues of the sacred leave the individual with a sense of obligation to achieve an authentic personhood. Modern individuals still feel obligated to develop an inner state of mind or spirit capable of sustaining the effort to live a life-time systematically oriented toward transcendent ends. They are no longer like Israelites returning from exile who still held on to a religion that required "submission to the chastisement of God, anxiety lest one sin against God through pride, and finally a fear-ridden punctiliousness in ritual and morals" (Weber 1964: 114). However, in modernity the individual is on his or her own, with no guarantee of being chosen or of achieving transcendence in the end. Thus what is called for is a secular type of spirituality that holds one responsible for arriving at a heavenly city at the end of the journey. No wonder that the modern individual is preoccupied with the development of selfhood; but for Weber, such self-concern is clearly a sign

of a deficiency of being. It is the lot of those who long for a sacred guarantee of their own being, but, lacking it, are caught in a concern about
what they will become either in this life or the next.

As Weber (1964: 212) put it, "Under the conditions of early, natural
agricultural economies, noble status is conferred, not just by wealthy
[sic], but also by a hospitable and charitable manner of living." Weber is
arguing that this aristocracy of the charitable not only became a fairly
universal religious obligation, but under the auspices of Christianity it
became necessary to develop a persistently charitable inner state of
mind and heart capable of generosity both to members of one's own
immediate family and also to others with whom one was associated only
by virtue of religious affiliation. That is, by developing an inward state of
religious commitment, one which requires the development of an independent and magnanimous spirit, Christianity created some of the conditions necessary for a universal ethic. That ethic, extended to the entire
social order and rationalized for application to many different situations
and contexts, raised the level of trust and obligation in work and politics
and extended the social basis for investment and credit, for commercial
endeavor and for political affiliation to progressively wider circles of citi-
zenry. As Weber (1964: 213) put it, "The relationships among brothers
in the faith came to be characterized by the same expectations which
were felt between friends and neighbors, such as the expectations that
credit would be extended without interest and that one's children would
be taken care of in time of need without any compensation."

Once affection, loyalty, and trust break out from the constraints of
kinship, however, they can extend to wider circles. One's fellow believers
become one's family, and, in the case of Christianity, religious identity
and belief trumped ethnicity and politics as a source of social trust.
Certainly this breaking open of the clans created the basis for the modern, Western city, and for wider circles of investment and commitment
among strangers who otherwise had no reason to trust each other.
However, that same ethic remained in chronic, prophetic tension with
the world.

Let us consider one source of this continuing tension. Generosity of
spirit requires a social character that is not only magnanimous but
authoritative and free-spirited enough to call into question the authority
and the constraints of every institution that would confine social trust
to its own immediate circles. In its origins, Christianity created a severe

tension between the free-spirited individual and the family; Weber (1964: 210) noted that it was necessary to "hate" one's parents in order to be a follower of Jesus. Generosity of spirit could therefore be subversive of the traditional restraints on magnanimity. Furthermore, there is something entirely secularizing about the radically Christian ethic of personal authenticity, especially in a world in which all that is offered to the individual is a set of roles to be played in a rather constricted present devoid of many possibilities that have been relegated to the past or the future.

The process of secularization, by constricting the range of possibility available in the present and by subjecting the present more radically to the passage of time, leaves the individual in the position of taking ultimate responsibility for a complex and rapidly changing social order that may have ultimate significance but has no clear ultimate meaning other than that brought to it by individuals themselves. Furthermore, Christianity located the sacred so deeply within the psyche that any external manifestation of the sacred could always be called into question: "an inner religious faith does not recognize any sacred law, but only a 'sacred inner religious state' that may sanction different maxims of conduct in different situations, and which is thus elastic and susceptible of accommodation. It may, depending on the pattern of life it engenders, produce revolutionary consequences from within, instead of exerting a stereotyping effect. But it acquires this ability to revolutionize at the price of also acquiring a whole complex of problems which becomes greatly intensified and internalized. The inherent conflict between the religious postulate and the reality of the world does not diminish, but rather increases" (Weber 1964: 209).

The intense qualification of the individual's own, inner being, then, has far more radical effects under the auspices of a "world-rejecting" religion like Christianity than it did when the aristocracy had a monopoly on unqualified self-affirmation. By setting "the co-religionist in the place of the fellow clansmen," Christianity undermined the basis of traditional authority; neither ethnicity or kinship could stem the flow of individual love and generosity or claim a monopoly on either loyalty or trust. What Weber (1964: 211) called "congregational religion" therefore "contributes very effectively to the emancipation from political organization."

In the modern world, then, it is hard to know exactly how causes are related to their effects. Explanations are always partial and open to revision. Modernity also makes it difficult to know what means are most appropriate for certain ends; what is right in one situation may not be right in another, and justifications are always contestable. Not surprisingly, modernity undermines confidence in any patterns, perceptions of which are always subject to interpretation and re-interpretation.

It is not only action however, that becomes problematical in the modern world; it is one's own being. Lacking the guarantees of an aristocratic sense that one's being is guaranteed by the order of things, and lacking the authorization that comes from having been chosen by a god, one's being, or at least a strong sense of it, is deferred until the time comes for divine promises to be fulfilled. The fulfillment of those promises, however, like the fulfillment of any other promise, is contingent on whether the one receiving the promise acts accordingly. It is one thing to be full of promise: quite another to fulfill that promise. Modernity required a character who was both the recipient of divine promise, full of promise, and capable of fulfilling that promise time after time.

If it is difficult in such a world to have a sure and definite sense of one's own being, intellectuals have intensified the difficulty. According to Weber (1964: 125), "It is the intellectual who transforms the concept of the world into the problem of meaning. As intellectualism suppresses belief in magic, the world's processes become disenchanted, lose their magical significance, and henceforth simply 'are' and 'happen' but no longer signify anything. As a consequence there is a growing demand that the world and the total pattern of life be subject to an order that is significant and meaningful." Note the dialectic here. The intellectual creates the very conditions that undermine a sense that one's being has a place in the cosmos; one's being itself becomes problematic. The intellectual thus is required to find meaning in a world whose complexity, ambiguity, and uncertainty on a cosmic scale make that very difficult indeed.

In such a world it is difficult to share the aristocratic sense that one's own being is rooted in the nature of things, just as it is difficult to have confidence, if not in one's own being, in one's eventual becoming. After all, one has no certainty that one has been chosen to transcend life in this world and to overcome death. Therefore there is little warrant to achieve a systematic ordering of life that conforms to or creates a universal sense of order. Not even the cultivation of an inner state of mind capable of sustaining the self in the face of radical uncertainty will be sufficient to place one's existential house in order before the end.

The varieties of individualism that have for so long concerned sociologists of religion, then, are signs of a deficiency of being. Individualism connotes a preoccupation with the self that afflicts all those who know they are not of the aristocracy but long for the aristocrat's assurance that his or her being is deeply rooted in the order of things. As we shall see, Durkheim would provide all individuals with precisely that assurance by demonstrating to them that their very individuality is simply an artifact of their membership in a social order: no social order, no selfhood. For Weber, however, such an easy reassurance is out of the question. That is because modernity engenders precisely such a self-concern: a deep uneasiness about the basis and nature of one's very being.

For a character to emerge as capable of bearing, embodying, or fulfilling promise requires a sense of continuity and development in the passage of time. However, secularization undermines the sense of a narrative progression from a beginning that continues through some sort of middle and develops into a story that culminates in an end. In this regard intellectuals have something in common with the lowest levels of the working class, the proletariat, for whom "Any thought of dependence upon the course of natural or meteorological processes, or upon anything that might be regarded as subject to the influence of magic or providence, has been eliminated" (Weber 1964: 100). Weber credited the working class with few illusions about its place in the larger society; workers knew that their future is in the hands of the people who make decisions about how and where to invest their capital or how high to set interest rates, and they also knew that the laws do not favor those who might lose their livelihoods and savings or even their lives. There was little chance that they would fulfill whatever promise their lives might hold, and little reason to think of creating an improved social order through continuous, systematic, and rational activity. Thus, for Weber (1964: 100), "the rationalism of the proletariat, like that of the bourgeoisie of developed capitalism when it has come into the full possession of economic power, of which indeed the proletariat's rationalism is a complementary phenomenon, cannot in the nature of the case easily possess a religious character and certainly cannot easily generate a religion."

In Europe the working class was secularized precisely because they knew that there was little continuity between the past, the present, and the future, and that the present was being emptied of possibilities, some of which were being relegated to the past, others deferred more or less indefinitely into the future. That is why the working class does not see the world as influenced by providence or magic half so much as it depends on "purely societal factors, economic conjunctures, and power relationship guaranteed by law" (Weber 1964: 100).

It is predominately the less privileged who are uncertain of their being. They are the ones who long for a future in which their worth will be recognized, either in this life or the next, if not for who they are, then for what they will have done. Weber (1964: 106) argues that "the sense of honor of disprivileged classes rests on some concealed promise for the future which implies the assignment of some function, mission, or vocation to them. What they cannot claim to *be*, they replace by the worth of that which they will one day *become*, to which they will be called in some future life here or hereafter." Hence the current levels of apocalyptic interest and enthusiasm reflect a lack of a sense of one's own being: a form of individualism as flawed as it is militant, without what Rousseau called "the sentiment of one's own being": a sense of one's self as having a being that is enduring and of unquestioned value, or as Weber put it more strongly, a sense of being that is "underived, ultimate, and qualitatively distinctive." There is thus a moral economy that links those who lack a strong sense of their own being with those who seem assured that they are indeed *sui generis* and of unquestioned worth. The latter are not filled with resentment at their own defective being, and the former, who are unsure, may identify with the aristocrat or warrior in making common cause against an enemy whose being lacks all validity and promise.

There is a strongly psychological foundation to Weber's thought, a point which is often missed by those who see Weber's work as preeminently sociological. In seeking to explain the religious contribution to modernization in the West, Weber did use a comparative and historical account focusing primarily on sociological factors. However, he is deeply interested not only in psychological concepts but particularly in the role of the unconscious. In terms that would not seem strange to Freud, Weber speaks of the relatively poor as harboring "a conscious or unconscious desire for vengeance." Because the distribution of wealth and power inhibits them, the resentful cannot act out their desire for vengeance against the wealthy and the noble; as compensation, therefore, they seek to score moral victories that in the end will enable them to turn the tables on those who have previously lorded it over them. Thus, as Weber (1964: 110–11) put it, "suffering may take on the quality of the religiously meritorious, in view of the belief that it brings in its wake great hopes for future compensation." The notion that unconscious drives for satisfaction, motivated by suffering, take on the form of religious claims to eventual privilege, was shared by Freud, perhaps in a common debt to Nietzsche.

References

(1964) [1922] *The Sociology of Religion*. Translated by Ephraim Fischoff. Introduction by Talcott Parsons. Boston: Beacon Press.
(1996) *The Protestant Ethic and the Spirit of Capitalism*. Introduction by Randall Collins. Los Angeles, CA: Roxbury Publishing Company.

Talcott Parsons

Talcott Parsons (1902–1979) lived through two world wars and a major depression in the United States, but his work emphasizes the ways that social systems manage to achieve a certain amount of consistency in the patterns by which people work and play, raise children and worship or vote. In theory as well as in social life Parsons had an eye for what he called pattern consistency; indeed he looked for ways in which the studies of Weber and Durkheim might converge on a single theory of action and the social structure of modern societies. At Harvard (1927–1974) for most of his professional life, Parsons has helped at least two generations of students make signal contributions to the field of sociology.

For Parsons, societies evolve along two main dimensions, space and time. As they do, religion emerges, develops, takes shape, performs functions, becomes more abstract as it covers more contingencies and situations, and finally emerges into a realm of its own in which, as a set of beliefs and values, it transcends the society. Once transcendent, religion gives the social order an enduring, open-ended present extending into both the past and the future. The gods become less capricious, the sacred less eventful, history more teleological, and the cosmos providential. Initially, the dimension of space is a tract of land, more or less unbounded, but always concretely specified: "traditionally established areas within which specific kin groups are conventionally entitled to hunt and gather" (Parsons 1966: 36). Small groups of hunters and gatherers wandered over tracts of land which their ancestors had given or promised to them. The dimension of time was personified in the ancestors, who lived at some point in the past before chronologies began and before time could be dated and counted. The ancestors could be superhuman and thus immortal, well beyond the passage of time, and they acted as guarantors of the timeless possession of the land by their descendants (Parsons 1966: 34). While "the founders had incestuous relations," [they] "decreed that their human descendants should be forbidden them" (Parsons 1966: 34). Thus incest remains a possibility retained as a memory: a possibility relegated to the past and hence imagined as no longer a threat or an opportunity in the present. Once religion constitutes the present as a limited set of possibilities, the remainders may be relegated to the past or deferred to the future.

Insofar as it is possible to speak of religion in this initial context, the symbolism is what Parsons (1966: 33) calls "constitutive," in the sense that the society was not easily separated either from its symbols or from the personalities of its members. In Parsons's language, these three aspects of the social system, the symbolic, the structural and the personal, were "undifferentiated" from each other (Parsons 1966: 33). Individuals would perhaps speak of themselves as actually being the symbols of their group. Thus, as Parsons (1966: 39) puts it, "the adult man directly *participates* in the world of the sacred by dramatically playing the part of a sacred being . . . the statuses of sacred object and 'secular' social unit have not been differentiated." Under these conditions, in which the sacred is as personal as it is practical and uncanny, the individual would have a sense of his own being as anchored in or constituted by a more potent, essential, and enduring being: a more vital presence.

Magic, as we have seen for Durkheim, is a set of largely alien and impersonal forces that come from outside a social system to disturb the people and the social relationships within a society. So for Parsons as well, magic is external to the social system, and it conveys the very possibilities that the society itself is designed to inhibit or altogether to exclude. As Parsons (1966: 40) puts it, "Religious beliefs and ritual practices are integrated with the social structure through common commitments (in the form of prescribed relational patterns) to either the largest significant collectivity or its segmental units – e.g. the clans. They promote the type of societal integration that Durkheim called mechanical solidarity. Magic is the ritualization of interests and activities which cannot be fitted into this framework, which are individualized in Durkheim's sense."

One of the advantages of this last quotation is that you can see in it, in a highly condensed form, some of the basic assumptions of the sociology of religion, at least among those influenced primarily by

Durkheim. Religion has to do with the collectivity: magic with the individual and his or her interests. Religion promotes solidarity; magic is divisive. Religion concerns the way a society identifies and reflects on its own self over time; magic concerns relationships with the environment. Religion excludes certain possibilities that are inherently disruptive to a social system; magic brings them back in. It is therefore imperative for religion, if it is to perform its function of promoting the continuity and solidarity of the society, that it manage the passions and longings, the memories and the hopes, that a society tends to exclude simply because they represent desires that the society itself is unable to satisfy or that might even tear it apart. Something has to give, if only on that one day of the year when the religious system allows the ghosts to come back or aggressive and sexual patterns to take to the streets and the fields, where they can find brief satisfaction before order once again is restored.

When Parsons says that in primitive societies individuals participate directly "in the world of the sacred," and that the sacred has not been "differentiated" from the secular world, he is inferring that the sacred is enmeshed in the everyday world and the mundane. The sacred is thus accessible to individuals, and it is immediate, however fleeting, in its impact on their psyches and their physical being. Individuals, furthermore, are tightly integrated into the social order, and they have a sense of their own being that is more or less defined by their age or their gender, by their family and kinship connection. These forms of identity are given to them at birth or are natural, and they are not something that the individual can readily alter; they are not a matter of choice or personal achievement, but are rather ascribed to the individual. Because they are ascribed, they are easily stereotyped. What boys or men, girls or women are supposed to do, comes quite literally with the territory. If you are born into a community that lives in a certain territory, much of who you are is already ascribed to you, just as much of what you must do is prescribed rather than a matter of choice or preference. The range of possibility is tightly constrained, and uncertain possibilities are thought to come from the environment in the form of diabolic, supernatural, or abstract forces of the sort understood and manipulated, if not entirely controlled, by magic. Parsons views individuals as largely socialized into a society from which they derive their sense of their own being.

In these primitive societies it is not only the psyche, and the individual's physical being that are tightly integrated with the social order. The social order itself is tightly integrated. Parsons (1966: 23, 25) speaks of the pattern-maintenance sub-system of the social order as defining the basic commitments of the society; it holds the clue as to what would be considered a good society and to the sorts of people and the kinds of behavior that are necessary to create such a society. Through the process of secularization, however, this system of values and of basic commitments becomes independent of the other subsystems that define the rules for relating the family to work and politics, for instance, and that prescribe the sorts of behavior that are required of individuals of various ages and genders, class positions and family connections. Parsons argues that "What we call the pattern-maintenance system of the society has *cultural* primacy in that it is the locus of direct relationship with the cultural system. It first becomes clearly differentiated from the other societal sub-systems as the latter establish themselves as clearly 'secular' spheres which, though legitimized in religious terms, are not directly part of the religious system. This process leads to the differentiation of 'church and state,' which was not fully achieved until the post-Roman phases of Christianity."

Thus Parsons links the process of differentiation directly to the formation of the secular. In the beginning is a social world in which it is impossible to separate the person from the social order or from the sacred objects that embody that order. Once the process of differentiation has set in, however, it is possible to speak of aspects of the social order that are secular: perhaps those concerned not with the continuity or tradition of the society so much as with its everyday processes for getting and spending, getting along and making do. The world of the expedient and the temporary, the utilitarian and the mundane, becomes relatively disenchanted in that it no longer embodies the sacred.

A second type of secularization thus occurs when a society loosens the grip of its beliefs and values on the way it conducts itself. That is, when the society has to evolve a special subsystem to attend to what Parsons calls pattern-maintenance, it is clear that behavior is no longer stereotyped and that individuals have some discretion over what they will do in a wider range of circumstances. Contingency makes it hard for stereotypes to work. The possibilities safely contained in the sacred, where appropriate behavior could be prescribed, are now let loose in a wide range of circumstances, and it takes a broader, and more elastic, frame of cultural references to give guidance and set limits. It is no longer enough to do the right thing on stated occasions. It becomes necessary to maintain a pattern in which a society's basic values are allowed to take shape in ways that have never been entirely prescribed or foreseen. It is still not yet a society that is as open and filled with contingencies and possibilities as a cybernetic system, but it is moving in that direction.

As the process of differentiation loosens the grip of the pattern-maintenance system on the other sub-systems of the society, there slowly emerges a surplus of possibilities. Individuals have more choices to make as their behavior is no longer prescribed by their age or gender or family connections so much as by values that are widely shared and deeply held by the members of the society. It is necessary to observe before acting and to reflect before communicating. Behavior is less stereotyped or prescribed than it is governed by values that are more general or abstract and thus less particular or specific than the old prescriptions. There are more degrees of freedom between values and actions, between individuals and their social roles, and between the roles themselves. As the society becomes differentiated into sub-systems, possibilities that were once excluded therefore have a chance to come into play. "Differentiation, particularly, produces cases in which the necessities for integrating newly differentiated sub-systems strongly indicate including otherwise excluded elements" (Parsons 1966: 23–24). As the church is separated from the state, for instance, it becomes possible for religion to enter the public sphere in the form of political activity. As kinship becomes separated from the economy, it becomes possible for corporations to style themselves as families. As the state becomes differentiated from the economy, it becomes possible for business to influence politics. That is, there evolves a surplus of possibilities, as every part of a society then becomes an environment for every other part of the society. In complex societies, the line between the social order and the environment is no longer clearly defined, and the society develops a complex set of internal environments. If, as Parsons (1966: 9) puts it, "a society is a type of social system, in any universe of social systems, which attains the highest level of self-sufficiency as a system in relation to its environments," then a highly differentiated, complex society is constantly engaged in exchanges with the environment which allow formerly excluded possibilities to be included. Business leaders then lobby politicians and write laws, as former government officials go into business. Religious leaders exercise direct influence in the government, and politicians display and promote their own religious beliefs and values.

Parsons (1966: 24) argues that the process of secularization continues "as greater distance emerges between the gods and the human condition." The distance of the gods is due, according to Parsons (1966: 24), to the process of "differentiation between cultural and social systems." As I have noted, beliefs and values become more general and abstract and offer less specific guidance to individuals and groups as they seek to live in accordance with the widely accepted notions of what is required of good members of the society. At the same time, Parsons notes other kinds of differentiation that create more uncertainty and free play in the relation of personalities and the human organism to the society. Individuals have more choices to make and are freer to reflect on how or even whether to live in accordance with dominant values. As Parsons (1966: 24) puts it, "A parallel process of differentiation can be traced between personality and society concerning the degree of autonomy of individuals." Similarly, individuals have more freedom, and cope with more uncertainty, as they choose how they are going to work, what they are going to do, and what they are going to contribute to the economy. All of this is happening, Parsons notes, at the same time as "processes internal to the social system" begin to separate from each other, and religion loosens its control over the polity and the economy. In this process, as we have seen, Parsons finds that beliefs and values become more general in order to cover more situations and contingencies. What they lose in being directly relevant to particular duties or conditions or problems they gain in applicability to a wide range of possible situations.

Parsons (1966: 23) is very clear, however, that "this process of generalization" is filled with potential pitfalls. He writes of "various groups" who are committed to the social values of a society "at the previous, lower level of generality." For them, "the demand for greater generality in evaluative standards appears to be a demand to abandon the 'real' commitments." These groups Parsons calls the "fundamentalists" (Parsons 1966: 23). They represent a real danger to a society that needs more internal complexity in order to adapt to a more complex environment. The danger is that the "fundamentalists" will refuse to accept the values and beliefs of a society as these evolve to include a wider range of possibilities. This refusal would keep individuals locked into roles that do not begin to satisfy the larger society's need for energy, skill, and knowledge in the economy or for commitment, loyalty and determination to carry out a wider range of roles and their related duties. As Parsons (1966: 17) puts it, "In relation to members as individuals, then, societal self-sufficiency requires – perhaps this is most fundamental – adequate control of motivational commitments."

There are other ways in which a society must function if it is to be self-sufficient. If a society is to have control over "motivational commitments" it also needs to control its territory well enough to establish "a normative order in a collectively organized population" (Parsons 1966: 17). It need not monopolize all the roles of individuals; people can have important roles outside of their societal communities. However, a society must make it possible for "individuals to meet their fundamental personal exigencies at all stages of the life cycle without going outside of the society." Parsons is most concerned about the way in which a society mobilizes the trust and loyalty, the commitment and the aspirations of its citizens. If the society is not the object of a serious moral commitment on the part of the majority if its citizens, it is in danger.

The danger is that the society simply will not survive. After enumerating the various ways in which a society must achieve a measure of self-sufficiency, Parsons goes on to warn that "Severe deficiency in any one or any combination of these criteria may be sufficient to destroy a society, or to create chronic instability or rigidity that prevent its further evolution." Societies that do not evolve, of course, are easy prey for their rivals and adversaries. Societies that are too rigid will not develop the science or the education, the technology or other communications, the political leadership or moral commitments that they need in order to mobilize their citizens to work, to engage in the development of the society, and if necessary to make sacrifices. It is clear that any society that fails to maintain and develop its religious basis will not evolve, will become rigid, and in the end will collapse or be destroyed. Fundamentalism thus represents not only a threat to the stability and order of a system but to its very survival.

If fundamentalism represents one danger to a society, however, secularization can represent another danger, and the two are closely related. Secularization is necessary if a society is to become "adaptively upgraded," in Parsons's terms, that is, more capable of responding flexibly and appropriately to a wide range of dangers and opportunities. To understand how secularization works in this way, we need to know what Parsons means by a cybernetic hierarchy. At the risk of some oversimplification, consider that hierarchy as beginning with what Parsons calls the "normative order." That is the order that integrates a society around a set of rules, and as we have seen, these can be more or less rigid and stereotypical or flexible and general. What makes these rules valid, however, is the "legitimation system," as Parsons calls it, consisting mainly of values that give validity to the rules of a society. It is good, for instance, to be honest, because honesty is the best policy: the value being the fair and efficient ordering of the social life of the nation. However, these values also need to be legitimated by what Parsons calls the "cultural system." A cultural system consists of general ideas, creeds, totems, images, or some other cultural production that grounds a society's values in an order that transcends the social order itself. The cultural system therefore always points beyond itself, because it embodies meanings that transcend the social order and are valid regardless of the fate or identity of a particular social system. In Parsons's view, this is a way of grounding beliefs, and the values they legitimate, in "ultimate reality." As Parsons (1966: 11) puts it, "a legitimation system is always related to, and meaningfully dependent on, a grounding in ordered relations to ultimate reality. That is, its grounding is always in some sense religious."

The process of secularization, then, undermines the system of legitimation by which a society's rules seem to be grounded in ultimate reality. There are many ways in which this process may loosen the ties that bind a society's normative order to ultimate reality, the most obvious of which is an increasing separation (differentiation) between the cultural system with its beliefs and creeds, images and totems, and the social order itself. Beliefs may become so general that they lack any specific or necessary relation to particular values, and the values themselves can no longer provide a firm grounding for the society's basic rules. People follow the rules, regardless of their values, and they hold their values, regardless of their beliefs. What Parsons calls the cultural system therefore loses its grip on the social order. Beliefs and values, rules and regulations float more or less independently in a sea of cultural options that lack any logical or necessary relationship to each other. One can follow the rules because to do so is expedient rather than right. One can do the right thing because it is one way to avoid conflict or surveillance, regardless of whether one considers the right thing to be good. Furthermore, one can do what is good regardless of whether one thinks it is true or has any lasting value that transcends self. One's choices and ethics may be expedient or situational, and one's values can be utilitarian or relative to the society one belongs to, and one's beliefs may support one's values but lack any transcendent authority.

It is precisely this loosening of the legitimation system that makes fundamentalists wish to return to a cultural system firmly grounded in what is taken to be ultimate reality. In such a system religion has a virtual monopoly on the sacred. Otherwise everything is relative to a local context and valid only for the time being. Parsons contrasts a society with such a surplus of possibilities with one that used to be self-sufficient with regard to its environment and hence more "primitive." In primitive societies a complicated network of prescribed patterns of behavior governed the relationships between the ages and sexes, and, of course, marriage, so as to avoid the possibility of incestuous relations. These prescriptions created what Parsons (1966: 36) called "an intricate network of groupings composed by variations on the themes of descent, sex, and age-grouping." As Parsons (1966: 36) put it, "Descent and marriage are so linked that those who belong in specific descent groups not only can but *must* marry persons belonging to specific other descent groups." Thus, this most primitive society was created by the symbols excluding one possibility above all others, that of incest, and these societies developed what Parsons (1966: 38) called a "distinctively prominent elaboration of precautions against incestuous marriages." Sacred taboos are reinforced by a variety of religious rules and ceremonies, beliefs and values.

In a primitive society the ancestors are both subhuman and superhuman. As the society is deeply intertwined with both the personality and the cultural system, so also the present is imbued both with the past and the future. The self is ontologically based in both nature and society by totems, whether plants or animals. Consider the carvings on a medieval cloister, that contain images of plants and animals of saints and sinners, of angels and demons. One's being is enclosed in a sacred cosmos, and there is no impassable gulf between the human and the noble or angelic, ordinary believer and the religious virtuoso.

This primitive form of social life is, as Parsons puts it, relatively "brittle." Everything depends on doing everything in the right way at the right time and the right place, and the right way to do things is relatively stereotyped. There is little room to maneuver or to negotiate, and little room for doubt as to what one is supposed to do or not to do. However, as societies expanded over larger territories, they encompassed a wider range of situations. Thus the prescriptions to be followed by individuals in specific situations had to become somewhat more general in order to apply to this wider range of contingencies. As prescriptions became increasingly abstracted from particular contexts, they became more general, lost some of their specific content, and became less stereotyped in order to maintain their general relevance (Parsons 1966: 35). They therefore have to be applied and specified to particular contexts. As individuals and groups come to understand their past as being somewhat removed from their present, and their present as being somewhat removed from their future, and as their society expands to cover people in unfamiliar places, religion emerges as a means of maintaining the society's sense of possibility over an expanded range of both time and space (Parsons 1966: 38), but the sacred begins to recover some of its immediacy to the person and the particular time or place while remaining both practical and yet mysterious.

In order to ensure the communication of prescriptions over this expanded territory and over longer temporal spans, societies employed written language. The use of written language, however, created a certain space between the cultural and social systems (Parsons 1966: 26). Symbols had a life beyond the time and place of their enactment. It was no longer necessary personally to enact, communicate, or perform the sacred in order to know what the sacred required. Because the written language was likely to be employed in a wide range of contexts beyond the one in and for which it was initially written, the language itself had to be sufficiently general to cover a wide range of situations and sufficiently abstract to be relevant to a wide range of contingencies. The spatial and temporal horizons began to recede, and the space and time over which religious prescriptions had to be applied began to expand (Parsons 1966: 26). Again, this gives the sacred more latitude to appear and to disappear in moments of immediate impact on and relevance to persons and places, times and occasions.

Up to this point it would be relatively easy to misunderstand Parsons as saying only or primarily that secularization is a process that is basically antithetical to religion. To be sure, secularization weakens the authority of religion and its influence or control over social systems. However, Parsons also traces fundamental processes of secularization to the religious bases of Western civilization. Of Israel, for instance, he says that its highly transcendent God in effect secularized the world of nature and human history. Israel "exalted divinity far above the level of archaic polytheism and gave it transcendence, unity, and coherence, so that the human level, being sharply differentiated from the divine, was thereby endowed with its own special independence and, indeed dignity" (Parsons 1966: 105). The world, then, was relieved of the over-whelming sense of possibility that is accompanied by the possible and immediate presence of the sacred. The present time, without the intrusion either of the past or the future, and devoid of interference from the subhuman and the supernatural, was an indirect outcome of tendencies embedded in biblical religion itself. The world was secular by divine fiat. A God whose ways are not the ways of humans is a God whose own transcendence creates secularity.

We have seen that the process of secularization turns norms and values that were once specific, closely tied to circumstance, filled with stereotypes about age and gender, and relatively inflexible into an independent moral order whose values are relatively general and abstract, and therefore able to cover a wider array of contingencies and circumstances; they are universalized. Now it seems, however, that this same process of secularization was carried by Israelite religion; indeed it was Israel's faith that turned religion into a force for secularization far beyond the boundaries of Israel itself, and long after Israel itself ceased to exist as an independent nation. As Parsons (1966: 102) puts it of this peculiar cultural complex: "first a transcendental 'legislator' god; second, a moral order prescribed by him; and third, the idea of a holy community executing his mandate, was able not only to survive the ending of a politically independent Israel, but eventually to become independent of the Israelitic community's dispersed units and be transferred to non-Israelitic societies and collectivities. This, I believe was Israel's great contribution to social evolution."

A transcendent God operating through a moral order that is binding not only on the community of faith but on societies beyond the immediate pale of salvation is a God who is self-limiting. The universe, therefore, and the larger society will not be flooded by unimaginable and uncontrollable possibility, although with this God all things are possible. It might seem that such a universal moral law would be as binding on the deity as it was on the people. After all, a whimsical god would be hard to follow, and one's sacrifices might be rewarded only by further loss or even punishment unless the law revealed by God were also morally binding on the deity itself. As Parsons (1966: 101) puts it, "some expectation of reward is required to ground faith as a crucial medium for motivating people to higher achievements." However, the transcendence of God in Israelite religion carried with it a further possibility, that God could not be held to any contract to deliver benefits to the people if they were sufficiently obedient to the law. God transcended even the covenant that was revealed through Moses, and which bound God to be the people's deity if they continued in His ways. Israel might be "chosen" by the will of God, but that opened up the possibility that they could be unchosen. At first, Parsons (1966: 101) argues, it was impossible for Israel to regard Jahweh as "morally free to treat His people as He saw fit, regardless of their behavior." Interestingly, however, Parsons (1966: 101) goes on immediately to say that an "orientation," as he calls it, to a God who transcends reasonable expectations of reward or punishment has been "prominent in the theology of Augustine and the early Church Reformers." Such a God, however self-limiting, remains the repository of all possibility.

In other words, Israel's faith was capable of encompassing a much wider range of possibilities. The faith was able to stipulate the necessity of trust even under conditions of extraordinarily high, even daunting, complexity and uncertainty. Under these conditions one could risk everything, even one's life, for a salvation that would not necessarily be forthcoming. However, the risks would be undertaken not in a spirit of gambling or religious roulette. On the contrary, the ethic underlying this orientation to high levels of faithfulness under conditions of extreme uncertainty and ambiguity was what Parsons (1966: 100) calls "religious individualism." Much as Max Weber spoke of the Protestant Ethic as being a discipline carried by individuals who placed themselves and their work, their wealth and their futures at carefully chosen risk, and who reinvested their gains over a lifetime of further productivity rather than squander or consume them, so Parsons (1966: 100) speaks of "the stream of Christian individualism."

As we shall see when we come to the work of David Martin, Christian individualism allows and even requires individuals to take personal responsibility for their relation to the world. This means that, with regard to citizenship, the individual subjects the state to moral scrutiny and judgment; it is up to the individual to decide how much to contribute or even to sacrifice, and to draw the line between obedience and defection. The strain of individualism in Christianity, inherited from Israel, also makes the individual responsible for his or her own faith, and thus individuals are required to repent, to convert, to believe, and to show forth the fruits of that redemption in daily life over a lifetime. They are responsible for the realization of the possibilities available to them in their context and situation.

However, this same tendency allows and requires Christians to believe themselves to be citizens of another kingdom whose possibilities transcend those of the kingdoms of this world, but they exercise that citizenship only by becoming citizens of this world. That is, they are easily moved and transplant themselves readily from one nation to another. They are mobile, upwardly as well as outwardly. All traditional forms of solidarity, then, whether a place or a family, an ethnic group or a nation, are subordinated to the fundamental obligation of the individual to be faithful to a call to a larger citizenship.

Paradoxically, this strain of individualism unites the believer with fellow believers in a worldwide people. Parsons (1966: 100) argues that "The people were defined both by having been 'chosen' and by having (in some sense) voluntarily associated themselves. Thus, mutual commitment, both to Jahweh and to one another, defined their solidarity." They were to be a nation within and also between other nations: a people whose final allegiance could be claimed by no autocrat, however divinely ordained or popularly elected. They themselves would be the reservoirs of surplus possibility outside the reach of any society's imagination and control. The nation, the polity, the laws of nations, a line of descent or a vast ethnicity: all these lose their grounding in religious legitimacy and become the object of a moral commitment to be freely chosen or rejected by the individual. Religion, Israelite and Christian, breeds and undermines secularity. It fosters secularity by focusing the loyalties and moral endeavor of the individual on the present, while deferring a large set of possibilities to a kingdom that lives primarily in memory and devout anticipation. On the other hand, the people of God themselves represent possibilities that are excluded from the beliefs and practices of a society, just as they themselves harbor memories and hopes of the advent of a kingdom that constitutes the basis of all possibility.

There can be little doubt that Parsons is seeking to explain, as did Weber, why the West became relatively modern, in the sense of being hospitable to open societies, inclusive political institutions, and market forces. In addition to crediting Israel with the notion of the people as a transnational moral community obeying a universal law under a transcendent deity, Parsons (1966: 103) credits ancient Greece with the notion of a people that "far transcended the city-state." Within the city-state there was "a *corporate* body of citizens which became (especially in the leading, exemplary case of Athens) a body of equals, though non-citizen residents were excluded and remained a 'lower class' " (Parsons 1966: 107). However, the people themselves were subject to a moral order that transcended the city-state and was rooted in Nature itself: a moral order to which the gods, often arbitrary and all-too-human themselves, were inevitably subject (Parsons 1966: 106). In this regard Parsons (1966: 100) finds them comparable to the Israelites, who also were a people who became "the societal community which bore the distinctive culture": a culture defined both by their voluntary commitment to their fellow-citizens and to a moral order that transcended that of the city-state or the nation. In Sophocles' treatment of the Oedipus myth, Parsons (1966: 106) argues, Athens achieved a sense of citizenship rooted in a moral order that transcended customary morality and kinship: "the *polis'* kinship-incest based archaic order had been superseded by an order based on 'civic' relationship." Here, then, was another step away from a rigid, stereotyped morality that circumscribed action, and was too inflexible to govern choices in a more complex environment of opportunity and danger. Athens, like Jerusalem, struck a blow against fundamentalism that enabled modernity, in the long run, to find a home in the West.

Conclusion

There is a paradox, or a dialectical theory, that runs through Parsons's sociology of religion. It is simply that religion has been a major source of the process by which societies (the societal community) and its basic standards and values become quite independent of religion. More specifically, Parsons (1971: 69–70) credits what Weber called "this-worldly asceticism" with a disciplined and rational approach to achieving in everyday life and in the larger society the implementation of values that derived from the religious tradition. The values were universal, in that they applied to everyone and covered a wide range of aspects of social life, from work and politics to leisure time and the family. They were "this-worldly" in the sense that they applied not to some eschatological or spiritual kingdom but to the social order in which individuals live and move and have their being: "oriented toward the building of the good society and not only toward the salvation of souls in the afterlife" (Parsons 1971: 69). The sense of a bearable but dynamic sense of possibility in an ongoing present open to but not mortgaged to either the past or the future was an achievement of Western religion.

Parsons (1971: 101) puts it this way: "We have traced the differentiation of the societal community and the pattern-maintenance system through many steps, especially the development of a normative order and the definition of a societal community not grounded directly in religion. The educational revolution is a further step in this secularization." Through the process of secularization, the societal community came increasingly to define itself in terms of its own beliefs and to govern itself through its own norms and values, however much these beliefs, norms, and values were indirectly associated with or derived from traditional religious beliefs in Western culture. As Parsons (1971: 99) puts it, "In a sense modernity began with the secularization of the medieval integration of society and religion, resulting in both the Renaissance and the Reformation."

Of course the process has not been smooth. As we have seen, what Parsons calls fundamentalism puts up a stiff resistance to the process by which norms become more flexible, and values become more general and abstract. In that process the societal community becomes equipped to make difficult choices in an environment that is increasingly complex, changeable, uncertain, and ambiguous. For Parsons (1971: 100), however, the old cultural order lives on, in which values were more specific than general, and that old culture may return in fresh outbreaks of fundamentalism and fascism: "The value specificity of certain older symbolic systems has hindered the establishment of a *moral* consensus that, at the level of total societal values, could have more integrative than divisive effects. We call resistance to value generalization 'fundamentalism.' It has been conspicuous in religious contexts, often linked with extreme social conservatism, as among the Dutch Calvinists in South Africa. Indeed, the Fascist movements of the twentieth century have on the whole been fundamentalist in this sense. We can also speak of a fundamentalism of the extreme left, from certain phases of the Communist Party to the current New Left" (emphasis in original).

References

(1966) *Societies: Evolutionary and Comparative Perspectives*. Englewood Cliffs, NJ: Prentice-Hall.
(1971) *The System of Modern Societies*. Englewood Cliffs, NJ: Prentice-Hall.

David Martin

David Martin taught sociology and the sociology of religion at the London School of Economics from 1962–1989. During that time, and as President of the International Society for the Sociology of Religion, he has become recognized as perhaps the most distinguished author in this field. Known equally for his long-term interest in the study of secularization and for his more recent work on Pentecostalism as a global religious movement with revolutionary implications from the ground up, Martin has made it clear that religious groups which seem to some sociologists reactionary or ill adapted to the modern world are in fact carriers of a modernity that is hospitable to the sacred.

David Martin is thus neither a cultured despiser of religion nor of modernity, and that makes him unique among contemporary sociologists. In an essay for a collection that I edited on the sociology of religion, Martin disclosed that his father was an evangelical Christian who preached of the coming of the Kingdom of God on the street corners of London. Rather than seeing his father as a reactionary who could not stand the onset of a secular rational, complex, fluid, and cybernetic modern society, Martin sees his father as an *avant garde* of a religious proletariat still often despised or at least ignored by sociologists. Thus Martin may be best known for his studies of Pentecostalism and voluntaristic forms of religion in Latin America, and more recently in Africa and Eastern Europe. He argues that the same movement or the same spirit that produced revolutionary enclaves in Bohemia in the late Middle Ages and became translated from one cultural periphery to another in Europe, the British Isles, and in North America, has taken very deep roots in the South. This type of the sacred requires individuals to take responsibility for their lives and to give a reason for the faith that is in them. Eminently reasonable, this Pentecostal faith separates individuals from the old social order that made them subservient to bosses and landowners, to illiteracy and addiction. Like the early Brethren of the Free Spirit, modern Pentecostals carve out niches for themselves where they can make a living and follow their own inner sources of inspiration and authority. No longer dominated by male models of machismo or by priests, they set their own houses in order, supporting their families often by entrepreneurial activity of their own, consult encyclopedias, save money for their own and their children's education, open themselves up to networks of mutual aid, and invest financially and spiritually in a future well beyond their lifetimes. Thus emancipated from traditional religion, they are open to possibilities on a global scale; indeed they are easily transported, not only by the Spirit but by such modern conveyances as air travel and the internet. Their social networks become global, and so do their interests and opportunities. They come and go frequently and easily across national borders as citizens of a transnational and sacred religious community of the Spirit. Apparently primitive in their religious ecstasies, they are exceedingly modern in their ability to think and do for themselves, to uproot and transport themselves into new situations, to take responsibilities for their lives and to seize their moments of opportunity.

The same voluntarism that makes these modern Pentecostals responsible for their faith, their livelihoods, and their lives, also requires them to think through churchly and political allegiances. Those who are expecting the advent of the Kingdom of God may sit rather loose to the kingdoms of this world, and these are notably what we call the church and the state. By taking responsibility for their faith, Pentecostals by-pass the institutionalized authority of the clergy, to whom they no longer need to make their confession, having a confession of their own. As for the state, any this-worldly political authority loses any form of traditional legitimacy and is known primarily by its fruits. It stands or falls in the Pentecostals' estimation according to whether it fulfills its promises and responsibilities: the same ethic by which they live themselves. That is, Pentecostals secularize the state by developing a sense of their own sovereignty and an allegiance to a kingdom not yet of this world. They secularize the church by developing their community of faith and practice. They secularize communities based on blood ties by developing their own sense of kinship in the spirit. They secularize communities based on time and place by breaking ties with the past, ushering in a new age, and moving about the world as if it were, as Martin puts it, their parish.

To put it another way, Pentecostals know from their own collective forms of enthusiastic worship what it means to create moments of a heightened sense of possibility. However, they sustain this sense of possibility by creating a present-time that is wide open to the advent of the future; the kingdom is always and everywhere about to come. They also create a sense of possibility in the present by recovering ancient forms of religious practice while freeing themselves from obligations carried over from a more recent past of feudal, patriarchal, or communal loyalties. The present becomes the long-awaited time in which possibilities for transformation, or at least for betterment are always and everywhere at hand. Such a view of the present also requires the Pentecostal to have a strong sense of presence: not only of the presence of the Spirit but of an equally potent and enduring personal presence. Such a personal presence has a strong will and is capable of making choices rather than of merely following custom or making the usual obeisances to those of higher status or authority. Voluntarism is born, and with a sense not only of personal freedom but of personal responsibility.

This ethic of responsibility also makes Pentecostals good candidates for receiving social and financial credit. Indeed, as Weber remarked a century ago, there is an intimate and dynamic link between this Protestant ethic and at least the spirit – if not the flesh – of capitalism. The struggles of the Pentecostal against the temptations of the flesh make them limited in their consumption, disciplined in their investments of time and money, and unlikely to be carried away by vain blasts of often Catholic doctrine. As Martin puts it, Pentecostalism is the option chosen by the poor for themselves, in contrast with Liberation Theology, which advocates the poor as an option for the faithful.

It is important to see in Martin's account an improvement over the traditional sociological narratives that pit tradition against modernity. In the 1960s it did appear that modernity would erode the last traces of religion as a source of collective identity and moral authority. As Martin (2005: 23) put it, "So far as authority was concerned, the figures of authority lost their capacity and will to impose and be imposing. *All* the main institutions were subjected to criticism and irony: politics, religion, the monarchy. It appeared that there were no examples of endeavor which might be held up for imitation and emulation. Each person sought a radical, individualized essence and self-fulfillment. That meant that all the ties of belonging loosened, including national identity and political identity."

To the extent that this is indeed true of the 1960s, individuals were not lacking in a strong sentiment of their own being. Their sense of themselves as enjoying a being that was as authoritative as it was underived seemed to trump all other sources of personal identity. This description also suggests that radical individuality has a way of disenchanting the social universe and of preventing social institutions from acquiring an aura, or even a patina, of the sacred. The social order becomes transparent to inspection. Pentecostals are secularizers. However, in the 1970s and 1980s, Martin (2005: 23) goes on to note, "The most notable survivor was evangelical Christianity, which took some elements of the expressive individualism of post-modernity but controlled them with a strong sense of moral obligation and loyalty to the community. Individual feelings were released but balanced and checked by moral disciplines and priorities." The universe may have been disenchanted, but, despite the views of Martin's colleague, Bryan Wilson, the social universe was not as yet wholly demoralized. There was a bond uniting individuals together in a legitimate social order, despite the advent of wholesale individual self-assertion and self-promotion.

To those who argued that modernity would deprive religion of its cultural monopolies and access to state power, as the process of differentiation made further advances and deprived religion of its control of various aspects of social life, Martin points out the successful adaptations of religion. He (2005: 21) notes that "religion flourished most abundantly under modern conditions where church and state were separated and where there was religious pluralism and completion." Differentiation allowed religion to develop its own identity and to substitute influence for authority. Pluralism, so far from weakening the plausibility of particular religious traditions and institutions, sharpened the competitive edge of their differences. In "countries where religion was the carrier of national culture," Martin (2005: 21) notes, religion served as a major source of cultural and community defense. So far from becoming relegated to the private sphere of leisure time and the family, religion entered the public sphere with spirited engagement with certain social issues, whether these concerned war and the economy or the fate of fetuses.

To summarize: In Martin's view, the truly modern form of religion is Pentecostalism, with its emphasis on voluntarism, on the individual's responsibilities in every aspect of personal and social life, on the separation of the self from its taken-for-granted social contexts, and on what Parsons called the "adaptive upgrading" of loyalties to the family and the ethnic or kinship group to the larger society and its major institutions. However, he notes that Pentecostals embody not only these modern, Protestant, rational, voluntaristic, and flexible forms of religiosity but also the more primitive forms of religion associated with indigenous peoples or unlettered social aggregates at moments of collective enthusiasm and highly ecstatic celebrations of corporate identity.

As I have suggested they translate the heightened sense of possibility encountered in their worship into a sense of possibility in the secular present, creating relative freedom from the past and gaining access to the future. In that reconceived present, they also develop a substantial sense of their own vital presence.

Martin typically blends a Durkheimian with a Weberian sociological perspective. On the one hand he credits Pentecostal religion with understanding and exploiting the collective forms of religious enthusiasm that exorcise deviant aspects of the individual psyche and make the individual fit for membership in a group that seeks to inhibit licentious, undisciplined or even incestuous activity. On the other hand, however, Martin, who sees his own work as carrying on a primarily Weberian interest in ascetic religious beliefs and practices that pit the individual against "the world," shows that religious asceticism is indeed alive and well among these Pentecostal, enthusiastic carriers of the Spirit.

Martin's reflections on the survival and transformation of traditional forms of religion in the modern world are part of his larger interest in the way Christianity endowed secularized Western societies with metamorphoses of the sacred. The voluntaristic forms of religious belief and practice within the collective celebrations of the Pentecostals are later waves of earlier religious movements of the heart that brought individuals out of their traditional and oppressive social contexts into a new social space in which they had a name, social credit, personal dignity, and responsibility for choosing carefully the objects of their political and religious devotion. Societies tied together by kinship and ethnicity, where the social space places the present in a continuous line of descent from the past, inevitably remain relatively closed to outside influences.

Unless threatened from outside by invasion or microbes, by alien ideas and currencies, these societies have little incentive to change, to become more complex in order to adapt to an environment with new risks and opportunities.

The most recent wave of religious voluntarism began in Western England during the awakenings of the early eighteenth century under the influence of evangelists like Whitefield, who created a new sense of possibility among the working class, and initiated a new set of tensions and responsibilities between the rural periphery and the political and cultural centers of Anglo-American societies in the British Isles and North America.

Clearly Martin considers social systems to be a subset of all the possibilities for social life and personal development that may be able to exist in a particular environment. How large that subset of possibilities may be depends on the kind of religion that informs the larger society or its peripheries. He argues that those possibilities are enlarged to the extent that the religious system incorporates both pluralism and voluntarism. The dynamism of Western societies, notably the British, has been due to a religious culture that combines high levels of collective enthusiasm with personal asceticism that link the periphery in creative tension with the center. This religious culture is responsible for a wide range of societies that have incorporated both more tensions and more possibilities for flexible adaptation to their environments than those in Europe that have been under the sway of religious monopolies or of a single ethnicity, especially when the religious and ethnic monopolies are closely tied to the powers of the state. These new possibilities and tensions are perennial social facts in societies where voluntaristic Christianity has taken root, if only on the social and cultural periphery. Referring to the United Kingdom, Martin (1997: 56) refers to "a complex relation between ethno-religion and voluntarism, not only on one periphery as in Romania but in four: Scotland, Wales, Ulster and Catholic Ireland." These peripheries have contributed to what Martin (1997: 57) calls a "complex interplay of establishment dissidence at work in the English 'centre' " as well as to a "complex interplay between ethno-religious pluralism and classical voluntarism."

Under the influence of Christianity individuals for centuries have been given a range of choices that unsettle their relationship to communities based on blood, race, or soil. Martin attributes to "the voluntary principle" a tendency among Christian groups and communities to take new risks and thus also to pose new challenges to conventional and traditional forms of authority. Voluntaristic religious communities recruit members from those who have been excluded from the body politic, and they give voice to people who have been muted. In the counsels of those who have become faithful by choice there are new opportunities not only to be heard but to exercise influence. These voluntaristic conventicles, then, may not only unsettle people by taking them out of their traditional confines in the family and ethnic group. They may pose unsettling challenges to the larger society. As Martin (1997: 58) puts it, "At the same time, the very existence of such voluntary bodies mediating between the mass of the people and the State has radical implications and these are extended by the further implications of organizational experiments in self-governance, lay initiative, popular preaching and participation, and – sometimes – local autonomy."

The incentive to change in response to a set of new possibilities comes, in Martin's view, from the constant pressures exerted by the languages and symbols of the Christian tradition. Martin (1997: 56) speaks of "the generic symbolic repertoire of Christianity [which] floats free of particular institutional attachments and of any ties these may have to political regimes." Like a cultural form of DNA, these words and images exert a continuous pull on the identity and aspirations, on the loyalties and allegiances, of an entire people. The pull weakens the grasp of the family and the neighborhood, the ethnic group and of prior generations on those living in the presence of these cultural forces. Particularly in its voluntaristic aspects, Martin (1997: 57) notes, Christianity "creates and implies social models based on variety by unhooking religion from state, territory, residence, and ethnicity."

Martin uses the image and doctrine of the Virgin Birth to locate, at the very basis of the Christian tradition, an imagery of contrarian and more expansive and inclusive devotion than is required or permitted by societies based on what he calls "consanguinity, contiguity, and continuity." On the one hand, Jesus is born of a Mary who is deeply Jewish, rooted in neighborhood and a village, a people and a place that have centuries of claims to loyalty and recognition, and intimate ties between the living and the dead. On the other hand, however, the Virginity of that birth foreshadows a radical break with race, blood, and soil: the opening of the most intimate and traditional communities to the possibilities contained in an unimaginable environment. Mary is thus pregnant with risks and dangers, opportunities and potential allegiances that may very well not only unsettle but dissolve the society based on kinship, ethnicity, and the ties between the generations both living and dead.

For Martin, the subversive aspect of Christian words and images fosters constructive and dynamic relationships between the social order and the voluntary, spontaneous tendencies of a people. Even an established Church, such as the one found in England after the civil war, could embrace free thinking, various kinds of churchmanship, and, in the end, both nonbelief and a passionate evangelicalism that centered religion not in London but in the heart of the individual. What Martin calls the Anglo-sphere found a way to keep its passions, which may have been messianic, from dominating its prose, which could be found both in the Book of Common Prayer and in the rhetoric of Parliament. The British could get their national act together by singing Handel's Messiah in churches both rural and urban, and the choir schools were one way in which talent was siphoned from the periphery to the cultural center, just as the chapel was a recruiting office for national politics. Similarly in the United States of America the local congregation could function as a party's precinct office where individual character and rhetoric could be honed and tested at the local level and social as well as financial credit accumulated for later expenditure. The English Enlightenment, as distinct from that of the continent, fostered a highly rational faith that, both at the local level and in the larger society, fostered personal self-discipline as well as inclusive forms of solidarity that lent themselves in the eighteenth century to creative forms of public charity and in the nineteenth and twentieth centuries to a liberal or, later, a welfare state.

The openness of the political and cultural center to the periphery provided a continuous supply of citizens who wished to bring their sobriety, self-discipline, concern for mutual support and welfare, as well as their attitudes toward violence, into the public arena. Martin (1997: 58) is careful to point out that the radical or even subversive temper of voluntaristic religious communities is, in the Protestant tradition, tempered by "The peaceable temper inculcated by denominations such as Methodism and Pentecostalism [which] includes in its scope personal conduct attitudes toward war, and attitudes toward civil power. Disobedience is at the very least civil." The openness of the periphery to the center enabled even the poor and semi-educated to take part in the high culture of the stage and the concert hall, and to sit at the church's high table not only for Morning or Evening Prayer but for the Eucharist: saying the same words and holding in common the same faith, open as it was to a wide range of interpretation, usage, and practice.

Martin (1997: 53) has in mind a range of societies. At one end are those like Britain, where religion is differentiated from the state, even if it is in some way "established." Religion is free to enter the political arena because no religious group has a monopoly on religion either at the center or the periphery. Pluralism at this end of the continuum may be due to the simple facts of competing ethnic groups, each with its own variety of Protestant or Catholic faith. However, pluralism may be due to a highly voluntaristic form of Christian faith which recruits individuals rather than ethnicities or kinship groups and which holds individuals accountable for their acts as well as their faith. Individuals thus take responsibilities in the local community that fit them for influential roles in the public sphere.

Participation in the larger society may well be mixed with protest, just as religious symbols, when used by the dominant regime for legitimation, may also be turned into a source of criticism. The role of symbols in the public sphere and their employment by the state is thus relatively open and fluid, and the symbols may enjoy considerable freedom from being interpreted literally or ideologically by those with the power or the interest to do so. Similarly, even when the public sphere recruits or even co-opts individuals, it cannot take their allegiance for granted. These societies, at this end of the continuum, are steeped in possibility. At the other end of the continuum are societies in which there is a strong link between religion and nationalism, between particular ethnic groups and the state, and if the periphery is different from the center in language or religion, its differences are enclosed in enclaves rather than allowed to engage the political or cultural center in dissent or protest. While the symbols and institutions of the periphery may find representation at the political center in the public square, they are placed less in opposition to the dominant institutions than on side streets, where confrontation can be symbolically avoided.

If the British example showed that religion could link the center to the periphery in co-operative and dynamic exchanges, and could integrate the nation around a religion that was both rational and emi-nently practical, religion on the continent has a different story to tell. At the opposite end of Martin's continuum from Britain, he finds Romania where "regimes of both right and left stitched the Orthodox Church in to the state apparatus" (Martin 1997: 55). Religion at the Romanian center, then, was "one major carrier of the national identity of the Romanian ethnic majority" (Martin 1997: 55). As such it lent itself to various kinds of romantic nationalism and reinforced tendencies toward anti-semitism, fascism, and "Marxist totalitarianism" (Martin 1997: 55). What possibilities there were for dissent were encapsulated in various ethnic and religious minority enclaves on its north-Western frontier, where Catholics, Calvinists, Lutherans and Unitarians, each with their own ethnic base, carried on their respective traditions. Their forms of voluntarism, according to Martin (1997: 55), were not "classi-cal" but a form of "quasi-establishment": a "legally ratified accep-tance." Instead of a steady flow of exchanges between the center and periphery, and a rationalized form of recruitment of local leadership into roles in the public sphere near the center, voluntarism and dissent remained encapsulated until conditions were appropriate for an abrupt and decisive intervention when a Hungarian Reformed pastor sparked the revolt that led to the down fall of the Ceaucescu regime in December 1989 (Martin 1997: 56).

Martin is expert on the history and current condition of religion in relation to the larger society in every country in Europe, but fully to under-stand his approach, we need to realize that Martin is a sociologist engaged in comparative empirical studies of social conditions that do indeed vary, and whose variation signals or even at times causes decisive changes in the relation of religion to society. Therefore we need to identify some of the factors or variables that he considers to be most useful in taking both an historical and comparative approach to religion and society.

One of the more important variables is the distance between the working and the middle classes of any country. Where there are opportunities for literate, sober and hardworking members of the work-ing class to enter the middle class, it is only a matter of two or three generations before the faithful become relatively comfortable and less disciplined, sometimes opting for avocational rather than vocational pursuits in everyday life, and suspending their belief rather than their disbelief, except, perhaps, in hard times. Where entrance to the middle class is relatively restricted, however, evangelical Christianity, ascetic and self-disciplined, or even Pentecostal and semi-ecstatic, survives in enclaves on the outskirts of the city, in the hills, or in relatively less populous rural areas.

Another equally strategic variable is the degree to which a religious culture is coterminous with the social and territorial boundaries of a society. In parts of Europe where the Reformation settled for a formula that designated the religion of the people to conform to that of the prince, it is possible for religion to define and shape national identity. It is also possible for religion at the center to be mirrored effectively at the social and geographical margins of the larger society. However, when the cultural center, and hence religion at the center, employs a language or is embedded in an ethnicity that is very different from that of the periphery, tensions develop between the elites and the marginalized sections of the populace. At the periphery one may find a more literal-minded, if less literate population than at the center. These give rise to various kinds of fundamentalism that concerned Talcott Parsons: pieties based on ethnicity, locale, and kinship that may resist inclusion in the more general and abstract values of the larger society. If one religious group or culture monopolizes the center, the stage is set for opposition to arise on the periphery, either from secularized movements or from divergent religious groupings. That is why we have seen Martin (1997: 56–57), speaking of "the whole territory which became the United Kingdom," argue that "we have a complex relation between ethno-religion and voluntarism, not only on the periphery as in Romania but in four: Scotland, Wales, Ulster, and Catholic Ireland. Each of these has in different ways and at different times counterbalanced the hierarchical powers of the English 'centre' and also nourished relatively egalitarian cultures. Indeed, in the case of the religious cultures of Scotland and Ulster, they combined with English voluntarism to help create the nascent culture of what became the United States."

I mention these variables because they affect the extent to which the social order could be open or closed to other possibilities: the possibilities represented, for instance, by the social periphery. Taken together, these variables determine to some extent whether religious voluntarism will be more or less tempered by "the principle of obedience," or whether religious symbols will be "deployed," as Martin puts it, for "legitimation" or for "protest, or whether a minority group will seek to divide or dominate the larger society. That is, pluralism, voluntarism, and symbolism inevitably "contribute to the dialectic of centre and periphery" (Martin 1997: 60).

Those who think of secularization as antithetical to religious interests will therefore find a very different perspective in the work of David Martin. Instead of seeing secularization as a process that produces a net loss for religion, whether in numbers and adherence or influence and authority, Martin speaks of what he calls "secular mutations" of religion itself; thus a secular seed in religion may develop into full maturity outside the walls of the monastery. Liberty, fraternity, and equality within the cloisters may become a revolutionary, secularist state or a state in which the religious and the secular share the same physical, social, and institutional spaces. Instead of thinking of secularization as a process in which religion becomes all too well-accommodated to secular authorities in the state or larger society, David Martin speaks of "transpositions" of religion from spheres normally thought of as sacred to ones considered more obviously secular. However, what once thrived under clerical auspices now succeeds more or less mightily under the authority of various ministries of the state.

With the notion of a transposition from the religious to the secular comes not only a loss of monopoly but a kind of continuity. Take, for example, Martin's (2005: 80) reference to a Scandinavian "secular mutation," by which he means "the way the inclusive scope of Lutheran monopoly in Scandinavia has been fused with and replicated by the inclusiveness of Social Democracy and the welfare state." True, in this transposition the ministries of the church become superseded by the ministries of the state, but there is continuity in the administration of humane and inclusive public concern. If such defeats for the churches are not successes, what are they? By success I mean simply the way a social system manages to replicate itself in other ways in novel contexts while keeping its cultural makeup, its cultural DNA. That is what Martin considers secular mutations, as if some social systems are more able than others to reproduce themselves in unprecedented ways under novel auspices in a wide range of contexts. These endings are in fact new beginnings: these defeats in fact novel successes. Secularization is always and everywhere, then, a form of religious change. Whether it is a form of religious decline is a judgment more often made by vested theological or ecclesiastical interests than by sociologists.

Not all secular mutations resist being understood as a defeat for the Church, and yet even in some dramatic examples of the loss of political authority and power by the Church, there is room for misunderstanding and varied interpretation about the nature of the mutation. Take, for another example, Martin's (2005: 80) comment on the effects of the French revolution: "the rigorous state monopoly exercised by the Catholic Church in France after the Revocation of the Edict of Nantes in 1685 was transposed into the monopoly eventually exercised during the Third Republic by the omnicompetent secular state." Secularization in this case represents the Church's move from the center to the periphery of the State, and its loss of monopoly on political power. An equally authoritarian and exclusive secular polity replaces the church and exercises a monopoly of legitimate authority, such that it even passes "laws restricting the operation of sects and cults." Why is this not a case of a successful secular mutation, by which the Church implants its DNA in a virus called the secular state which then proceeds to inhibit the religious organizations that lack the legitimacy of the traditional Church itself?

One way to read Martin, then, is to see the presence of the past under various modern guises. In Britain, for instance, Martin (2005: 80) notes a tension between formalism on the one hand and on the other an evangelical emphasis on what he calls "heartwork." That same tension exists in what Martin (2005: 80) calls "the flexibility of the political system and its concept of a loyal opposition." That is, the social system contains within itself the principles of its own negation and holds them in creative tension with each other: a characteristic that Martin (2005: 80) traces back to the "accepted rivalry of Church-State establishment with religious nonconformity." However, even this internal competition and rivalry was only a later and highly evolved form of an earlier "attempt of the Reformed Anglican Church to accommodate and 'comprehend' an inclusive middle" (Martin 2005: 80). For Martin, then, the present contains highly evolved and apparently secular forms of social tension or even conflict between possibilities that have been located more or less in the political and cultural center or on the social and geographic peripheries. Call these forms of tension dialectical, since the formalism and tolerance of the center respond to and make possible various sources of opposition on the periphery without which the center would not be central or the periphery peripheral. What Martin calls the "donation of history" may endow a society with a legacy of voluntarism. The nation may embrace a central tendency both in religion and politics to base its institutions on the freely exercised choices of its members. However, the "donation of history" is a tradition, as in Romania, where to be an ethnic Romanian meant that one was also, practically by definition, and with an historical inevitability, a member of the Orthodox Church.

Secularization typically reduces what is given or traditional, obligatory and inevitable, to a matter of mere choice. Whatever is optional, including one's faith, becomes *merely* optional, no matter how much one believes that one's choices are predestined or that one is choosing to be a member of a people who have already been chosen. This secularizing tendency among voluntary religions is therefore pitted against the kinds of solidarity that Martin associated with ethno-nationalism, where one's faith comes along with one's kinship and territory. Returning the compliment, or insult, of secularity, religion that is based on the donations of the past tends to reduce voluntarist religions to the realm of the merely transitory and individualistic and thus to deprive them of their claims to transcendence. Conversely, voluntaristic faiths may counter the claims of an ethnic-religion to historical transcendence by relegating them to the past. Both the voluntarist and ethnic forms of religion in the end fall back on the same temporal strategy of secularizing their rivals by assigning them to a world that either is passing away or has already past.

As a case in point, Martin (1997: 75) describes Romanian ethnic-religious nationalism as attacking its religious rivals as "an outdated social formation, based on pre-scientific superstition and on class contradictions and likely to divert people from their true and proper loyalty." It may be difficult to imagine how Romanian orthodoxy, itself steeped in a traditional form of religious and ethnic identity, could stigmatize its Hungarian, Reformed, and Baptist rivals in the Romanian Northwest as "Hungarian revanchism," but the ideological ploy was performed with the aid of communism. Under Ceausescu the Romanian communist party "united itself to a local nationalism as a defense against Russian communist imperialism," (Martin 1997: 74) and in so doing elevated itself from the secular to sacred, from an historical novelty to the guardian of a sacred national ethnicity, and as the protector of an Orthodox faith that could survive only on a highly secured, one might even think of it as an insular, national territory. There Orthodoxy and nationalism could protect themselves against the extremes of Reformation religiosity whether in the form of Calvinism or Baptist voluntarist religion. It is as if Martin had found a Romanian Henry the VIII who was capable of protecting the faith and the nation at the same time against the threats of secularization from both domestic and international sources.

The sacred, in this case Romanian nationality, took refuge in the sanctuary of religion under the auspices of Russian Orthodoxy. In turn, religion borrowed new life from the sacred over which it acquired a near-monopoly, except for the Protestant communities in the northwest. However, this heightened form of cultural defense against outside, Russian influences could also be deployed against the sources of cultural competition and subversion in those parts of Romania where other ethnicities flourished, notably among the Hungarians in the Romanian northwest. There, also, survived the voluntarist forms of religious community, especially among the Baptists and the Unitarians. Martin (1997: 75) thus argues that "The effect of communism in promoting organicist reactions against pluralism is actually improved by its progressivist credentials. Thus, movements for change in Transylvania, could be condemned as Hungarian revanchism and the bourgeois variety of nationalism. Religion could be suppressed, more especially non-Romanian religion, on the ground that it was an outdated social formation."

It would be easy to miss the point that Martin is making. It is that if we are to understand how Christianity can lend itself to the most brutal and reactionary exercises of state power, we need to understand also how it is that rational, Enlightenment philosophies such as Marxism can, when joined to indigenous ethnicities with access to a monopoly on state power, produce the most ruthless of "countervailing pressures," and become "the vehicle of oppressive power and totalitarian national integration."

It would also be easy to miss the larger point that the overlapping of two quite different social systems, one internal and the other intensely national, one bureaucratic-rational and the other thoroughly ethnic-religious, is capable of introducing tendencies toward secularization in which one side inevitably is stigmatized with temporality. Thus, with the ideological armor of Romanian communism it was possible to brand the Reformed Hungarian enclaves in the northwestern area of Romania as reactionary survivals from the past.

The intrusion of an alien social system into a self-contained social order thus intensifies, perhaps to the breaking point, the internal tendency of any social system to divide into sacred and secular elements. Every society with any claim to continuity among the living and the dead relies on tradition to reinforce sacred memory and on ritual to reenact the beliefs and practices of the society so that they come alive in each successive generation. Inevitably, therefore, these traditional elements of social order regard those concerned with local and particular interests, with individual preferences, and with the requirements of everyday life as secular. However, when the sacred center of a society is guarded by an ethnic group in competition with competing ethnicities on the social or geographic periphery; and when these marginalized ethnicities carry religious beliefs and practices different from that carried by the dominant ethnicity; and when differences in language between the center and periphery are also at play, the religious-national center seeks to secularize the periphery, just as the ethnic and cultural periphery seeks to secularize the center. Each is likely to consign the other to the world of the temporary, the temporal, the passing away, or the past.

In some of his most recent works Martin invokes the notion of "the sacred," and it appears that the sacred lives well outside the reach of the institutions and organizations that make it their business. Indeed, to understand modernity it is necessary to trace the fate of the sacred in a wide range of countries under an equally wide range of social conditions. Martin (2005: 77) writes, for instance, that "religion and ethnicity either divide the sacred between them, or the sanctity of faith and nation are partially merged. So one needs to understand both how the sacred may occupy rival poles, and how it may partially migrate to occupy a new national space. One also needs to be cautious about projections concerning the demise of sacred nationalism or the sacred nation-state."

Religion thrives to the extent that it can mobilize, coordinate, control, interpret and monopolize the sacred. For instance, Martin is interested in the ways in which the survival and strength of the Church in Europe and the United States of America has depended on its willingness to cooperate with or to co-opt the nation-state, especially when that state has been dominated by secular or even secularist elites. Secular elites would not necessarily be antagonistic to religion but willing to let religion compete in the cultural marketplace, whereas the secularist elites would create a political and cultural center relatively immune to religious influences. "Secularity," Martin (2005: 81) notes, "I treat as a condition and secularism as an ideology." Secularization, I would add, is the process by which religion loses its ownership and control of the sacred.

In some countries, Martin (2005: 81) points out, Catholicism was "hostile to the birth of a modern nation-state: in France and in Czech lands, Catholicism was perceived as hostile; in Poland, Lithuania, Croatia and Slovakia, the situation was quite the reverse." That is, in some countries Catholicism was more likely to have been rooted out of the political and cultural centers if it were seen as antagonistic to a secular nation-state, whereas in other countries the Church was deeply embedded in an ethnic nationalism that held the nation itself to be sacred. It is in what Martin calls the "Anglosphere," as well as in Scandinavia and Holland, that a moderate, domestic, fairly rational accommodation exists between the Church and the nation-state. Martin (2005: 79) argues that "these three civic cultures, each rooted in Protestantism, between them pioneered a model of (relative) pluralism, tolerance, federalism, and philosemitism. They reduced the height and scale of human and divine sovereignty and emptied out some of the potency of the sacred concentrated at the heart of the city." That is, the secularizing tendency of Western religion seems to have had wider scope and more lasting effects in the Anglosphere, as Martin calls it, and in the maritime empires of Britain and Holland, as well as in Scandinavia than in the rest of Europe, where a Catholicism entrenched in the state was repudiated by a revolutionary, secularist political center in revolution (Paris) or where a Catholicism deeply embedded in communities defined by ethnicity and language became a vehicle for a sacred nation or nation-state. Secularization, in the form of ideological secularism, was indeed the enemy of Catholicism in "the cases of successful secularist indoctrination by the state, in France, the Czech Republic, the former East Germany and Estonia. This is the obverse of religious nationalism, because the success of counter-indoctrination by an ideologically secularist state, whether radical liberal or Marxist, depends to a great extent on whether the Church has been aligned with or opposed to the mobilization of national feeling and the nation-state" (Martin 2005: 77).

Although secularism attacked religion in the case of Catholicism, especially where the Church was opposed to the nation-state, in the rest of Europe there was a creative tension between the secular and the religious. It was creative in the sense of the dialectic, with religion defining and shaping the secular, and the secular in turn defining and shaping religion, until they become similar enough to be mirror images of each other rather than the one superseding or eliminating the other. Martin (2005: 78) puts it this way: "Christianity embodies a dialectic of the religious and the secular which more easily generates secular mutations of faith than straightforward replacements and displacements." In some cities, notably Paris and Rome, the church is more visibly represented as the arch-rival of the sacred nation, whereas in Berlin, Amsterdam, Edinburgh, and London the Church is on easy terms with the institutions representing the nation's art and higher learning.

Secularization revisited

Even religion, Martin (2005: 128–30) argues, became highly rationalized; one could as well be rational about one's religion as about one's atheism. "Such a religion requires little or nothing by way in institutional or clerical mediation, and it is likely to view miracle as arbitrary interference with the law," (Martin 2005: 129): an unwarranted intrusion of unauthorized possibility. Thus nature was part of the process of differentiation. As nature became increasingly natural, Martin (2005: 128) notes, "The emerging autonomy of nature includes both a disenchantment rejecting the operation of occult forces and a rational religiosity complemented by a rational atheism": a process that made possible the differentiation of the worlds of business and politics, the family and education.

Few understand as well as Martin just how secular religion itself can become, especially when it is thoroughly rationalized. The world ceases to be mysterious, and it becomes a source of information about the purposes and operations of the divine. One can get back to origins through the study of the elements of nature and of the processes of evolution; one can also get back to origins through a study of the various tendencies, traditions, literary strands, and textual sources in the development of the Bible.

It is not surprising, therefore, that Martin (2005: 130) speaks of a "*religious* frustration with an over-intellectualized and chronically moralistic Christianity." Mystical tendencies in art and poetry then come to evoke the solitary individual standing in sacred places against a sublime background of exalted landscapes: an image of God restored to a no longer entirely secular and unambiguous nature (Martin 2005: 130). The modern environmentalist movement, in which good and evil are pitted against each other in the world of nature, and some places retain the innocence of a lost paradise, while others embody the effects of desecration, is a case, Martin (2005: 130) argues, in which it is possible to discern "either extravagant metaphor or massive echo of a Christian repertoire."

Like nature, the Bible then becomes a source of information about God: not a presence in relation to whom one adopts appropriate postures of expectation or submission. As religion becomes increasingly rationalized, the Scripture may be edited to remove the passages that seem arbitrary or extreme, in a word, irrational. The tradition itself may also be edited so that the pieces of belief become intelligibly and systematically related to each other. Theology becomes at least as systematic as it is dogmatic. Once codified in a set of propositions about God, faith can be had without immersion in anything more than the text itself. The ends toward which human life must be devoted can be spelled out in confessions that are easy to read and unambiguous in their content. One does not have to ponder in one's heart too many mysteries when they are spelled out in the various confessions. Similarly, the rationalization of religion removes some of the doubt and uncertainty about the right thing to do. Instead of a word from the Lord on specific occasions, rationalized religion offers a set of principles, stated more or less abstractly, that can be applied to specific contexts and to particular situations.

Martin extends the discussion of secularization to include philosophical questions about the relation of religion to modernity. Borrowing from Taylor's "account of the humanist dependence on an unacknowledged Christian ontology" Martin (2005: 126) argues that "Belief in progress is millennial expectation transmuted, while the unique status of man is a version of the *imago dei*." It may be that the connection of a man with some divine being is unacknowledged and unrecognized, at least in a highly secularized culture. The result of this misrecognition, however, is that humans are out of touch with divine being, or in more secular terms, with Being itself. It is a point made nearly 50 years go by Charles West, and it still stands.

To be out of touch with Being is indeed a stage of advanced secularity. It is to move, according to what Martin (2005: 127) calls one "master narrative", from the "childhood of humanity" to "secular reality in its maturity." The child lives in an enchanted universe of presences, of beings that come and go on their own, at will, and of a Being that permeates everyday life with its own unseen mystery. The secular human being, mature at last, lives in a world in which the only unseen hand is that of the market, and the only beings who come and go at will are individuals with minds and wills of their own. Their beings matter, if only to themselves. As Martin (2005: 127) puts it, "Unlike George Herbert, who saw another world 'as through a glass', we have a single eye for a single reality." To live in a world with a sense of Being but without access to Being is to live in extreme existential loneliness. Of course, no matter how religious one may be, one may feel out of touch with Being. Hindus know that God may not answer their prayers and may not come when called. Christian saints have dark nights of the soul. The window to secularity is always open, even in the heart of the monastery. However, the possibility of living in a world empty of Being was intended to be excluded by the sanctuary and the cloisters. The monastery was a place where a divine presence once defined possibility, the present was calibrated by the monastic hours, which continued in an endlessly repeated cycle rather than marking a present that was continually passing away. There personal presence was both possible and obligatory. In the secular world, by contrast, the divine presence was known by the absence of any possibility other than the sequence of hours and days, the present was merely temporal and therefore always in the process of passing away, and personal presence was uncalled for. Martin's work alerts the sociologist and the historian to the ways in which secular time came to be marked with the regularity and taken with the seriousness of monastic time, in which personal presence was called for through the doctrine of vocation, and where social systems took on the aura of possibility formerly contained in the abbey and the cloister.

Martin's work is also a reminder of how much has been lost in this mutation or transposition of the sacred into the midst of the secular. Martin (2005: 126), drawing on the works of Ernest Gellner, names a few, "the rejection of 'supernatural' or spiritual explanations of phenomena in favour of the structure and activity of matter; determinism and relativism; empiricism in epistemology; hedonism and/or egoism in psychology; belief in reason as the arbiter of existence; utilitarianism in ethics; utilitarianism and/or democracy in politics; pragmatism in the theory of truth; and a belief in the power of education to improve the human condition." What all of these have in common is a flat, one-dimensional view of the material and social universe: an emptying of possibility and presence both from large scale societies, their dominant institutions and from the routines of everyday life. This world is not permeable to influences from another world. There is only a world in which people do what they can to affirm their own beings, to get what they need, to get along in life and with each other, and to justify themselves and their actions as best they can. Even the social order itself is a work in progress, and nature is a mute witness to species that did not adapt in time or make the grade.

References

(1997) *Does Christianity Cause War?* Oxford: Clarendon Press.
(2002) *Pentecostalism: The World Their Parish*. Oxford: Blackwell Publishers.
(2005) *On Secularization: Towards a Revised General Theory*. Aldershot, UK: Ashgate.

Bryan Wilson

Bryan Wilson was a Reader in the Sociology of Religion at All Souls College, Oxford University, for the majority of his professional life. Born in Yorkshire, England, he became a devoted scholar of religious movements on a global scale. His study of millenarian movements, *Magic and the Millennium*, remains a landmark study in the field, and was followed by his other studies on the sociology of sectarianism and of new religious movements. His theory of secularization has long been adapted by two generations of students, but remains essential to the field.

Religion, for Bryan Wilson, always defeats itself by its own successes in creating a lasting presence for its adherents. Originally offering its adherents a form of heaven upon earth, religion becomes preoccupied with the mundane in the present. It becomes secular. The more religion succeeds in taking root and in outlasting its rivals, the more involved it becomes with the present. Religion may offer individuals access to the transcendent, but it inevitably enmeshes them in a series of obligatory procedures for the time being. While religion may offer its devotees a form of liberation, religion, the more it succeeds, always and everywhere provides them with new disciplines to be performed in the present. Whereas religion may promise a social order that is not of this world, it tends, with increasing success, to unsettle earthly kingdoms and to give individuals and groups a chance to shape and settle a social order more of their own design and to their own liking. "Millennialism," writes Wilson (1975: 494), "always promises social transformation, and although always erroneous, it nonetheless creates a new conscious expectation of social change. Sometimes it prompts men to begin to make the millennium. The new age does not come, but the effort of work, organization, and the futuristic (or restorative) ethic has important consequences."

Whatever immediate access to mysterious sources of transformation and healing a religion may offer, its adherents soon learn that they may have to wait for complete access to salvation, and that there are things they must do in the mean time. The present, previously emptier or more unbearable, now becomes a time in which there is work to be done, rules to be followed, examples to be emulated, accounts to be given, stories to be told, judgments to be made, failings to be atoned, and gains, finally, to be calculated. As the present becomes more open to the past and to the future, stories acquire high levels of continuity and development. From the moment the sacred begins to stir in the form of new religious movements, it creates a present open not only to the past but to the future, and in doing so the present begins to acquire secularity not only by foreshadowing the one to come but also by being part of the age that is passing away. Religion envisages a new order of things that generates hope and radical commitment, and from them religion fashions procedures and routines that are always more secular than the original vision. As Wilson (1975: 494) puts it, "Even in restorative millennialism a new basis of social identity is created: in futuristic millennialism, the tendency is toward the establishment of a more rational order, as men themselves begin to take on the powers once ascribed to the gods, and to construct their own social institutions – not perfectly but with growing self-consciousness."

For Wilson (1975: 502), there are still magical or millennial aspects of religion in modern societies, but they have become more marginal and secularized, with less emphatic claims to the miraculous; prophecy has become more "forth-telling" than "foretelling" (Wilson 1975: 503). What for Martin, then, is the dominant mode of Christian activity, the global Pentecostal movement, is for Wilson a tendency found only on the fringes of society and of Christianity itself.

The fringe aspect of miraculous or millennial religion is due to the characteristic of what Wilson (1975: 502) calls "advanced societies," in which "social relationships are predominately organized according to empirical and rational principles. Modern men expect their blessing mainly from the welfare state, scientific medicine, the development of technology, the availability of education, the operation of impersonal legal institutions, and disinterested agencies for the maintenance of social order." Of course, we need to remember that Wilson was writing this book during the 1960s in which he had become well aware of very powerful mass enthusiasm moving an entire generation to undertake unprecedented action, expose themselves to novel risks, and to seek innovative forms of emotional expression and political activity. It is in the context of a heightened sense of urgency and expectation in a newly meaningful present-time that we are to understand Wilson's (1975: 503) comment that millennialism still survives in advanced societies "in highly secularized form, in the spasmodic socio-political enthusiasms that capture the minds principally of the young." The Now generation, as it was called, found itself living in a present that was both unprecedented, in their view, and the threshold of a New Age.

No doubt Wilson was fully aware of the irrational aspects of some of the social movements of the 1960s, many of which had clearly religious dimensions even if they lacked orthodox beliefs, practices, and dispositions. In Wilson's (1975: 500) view, movements with magical or millennial elements "never constitute impressive demonstrations of intellectual reconstruction." That is because emotions and values become embedded in the way people see and describe their social worlds, as well as in the way they interpret and explain them. Rationality, we can infer from Wilson's discussion, requires the ability to separate description from interpretation, explanation from evaluation, ontology from theory. However, these distinctions can easily be lost in religious enthusiasm as well as in the enthusiasm of young people seeking immediate access to social power and opportunities to speak with uncommon authority. This intermingling of description with interpretation and explanation, and of theories with ontologies and moral judgments, is typical of times that generate religious enthusiasms.

What sorts of times are those? It is clear from Wilson's argument that the primary characteristic of times that generate religious or quasi-religious movements is novelty. The unprecedented puts individuals and groups in situations that are so new that customary ways of thinking and feeling, acting and reacting no longer are comforting, useful, or effective. Of course, religious movements themselves disrupt social relationships, arouse longings that are difficult if not impossible to fulfill, and intensify demands for social justice that may have radical or even revolutionary implications. But for Wilson (1975: 501) the causal chain works the other way, from social to cultural and religious change. "The causes of new movements are laid in the unprecedented disruption of social circumstances . . . in the early stages, in the ecstasy of

millennialism, in the first new hopes for new miracles and new therapy
. . . it is the breakdown and abandonment of previous assumptions
and codes of discipline, of earlier norms and goals, rather than the
institutionalization of new ones, which is more impressive." In a novel
situation, all the old constraints and habits seem futile or as unnecessary
barriers to fulfillment and satisfaction and the time is coming for entirely
unprecedented satisfactions of old longings. The present becomes a
time for all to present themselves, their longings and demands, before a
high tribunal about to usher in a new dispensation.

There are thus various kinds of present, and to understand the role
of religion in social change we would need to at least keep in mind the
various possibilities, from a present that seems relatively empty to one
that is fraught with possibility, or from one that seems to embody
aspects of the present and to intimate the future, to one that seems
to represent a novel situation, a sharp break with the past, and
a precipitate advance into the future. To summarize Wilson's view of the
situations that seem to accompany and stimulate new religious movements, we might say that they confront societies with new threats of
chaos, and they place evil in sharper contrast or confrontation with
the good. In a novel situation, as Wilson has told us, social habits wear
thin, old constraints are loosed, and people act out their emotions and
desires in novel ways. Chaos could replace order and becomes at the
very least a more palpable threat. In the same way, Wilson suggests,
longings for salvation are intensified. Salvation offers the healing of
illnesses, recompense for suffering, justice for grievances, reconciliation
for conflicts: the very embodiment of the good over and against the ills,
the evils, that tear apart societies and the human psyche. However, as
demands for salvation increase, so does the opportunity for irrational
thinking and aspiration. As Wilson (1975: 500) puts it, "We need not
ignore the fact that men (no less in simpler societies than elsewhere)
are capable of compartmentalizing experience, of seeking salvation
according to certain intimations which do not – even according to their
own stands – really finally 'make sense.' "

Some forms of the sacred indeed pose a threat to other forms of the
sacred, especially to those that are more traditional, or embedded in
the structure of the community, or given a more formal and continuous,
but highly institutionalized life in the organization of religious communities and denominations. Wilson (1975: 159) notes that the Christian

missions in Africa offered "a permanent, independent, self-sufficient, externally supported organization," and that tribal communities also offered their own forms of sacred authority. However, religious movements and cults provided rival forms of the sacred that could "promote a steady erosion of the existing legitimation of traditional authority" (Wilson 1975: 158). Because mission churches often lacked "the very things Africans sought in religion," (Wilson 1975: 160) religious movements and their associated cults might set up rival forms of the sacred. Some offered a leader who was capable of dispensing holy water or healings at a central shrine, while others offered more informal access to healing and to various kinds of spiritual experience such as visions (Wilson 1975: 161–62). It was not only missions that suffered a loss of the sacred through these movements; the same religious innovations could also pose a threat to traditional, communal sources of the sacred. Wilson (1975: 162) recounts one movement in which "old cult objects were de-sacralized, and traditional artistic endeavor and traditional religious practice were equally condemned." Thus the process of secularization occurred not only when religious institutions became more formal and rational, their practices more objectified, rational, and instrumental, and their teachings more general and abstract. Secularization also occurred when new forms of the sacred directly cometed with traditional or institutional forms of the sacred such as those found in African communities and in the mission churches themselves.

For Wilson all of this is true despite, as well as because of, the fact that there is something fundamentally irrational about religion. Religious visions may make leaps of faith that predict far beyond the reach of ordinary and reasonable levels of inference from observable data; religion prophesies rather than predicts and thus provides access to a future-present.

Religion, for Wilson, is based on a fundamental misrecognition of the facts. While facts never speak for themselves, religion gives them a voice that is far more oracular than it is scientific. Religion describes things, interprets and explains things in ways that are not empirically justifiable. It may make connections between events that are not connected, and miss connections that, to a twenty first century observer, are obviously related. Religion may take the succession of events and turn it into a story, or from a study infer moral relationships between means and ends that cannot be justified by any rational procedures.

The sacred may link causes with effects in ways that defy the canons of rational prediction. The sacred generates mystery, and, with mystery a heightened sense of possibility in the present.

Indeed, Wilson argues that charismatic religion creates a new present, with novel relations to both the past and the future, and with novel relationships between means and ends, causes and effects. In what Wilson aptly terms charismatic demand, religion endows a sacred person or at times a sacred object with possibilities for personal transformation or a revolutionary transformation of the social order. The first set of possibilities belongs to the province of magic: the second to millennialist religious movements. Magic endows the sacred person with an uncommon presence: authoritative, autonomous, and underived, and beyond question, capable of commanding assent and receiving obedience. Charismatic demand arises when a wide range of social conditions are sufficiently unsettling, unsatisfying, or threatening to undermine individuals' confidence in their own survival or in their ability to maintain their own presence, their very being. What they need, and what, if their charismatic demand is satisfied, they receive, is access to a source of charisma, or grace, that, offers them release from suffering and undergirds their being.

Charismatic endowment, once conferred by a following of believers, enabled an individual to claim to be a source of extraordinary magical or millennial significance. If his or her significance were magical the individual would be endowed with sacred potencies: the gift of healing, for instance, or of clairvoyance, of prophecy and prediction. The charismatically endowed would confer to his or her followers this sense of their own being as underived because they now are in direct contact with a source of ultimate authority. In his or her presence they acquired a presence of their own: a being that mattered. By being thus endowed, the followers of the charismatic leader could undertake new risks in the name of new possibilities. That is, their taste for novelty and their capacity to endure the unprecedented would be vastly enlarged. They could live in the present, free from the past, open to the future. If the charismatic endowment were of a more millennial variety, the charismatic leader would either announce or embody a new social order. His or her followers, then would be an *avant garde* of a spiritual elite that would, in the end times, be authorized to initiate and lead a new society: one in which the gifts of the hitherto marginal were central to the social system.

The sacred often shuffles the deck of possibility so that a new deal, whether for the individual or the larger society, is in order. Thus the sense of time itself becomes disarranged. The present is not what it used to be and foreshadows a future-present that will include formerly excluded possibilities and new presences. Hitherto impossible conjunctions will seem to be quite expectable. For instance, in the name of a future that represents a sharp break with the past, the ancestors themselves would return. Religion, however, tames the sacred.

To understand Wilson's approach to the study of religion we cannot do better than to track carefully his discussion of a social movement in some of the islands of Melanesia after the Second World War. Originally colonized by the Germans in 1912, the islanders became less warlike; they learned some English from Australian colonists, used European money, and became aware of possibilities for cultural and social change. This awareness was heightened during the Second World War through contact first with Japanese, then with American soldiers. The Americans' racial diversity and friendliness, as well as their impressive machinery and equipment, aroused new hopes for social and cultural transformation. Particularly burdensome on young men had been the price customarily paid for brides; it was like a mortgage that required many years to pay off and kept the young not only saddled with debt but under the control of their families and especially of men with seniority. Traditional roles in village life became less appealing to younger men, as did the type of Christianity the natives had learned from missionaries. Both native and Christian religious beliefs and practices seemed to keep them in their place, require them to expend what money they had on feasts and brides, prevent them from pursuing new forms of work and ways to acquire wealth, and to stifle cooperation among the natives themselves. Even before the war, leaders like a young man named Paliau had sought to create new ways in which the young could borrow capital, resolve their own conflicts, pay their taxes, think for themselves, free themselves from the influence of missionaries, and govern their own villages. As Wilson (1975: 479–80) goes on to recount, "Individuals arose in different places whose excitement at the prospects of the new movement led to dreams of the coming of cargo, to be brought by Jesus and the ancestors. Old goods were to be destroyed – canoes, the church, everything that spoke of the past: even the money which had been collected in the movement was thrown away at Mouk, a village on Baluan. . . . Visions occurred, lights were seen, and planes, cars, and other supernatural manifestations presaged the early return of the ancestors." Along with Paliau's movement to renew and reform village life, then, emerged a cult with ecstatic and millennial overtones. Villagers shook in ecstasy, but they also marched in order toward a new day. At times the cultic aspects of the movement dissipated, and leaders emphasized the development of literacy and self-discipline, especially under Paliau's influence; hard work and organization were expected to usher in a new day of cooperation among the villages and of increasing material well-being. At other times the cultic aspects of the movement displaced the more rational activities and expectations, with an emphasis on the coming of Jesus on "the Last Day, which was set for Easter Day, 1954, when the world would be leveled out into a park-like condition. Drilling, uniforms, proper procedure at meetings, with one thing decided at a time, (a point Paliau had persistently made) were part of the instructions of the ancestors" (Wilson 1975: 481). There was thus an alternation and a mingling of ecstatic and millennial expressions of intense desire and anxiety; emphasis shifted back and forth from work to celebration, from marching to having orderly meetings. Sometimes the focus was on the return of the ancestors: at others, expectation shifted to a Christian Eschaton. In some periods it was the marginal members of the movement who took center stage in their demands for reassurance and recognition; at others control seemed to be more in the hands of elders who understood proper conduct and how to negotiate with Australian officials.

Wilson (1975: 483) summarizes the movement in a way that indicates his extraordinary grasp of the way that the sacred often carries and conceals the secular: "In Paliau's teaching there was a general secularity which, although he too was affected by the cult ideas, generally led away from magical expectations, and emphasized the acquisition of discipline and skills as the way to reach a social order. That these procedures should have been mistaken for magical instrumental means to bring the millennium into being is not itself surprising, considering the very limited knowledge of Western civilization that was available to the natives from the type of cultural contact that they had experienced."

Clearly, for Wilson (1975: 483), secularity is a term that covers the sorts of rationality that are associated with "the conjoining of end and means" with adequate understanding of the relationships of causes to effects or, I would add, of performances to qualities. However, although it is a mistake for villagers to assume that marching in military drill formation will bring prosperity or make the crops grow, still it is necessary to acquire social disciplines on the way to transforming a social order from ineffective and episodic outburst of enthusiasm to continuous and effective work and politics. Even for an observer as experienced and as astute as Wilson, it is not always simple to separate the sacred from the secular, the rational from the irrational or nonrational, and the instrumental from the merely expressive. That is because the novel and open-ended present created by a charismatic movement, the relation of ends to means and of effects to causes, and of the present to the future, is itself unsettled and ambiguous.

Because what is on the ground is usually far more subtle, variable, and complex than any conceptual framework, Wilson is exceedingly careful in his application of a typology to a charismatic movement or institution. There were aspects of the social movement led by Paliau that were at times millennial, but they were often simultaneously also purely present-oriented, whether they were ecstatic or focused on wonder-working through magical means. The latter type of movement Wilson (1975: 484) calls "thaumaturgical," and it is magical because it includes "belief in empirically unjustified practices and procedures which affect personal well-being." With regard to millennial movements, Wilson (1975: 484) is careful to say it is a "misnomer if the strictly Christian implications of the word are borne in mind." Millennial movements are what Wilson (1975: 484) calls revolutionist, because the intended transformations are not, as in magic, largely personal and restricted to the individuals or their families and communities. The "revolutionist response," according to Wilson (1975: 484) "is always social – tribal or ethnic – and rarely localized to the merely communal." These terms, the revolutionist and the thaumaturgical, along with the notion of cargo cults like Paliau's movement, have the advantage, according to Wilson (1975: 485) of being "close to empirical data, initially in the self-conceptions of the votaries themselves." They have the further advantage of lending themselves to cross-cultural comparisons and analyses, in a way that terms more closely related to specific religious traditions, like Zionism and messianism, do not. Both types of social movements, the revolutionist and the thaumaturgical, can be distinguished from other types of movements whose "orientations are steadily subordinated to apprehension of the rational measures instituted to bring about an improvement of social experience" (Wilson 1975: 485). However, in subjecting social movements to the criteria of rationality, and in rooting rationality in the way religious conceptions fit the data yielded by an empirical investigation, Wilson is merely applying the same standards that he uses to evaluate his own sociological investigations. As a sociologist, Wilson (1975: 484) notes, he is continually "reminded of the limitations of his conceptual apparatus in embracing the complexity of the world," a dilemma he shares with the most devoted adherent of a new religious movement.

There is a paradox at the heart of Wilson's view of religious movements that offer some variation or combination either of magic or the millennium. One type of millennial movement, the revolutionist, is "occasional, episodic, and unenduring" (Wilson 1975: 492). It clearly lacks staying power and will not stand the test of time. It is clearly rooted in and limited to the present. In fact, not only is the revolutionist response "transitory," argues Wilson (1975: 492); "it is also incapable, in its own terms, of attaining any measure of success" (Wilson 1975: 492). That is because the millennial movement cannot initiate its own future but must await decisive action by some "external agency," and the transformation is not slow or incremental, to be arrived at in a series of reasonable or orderly steps, but a cataclysm that changes everything, including the conditions under which any actions could be undertaken. The millennial movement is inherently secular and temporal, precisely because it anticipates a future-present that is radically different from and will displace the actual present, and yet it is sacred.

Given his critique of millennialism, it is understandable that Wilson (1975: 492) argues that thaumaturgy "is not only the pristine religious orientation, it is also more persistent than millennialism. The many little failures of magic are less disturbing to believers than the one big periodic failure of the millennium, and are more easily explained away. Given the localism implicit in tribal societies, the lack of consciousness of social structure, the persistence of a world-view expressed in a personal idiom, it is understandable that magic should be the acceptable means for the solution of problems" (Wilson 1975: 493). Wilson's view is entirely consistent with sociological critiques of the counter-cultural social movements of the 1960s that also promised social transformations, but that based the promised transformation entirely on changes in the individuals' own consciousness and personal habits. Lacking any coherent view of the social order or any rational program for social change, much of the counter-culture of the 1960s required only that individuals undergo personal transformations, changes in their personal routines, or enhance their own consciousness in ways that would assure them of their ultimate grounding in a cosmic order that stands above history and any particular social system. Speaking of thaumaturgy, Wilson (1975: 492) argues "The thaumaturge, it is true, also claims to be able to affect external circumstances and makes few direct demands of his client, but thaumaturgy does affect mental attitudes, reassures men, confirms their diagnoses (in witch-finding), utilizes trickery and self-confirming devices (in ordeals), and normally escapes objective test." Thaumaturgy and magic thus create a presence by transforming and confirming the believers' experience of their own presence. They are primitive forms of the sacred.

Wilson is not saying that even these charismatic movements lack all significance for social change. Paradoxically, it is charisma that gives the impetus to individuals to understand and assert their own agency. Under the influence of charisma, even the social order seems to be changeable and responsive to the enhanced presence, to the wishes and actions, of ordinary human beings. What seemed to be given and unchangeable appears, under the impact of religious movements, to be subject to change and thus to the passage of time. It is as if the sacred creates out the sphere of the present, of the mundane and temporal, and opens that sphere to the play of human desire and interest. On the contrary, "Even in restorative millennialism a new basis of social identity is created: in futuristic millennialism the tendency is toward the establishment of a more rational order, as men themselves begin to take on the powers once ascribed to the gods, and to construct their own social institutions – not perfectly but with growing social consciousness. . . . It is within religious phenomena that secularization must first appear" (Wilson 1975: 494, 497).

Wilson (1975a: 87–90) is very clear that the sacred itself is a primary source of secularization. On the one hand the sacred defines what is extraneous to the social order and what is, therefore, temporal and expendable. Speaking of a mythological figure among the Tanna Islanders of the Pacific, by name Jonfrum, Wilson (1975a: 87) notes that on his return, whether as a god or a "western type superman," he would "cause the whites to leave, render European money useless, and restore to the Tannese their youth. Work and sickness would cease, old customs would be restored, and the mission, the government, and police would be obliged to leave, together with natives from other islands. . . . A run on the stores occurred, and the chiefs kept their people away from the Presbyterian mission services, and kava drinking and dancing – prohibited by the mission – were now freely practiced." If it were not for the anticipated appearance of the sacred in the form of this Jonfrum, religion would not number among the various influences, institutions, and practices that are extraneous to the social order and hence slated to pass away. The sacred determines what it is that will – and will not – stand the test of time. The temporal, the present that is here only for the time being, thus includes the sacred, and it may in fact deprive much, like the Presbyterian missions and their services, of any claim to the authority of religion.

To be sure, the sacred may well reinforce whatever is extraneous to the social order. Thus, at first sacred practices may seem at best strategic or instrumental, practical or self-interested on the part of individuals, rather than functioning to reinforce and express the central beliefs and values of the society itself. As we have discovered in the passage just quoted, moreover, the sacred may threaten people and institutions "from away": a government that comes from some distant source outside the village, or missions that are clearly from another culture altogether. In fact, it would appear that the demand for creating and defining the sacred increases, the more that extraneous influences, especially those from outside the society, tend to infiltrate a society, reach down to the local level, and influence everyday life and the face to face interactions of the indigenous people.

However, we need to remember that a practice may well be sacred regardless of whether it may arise from some mundane or practical, as opposed to some highly ritualized or essential activity, or whether it is imported or imposed from the outside. Rather, what makes a belief or practice, a person or custom extraneous and therefore secular depends on the role of religion in determining what is quintessential and lasting to a social order and what is extraneous, superfluous, and of merely temporal significance.

For instance, the presence of a charismatic leader endowed with supernatural power makes it very difficult for an other to claim to possess that power. Such claims are difficult at best to substantiate, and followers of charismatic leaders are as easily and quickly disenchanted by a lack of success on the part of the leader as they are ready to be enchanted by such a figure's extraordinary presence, prowess, or claims. Furthermore even leaders who claim to have at best only a second-hand endowment of charisma derived from a mythical or transcendent source are capable of preserving whatever sacred residues might be possessed by local religious institutions, traditions, and governments. Speaking of the Jonfrum movement in the Congo between the two world wars of the twentieth century, Wilson (1975a: 90) notes that "the claims of its actual leaders were, of course, met, because natives discovered the extent to which, once they withdrew their consent to being controlled by the government agent and the mission, they escaped control, and could indeed revert to prohibited practices such as drinking and dancing." Their presence and hence their being mattered. Under the impact of the sacred, the social order and even religion itself begin to collapse.

It may seem at first that Wilson's theory of secularization stands commonsense on its head. It would seem to be taken for granted that the sacred tends to cast an aura of the extraordinary or the supernatural over the ordinary, and indeed it does. However, the sacred may have little room for rivals and substitutes; they cannot all be the real thing. When a charismatic leader appears, whose claim to the sacred seems beyond doubt at least for the time being, other forms of the sacred lose their power to enchant. Wilson (1975a: 98) puts it very clearly: "with the emergence of a charismatic figure, a wide range of practices and procedures, even though they are sacrally reinforced, may be suddenly abandoned and superseded." One presence overshadows the other.

The secularizing consequences of the sacred are all the more remarkable because the sacred itself is not only quintessential but temporary. On the one hand, it claims by its very being to be above the ordinary, set apart, exceptional and, by the definition I would use here, quintessential. Without its presence, nothing is as it appears or should be. On the other hand, the sacred is always prone to losing its own claims to transcendence; it is, I would suggest, at best subject to conditions and change. There are various ways this same statement could be made, depending on the social conditions in which the sacred is found. Other than the binary distinction between the quintessential and the evanescent, a number of others may define the internal contradictions within the sacred itself: the everlasting and the temporal, the transcendent and the immanent, the extraordinary and the ordinary, the unconditional and the conditional, the necessary and the impossible, the imperative and the optional.

Thus the sacred contains within itself the principle of its own undoing or negation. Speaking of charismatic figures, Wilson (1975a: 93) argues that "the specific prophecies of the charismatic leader normally fail; the type and range of the illness that he can miraculously cure are limited; the essential miracles are heard about rather than seen; the expectations of his followers are always eventually disappointed." That is, contingencies, accidents, constantly interfere with the revelation and effectiveness of his presence. The heart of the revelation remains undisclosed; the prophecy of a coming day of redemption fails, and the future is once again deferred.

The present becomes inevitably disappointing, a passage into the past. Under religious protection, the sacred is less affected by the passage of time, freer from contingency and accident; it is not to be negotiated or revised, and will never be merely optional. Nevertheless, there is no revelation that is complete and no prophets without those who fail to give them honor in their own country. Inevitably, then, the contradiction within the sacred becomes externalized, and circumstance or the passage of time, disbelievers or outsiders, those who are shortsighted or whose horizons are limited to their own immediate context and self-interest, inevitably ignore, fail to understand, or betray the presence of the sacred.

Wilson (1975a: 94) argues that in the simplest societies it is possible to imagine someone whose presence is so commanding that he or she elicits total respect, even faith itself: "Thus it is in simple societies that there obtains that basic condition of human consciousness on which the emergence of a charismatic figure depends." In these societies individuals remain persons as such, not people who are performing roles; their total person is therefore never fully reduced to a single role or its performance. The sacred person is embodied in someone who is the most extraordinary in some regard, whether for his or her capacities to heal or speak, or to hunt and fight. However, as Wilson goes on to argue, in such societies "there are few, if any, extraneous influences to promote change – [thus] it is difficult for any individual to rise far above the generality" (Wilson 1975a: 94). Thus it is difficult to know when one is in presence of the sacred as opposed to the merely contingent or accidental, since there are relatively few contingencies or accidents, and only the truly extraordinary individual can embody what is quintessentially human or divine.

Thus Wilson develops several factors or variables that are conducive to the formation and emergence of the sacred. The more a society becomes differentiated between its core values and practices, on the one hand, and the mundane and purely practical on the other; the more outside influences from an alien society penetrate and overlap with everyday life in an indigenous community; the more disruption there is in everyday life, so that individuals develop basic anxieties about the present and the future: the more that the present is ephemeral or problematic, the more will the sacred emerge.

To put it another way, the greater the surplus of possibilities beyond what a society may understand and realize, the greater the demand for the sacred to define the present and embody presence. You would expect Wilson to argue, then, that in societies where there are relatively few possibilities for individuals to distinguish themselves from each other, there would be relatively little demand for the presence of a sacred person whose very being defined the quintessentially social, human, or divine. That is precisely Wilson's (1975a: 85) point when he argues that "The lack of profound differentiation between individuals in Melanesian societies, and the low degree of specialization, perhaps make it inevitable that the typical movement should celebrate, not so much the individual of high standing, as the ancestors as a collectivity." It is the ancestors who embody surplus possibility, not the extraordinary individual.

When a society undergoes a process of differentiation, the core of the social system separates from what is relatively extraneous. The central values of the social order are then separable from the interests of those who pursue them. Without such basic, inner differentiation, the novel and the unpredictable seldom arise, whether because order remains uninterrupted or because there is so little order to interrupt. Until there is some differentiation between the basic beliefs, practices, and rituals of the social order, and everyday life with its relatively accidental, contingent, and unpredictable occurrences, there is little demand for a charismatic figure to define the present or to embody effective presence. As Wilson (1975a: 94) puts it, "We may suppose that without the impress of external events, the growth of anxieties, the disruption of normal life, there would be little demand for a man of supposed *extraordinary* supernatural power, and that it would be difficult for such an individual to arise." That is, until there are more possibilities than can be predicted, accounted for, or prevented by the social order, the present will not be problematical.

In Wilson's (1975a: 96–97) view, furthermore, if there were no surplus possibilities or if the present were neither disappointing or anxiety-laden, there would be no need to provide elaborate justifications for a god whose prophecies fail. Indeed, an entire religious tradition may be understood to be the elaboration of explanations and justifications for the failure of a charismatic figure to be a presence effective enough to anticipate or cope with various contingencies.

To protect the sacred from contingency, many religions provide their deities with a measure of transcendence. In Wilson's view, Christianity, in continuity with Judaism, far exceeds other world religions in this respect. "In general," writes Wilson (1982: 74), "even though God is still thought to be susceptible to human dispositions and supplications, divine power is not expected to be manifest in the world: nature and supernature are markedly distinct." The more that God's ways are distinct from human ways, therefore, the more the world is secular. Indeed, that is one way in which Christianity, and before it Judaism, contributed to the process of secularization, by removing the presence of the sacred from the contingencies and accidents of this world. As Wilson (1982: 74) puts it, "The world is profane – and in the Christian conception, sullied by sin – and the deity, remote from this profanity, may be reached only because of his mercy." The present is thus not lacking in possibility but cannot be either anxiety-laden or disappointing.

Of course Wilson recognizes that within the Christian tradition there are many strands that have reenchanted the natural and social world by making them places where the sacred can indeed be found in the ordinary. The saints provided links between the human and the divine and were sources of help in the contingencies of everyday life. He also notes that "the contemporary enthusiasm for charismatic renewal" introduces the transcendent into the immanent and makes this world a scene of greater enchantment. However, "in general," Wilson (1982: 73) notes, "the effectiveness of Church organization and control has been such that untoward evidence of the operation of divine and supernatural forces at work in the world have been subject to rigorous scrutiny." It may seem that Wilson is enjoying a bit of irony at the Church's expense here, by making the Church a guardian of the secular world against intrusions from the divine, but he is also noting, as did Durkheim, that the sacred requires protection from its opposite, as the secular, if it is to remain secular, requires protection from the sacred.

Because of its monotheistic traditions, Wilson (1982: 74) goes on to note, Christianity has been notably inhospitable to competing sources of the sacred. Whereas various kinds of Buddhism or Hinduism offer believers a way to find the sacred in the midst of the profane, Christianity tends to draw a sharper line differentiating the two. As Wilson puts it, "Christianity (where alternative and lesser sources of spiritual help were inadmissible, especially in Protestantism) led to secularization." The present remained transient and mundane.

The secularization of Western society proceeded under the influence of Protestantism, Wilson (1982: 75 ff.) argues. Thanks primarily to Calvinism, a "new work order which burgeoned under capitalism" (Wilson 1982: 76) made everyday life and labour a means, first of all, to the glorification of God and soon thereafter a way of assuring oneself of the very salvation that was inherently beyond the reach of any human effort. Humans were left to rely upon themselves for self-improvement and for bettering their own condition, "since God was no longer active in the world, and the church had no role save that of teaching God's law and of offering men spiritual guidance" (Wilson 1982: 76). Because the present was devoid of surplus possibility, to glorify God required a certain element of self-mastery; emotions were to be brought under control, purposes declared, and responsibility taken for the course not only of one's everyday actions but of one's life. The same mastery was to be extended over the world of nature, and science became a vocation, a calling, to "demonstrate the glory of God by discovering the wonders of the physical world" (Wilson 1982: 77). Eventually, of course, both science and capitalism developed their own motivations and standards, procedures and policies, and they became their own sources of both inspiration and authority. However "the culture of Western society was now transformed" by a Protestant Reformation that had effectively driven a powerful wedge between this world and the next. The transcendence of God was firmly established, and everyday life was left largely to its own devices. The present lacked surprises and enchantment.

In this same process, religion not only was a carrier of secular values and a force leading to the secularization of Western societies; it also became highly secularized itself. Wilson (1982: 80–81) points to the diminished role of the priesthood and of worship among both Protestant and Catholics. Lay ministries now supplement and support clerical ministries, and the priesthood is far less oriented to the mysteries of worship than to the effective management of local religious institutions. As Wilson (1982: 80–81) puts it, "The priesthood and its functions became demystified – reduced to the role of ministry. . . . Instrumental values and the accompanying attitudes of mind, having become the dominant mode of Western culture, have exerted their influence on religion, which instead of shaping secular values, as once in large part it did, is now increasingly shaped by them." The present is not filled with mystery or with surplus possibility. The presence of the individual, the total personality, is muted by the restriction of the individual to the performance of roles.

Secularization and the decline of Western civilization

Wilson's (1982: 31) view is that, left unchecked, the process of secularization entails the eventual breakdown of large scale societies. If it is true, as Wilson has argued, that secularization frees most areas of social life to become rational on their own terms, to develop their own resources, to engineer their own models, to follow their own procedures, and to police themselves, rationality loses its basis in anything beyond itself. There is no end in sight, and thus nothing to which people may give themselves: nothing for which they may be asked to sacrifice themselves. All of social life becomes an object of self-interested calculation, and, as Wilson (1982: 51) puts it, "Modern society rejects religion on intellectual grounds, and fails to see what the cost might be in terms of the emotional sustenance that men need in order to live."

Just what that cost may be, if properly calculated, is itself incalculable but extreme. At the very least, Wilson (1982: 51) argues, "there are unexplored elements of 'input' on which a modern society depends but which it does nothing to service." Some of this "input" is what Wilson (1982: 51) calls "residual disinterested goodwill and social obligation." These residues of good intention were created in small communities in which people where valued as individuals and to which they made real contributions over a lifetime; in these communities people learned to participate and to care for each other (Wilson 1982: 51–52). They were real presences.

As these communities dissolve in a process that subsumes community life under society-wide standards and substitutes rational for religious controls, people participate less and care less for one another. As a result, they neglect to do the hard work of keeping local communities and their institutions vital. They begin to fight and to hurt each other; violence in everyday life increases, as does discouragement or even despair. People neglect not only their communities but their natural environments; it is as if when there is no end in sight, only means, anything goes, and there is no real tomorrow. One lives in an endless present without meaning or hope. As Wilson (1982: 52) concludes, "Unless the basic virtues are serviced, unless men are given a sense of psychic reassurance that transcends the confines of the social system, we may see a time when, for one reason or another, the system itself fails to work, because men lack the basic dispositions to 'give themselves' for the benefit of each other."

Under these conditions, we might expect a society to manufacture a sense of crisis in order to mobilize the commitments and motivations that otherwise would remain focused on individuals and their own immediate interests and commitments. A society would have to generate at least a quasi-religious worldview that would pit chaos against order, evil against the good, in order to provide secular challenges commensurate with the incentives and warnings formerly provided by religion. Society itself would take on a sectarian character, as if pitted over and against a world that was full of great possibility and yet great danger. Only in this way could a society hope to elicit the enthusiasm and evoke the commitments that formerly had been sustained by religion itself.

The need for such a sectarian social order becomes clear as Wilson (1982: 86) describes how secularization resulted in the breakdown of morality in Western societies: "When in the West, religion waned, when the rationalistic forces inherent in Puritanism acquired autonomy of their religious origins, so the sense of moral propriety also waned – albeit somewhat later, as a cultural lag. Following the decline of religion, although not explicitly and directly as a consequence of it, came a process of moral breakdown, and the so-called 'new morality' or 'permissive morality' was born." Wilson goes on to point out that there is no consensus on how to raise or what to teach children about proper behavior, just as there is a "genuine concern about the role of morality in contemporary culture" (Wilson 1982: 87). Permissiveness, uncertainty, disagreement, even conflict about how to live and what to live for become the fate of societies that lack the bonds linking religion to morality, and morality has to find its own support and justifications outside of any taken-for-granted or authoritative context. There is no unified sense of the past, of traditional culture, just as there is no common future of collective aspiration.

It is not only that societies become confused as moral questions become increasingly contentious. It is that societies themselves lose the distinct traditions within which it is possible to think and to argue about morality. There is no context outside of a rationalized science or technology within which to raise and resolve moral questions, and both science and technology are simply unable to authorize answers that will command the consent that is necessary if individuals are to subordinate their own separate interests and goals to a larger, collective view of what makes life worth living. Wilson (1982: 88) warns us that "western culture lives off the borrowed capital of its religious past." And that "the consequences, not only for the arts and for high culture, but also, and perhaps more importantly, for the standards of civic order, social responsibility, and individual integrity, may be such that the future of western civilization itself may be thrown in jeopardy."

References

(1975) [Heinemann 1973] *Magic and the Millennium*. St Albans: Paladin.
(1975a) *The Noble Savages. The Primitive Origins of Charisma and its Contemporary Survival*. Berkeley, Los Angeles and London: University of California Press.
(1982) *Religion in Sociological Perspective*. Oxford and New York: Oxford University Press.

Peter L. Berger

Born in Vienna in 1929, Peter Berger received his doctorate in 1952 from the New School for Social Research in New York City. After teaching at several campuses, including the New School and Rutgers University, in 1981 Berger took the post of Professor of Sociology and Theology at Boston University, where he initiated the Institute for the Study of Economic Culture.

To understand Berger's sociology of religion it is wise to start with his ideas on secularization. These provide an overview of his general theory on religion in the Western world and its relation to modernity. However, sometimes Berger is writing about secularization as it affects religious institutions from within: an inner secularization of which the churches, for instance, themselves may be the agents and of which they may remain largely unaware. Sometimes Berger is talking about the secularization of the nation-state itself: a topic that involves not only what is often called civil religion, but the general legitimacy of the state itself. Still on another level, Berger may be speaking of long-term processes that have been carried by and that have in turn affected Western civilization.

It is well to keep them separate, even though in any given work Berger may treat them together. For instance, Berger (1977: 157–68) wrote, in an article devoted primarily to secularization at the level of religious institutions and of American society, that "My own tendency is to think that secularization has been a long-lasting and fairly even process, and that nothing drastic happened to the American religious consciousness either after World War II or in the most recent decade [the 1960s–1970s]." However, despite his reference to American society, in this sentence it is likely that Berger is also referring to processes broader in scope and long antedating American society and culture. For instance, speaking at the level of Western civilization, Berger (1990: 111) writes of "an immense shrinkage in the scope of the sacred in reality." It is an idea that derives from Max Weber's notions about "disenchantment" and the way in which Protestantism eliminated "mystery, miracle, and magic" from Western culture and from the psychology of the individual (Berger 1990: 111). We will return later in this chapter to other arguments that Berger has made, which root secularization in a process that begins with the very origins of Israelite religion.

Speaking at the level of American society, Berger focuses specifically on two aspects of religion: the general legitimacy of the nation-state and its institutions; and civil religion, or the nation's religious consciousness of its own identity and history. With regard to the nation-state and its legitimacy, Berger (1977: 159) argues that the 1960s and the 1970s presented what amounts to a genuine legitimacy crisis in the United States: "We have been passing through a process that sociologists rather ominously describe as *delegitimation* – that is, a weakening of the values and assumptions on which a political order is based. We have been lucky, I think, that this malaise of the political system has not so far been accompanied by severe dislocations in the economy; I can only express the hope that our luck continues to hold." Berger does mention various events that contributed to this legitimation crisis; clearly protests against racial discrimination and the war in Vietnam eventually called into question the state's ability or willingness to honor basic American values, as in the Watergate crisis which felled the Nixon administration. However, Berger (1977: 158) also points the finger at secularizing political elites themselves, e.g. "the more openly acknowledged secularism of that portion of the college-educated upper middle class that finances what it considers good causes – in this instance, the cause of pushing secularist cases through the courts." Not only did these secularizing elites succeed in getting prayer out of the public schools but have resisted the payment of public funds to church schools and to other church-related institutions. As a result, Berger (1977: 159) argues that "the legitimacy of the American political order faces the gravest crisis since the Civil War."

It is not only the political system that has been secularized and endangered in this process but the nation-state itself. In Berger's view, the nation has been undergoing "a weakening in the plausibility of its own creed, quite apart from the relation of this creed to the several churches." What he has in mind is the removal of the phrase "Under God" from the pledge of allegiance, and the more general sense that this nation serves a providential purpose and operates under a divine mandate. As a result, Berger concluded in the late 1970s, the nation may be facing either an international breakdown of its authority and influence, or an attempt to impose by state power the values of a fundamental or conservative right-wing, or an internal movement that would revitalize and update the nation's confidence in its own beliefs, values, and institutions. Berger saw little hope for the last possibility, which leaves the first two possibilities relatively intact and of obvious relevance to the present. Over and above the loss of confidence in the American civil religion, and possible attempts to revive it with a right-wing version of national messianism, Berger's comments point to a deflation, as others might call it: a delegitimation, in which American institutions, especially the government and political elites, undergo a loss of trust and credibility, even a loss of authority in the estimation of the American public. Religion loses control of the sacred.

It is very possible, however, that Berger reserves his most stringent comments for the level of religious institutions, that is, the churches and religious denominations. Speaking at the level of religious institutions, however, Berger (1977: 154) spoke of the churches in the United States in the post World War II era as having undergone an "invisible secularization" (emphasis in the original). Berger (1977: 157) goes on to speak of secularizing "theological movements" which were eager to "divest the churches of their traditional contents and to replace these with a variety of secular gospels – existentialism, psychoanalysis, revolutionary liberation, or avant-garde sensitivity." *By referring to "secular gospels," of course, Berger implicitly notes how difficult it is to differentiate the sacred from the secular, just as it is difficult for traditional religions like Christianity to maintain a monopoly on or control over the sacred.* Of course, this process of inner secularization is not new. Berger notes that the Reformed tendency in Western Protestantism is inherently secularizing, in the sense of tending to demystify the sacred, and Berger (1990: 111) argues that "The sacramental apparatus is reduced to a minimum and, even there, divested of its more numinous qualities." The Eucharist commemorates or, at the most, reenacts the Last Supper without creating a food that bears within itself the person and presence of Jesus of Nazareth. As Wilson pointed out regarding modern societies, they become disenchanted as roles replace personal presence with role-performances.

Of course, it is not empirically necessary or true that, as religion decreases the scope of the sacred within its own beliefs, institutions, and practices, the sacred is similarly diminished in scope outside the provinces and control of religion. *As religion becomes increasingly secularized, the sacred may take on new forms and vitality in a wide range of social contexts well outside the scope of religion itself*. The nation-state, for example, may remain secular and yet become sacralized without enjoying any religious legitimation or having any identity with traditional religion.

Although church-based or church-related religion may be on the decline in Western Europe and, increasingly so in Spain, Italy, and even Greece, it is clear that religion of a more generic or populist nature is alive and well. That is, as religion becomes one part of a society instead of its overarching "sacred canopy," to use Berger's excellent title, the sacred thrives outside the auspices of traditional religion. In one of his most recent discussions of secularization, Berger (1999: 10) therefore has suggested that "A shift in the institutional location of religion, then, rather than secularization, would be a more accurate description of the European situation." The sacred takes on a life of its own.

Berger's point in *The Sacred Canopy* is primarily historical and operates on the level of the civilization rather than of the nation-state, its culture, or of particular religious institutions. He (1990: 112) notes that, in opposing Catholicism, Protestantism disrupted the "vast continuity of being between the seen and the unseen." It did so by substituting the Word of God, to be found in the Bible and in preaching, for a universe permeated by sacred presences. Whereas for the Catholic, as Berger (1990: 113) puts it, there is "an ongoing linkage of human events with the sacred forces permeating the universe," and this linkage is recreated through ritual, Protestantism "narrowed man's relationship to the sacred to the one exceedingly narrow channel that it called God's word."

However, as Berger (1990: 117–18) goes on to note, Protestantism was not the first highly secularizing religious formation in Western history. On the contrary, the religion of ancient Israel emphasized humanity's "*dis*continuity not only with God but with the rest of creation" (Berger 1990: 117; emphasis in original). Thus, Berger (1990: 118) argues, "the transcendentalization of God and the concomitant 'disenchantment of the world' opened up a 'space' for history as the arena of both divine and human actions." The secularity of the modern world is thus a direct result of a religious tradition that elevates the deity out of this world and insists on divine transcendence. Berger (1990: 123) allows that in the period of history in which Christendom created a balance between the sacred and the profane, there was some continuity of being between this world and the next. However, with Protestantism's expansion " 'the world' could all the more rapidly be secularized in that it had already been defined as a realm outside the jurisdiction of the sacred properly speaking."

It is in this context that we are to understand Berger's later (1999: 13) comment that "The critique of secularity common to all religious movements is that human existence bereft of transcendence is an impoverished and finally untenable condition." The religious movements so widespread today, which Berger sees as living proof that secularization is no longer a dominant tendency either in Western societies or more globally, are on this view a response to an earlier secularization that was itself the expression of dominant tendencies in Western religion. However, it is not clear whether or not those religious movements will have effects outside traditional religious institutions, revivifying the nation's civil religion or adding to the legitimacy of the nation's political elites.

Properly to understand Berger, then, we need to know whether, on the basis of more recent developments in religion and society, he is reversing his long-standing historically oriented thesis on secularization at the level of Western civilization. That thesis is based on a review of several thousand years of religious history.

However, it would seem, in some passages, that Berger is arguing, on the basis of developments over the last 20 or 30 years, that that thesis has been falsified. Speaking of the resurgence of conservative religion not only in the various branches of Christianity but in Buddhism, Islam, and Hinduism, Berger (1999: 6) writes, "taken together they provide a massive falsification of the idea that modernization and secularization are cognate phenomena. At the very least they show that counter-secularization is as important a phenomenon in the contemporary world as secularization." Arguing that contemporary religious trends appear to oppose secularization, he seems to be arguing both that secularization has been a dominant trend and that now it is being reversed by a resurgence in religion. Noting that it would be difficult to account for religious movements opposed to secularization if the dominant trend were indeed a decline in secularization, a desecularization, Berger (1999: 7) comments that "In that sense, at least, something of the old secularization theory may be said to hold up, in a rather back-handed way."

Of course, there is no inconsistency or contradiction here at all if one takes Berger's thesis on desecularization to apply to the vitality of religious institutions and movements, and only secondarily to possible changes at the level of the nation-state, without being extended, as yet, to the level of Western civilization, which may be far more resistant to short-term fluctuations in religiosity. It is therefore not clear that Berger is abandoning his former thesis that Christianity has been a major force for secularization at the level of Western civilization regardless of the smaller historical cycles at the level of the nation-state and its culture. Furthermore, the religious movements that Berger mentions as reversing the trend toward secularization at the level of the nation-state and its culture also have major secularizing effects and tendencies. In *The Desecularization of the World*, Berger argues that some of the most energetic and successful religious movements, Evangelicalism, for instance, create "schools for democracy and social mobility" (Berger 1999: 14). Not only is this true of Christian Evangelicals but of some forms of Roman Catholicism and of Islam (Berger 1999: 16–17). Thus what appears to be a force for the desecularization of modern societies is stimulating the growth of the very institutions that encourage people to think for themselves, reject tradition, take control of their societies, engage in novel practices, and become more systematic and rational in their social practices: in a word, more secular.

In his historical approach to secularization at the level of Western civilization, Berger was arguing that the secular world was a creation of Christianity's own tendency to separate the sacred from the profane. As we have seen, if God alone is divine, then the rest of the world, nature and all of humanity, is necessarily secular. If only the Word of God is sacred, then all other communication is by definition secular. If indeed only the Church is a truly sacred institution, all the more reason, then, exists for the world to be secular. As Berger (1990: 123; emphasis in the original) puts it, "The concentration of religious activities and symbols in *one* institutional sphere . . . *ipse facto* defines the rest of society as 'the world,' as a profane realm at least relatively removed from the jurisdiction of the sacred."

A great deal depends on the phrase "properly speaking" in the last sentence of the preceding paragraph. So long as the Church has had a monopoly on what it means to speak properly of the sacred, then by its own definitions "the world" could be defined as secular. With the development of the anthropology and sociology of religion, however, in the twentieth century, discourse about the sacred takes on a new turn. It becomes an empirical question as to whether any particular religion or even religion itself has control of discourse about the sacred or sacred practices. The sacred may or may not be found within the precincts of the institutional church, and the institutional church may or may not have a monopoly on what passes for the sacred. But these questions lie outside the immediate scope of *The Sacred Canopy*. As Berger (1990: 108) puts it, "We cannot here pursue the interesting question of the extent to which there may be, so to speak, asymmetry between these two dimensions of secularization, so that there may not only be secularization of consciousness within the traditional religious institutions but also a continuation of more or less traditional motifs of religious consciousness outside their previous institutional contexts."

Let us take both points together as we examine Berger's recent essay in the *Desecularization of the World*. That there is indeed a "secularization of consciousness within the traditional religious institutions" becomes clear when Berger (1999: 12) speaks of conservative and populist religious movements as "linked to non-religious forces of one sort or another, and the future course of the former [the religious movements] will be at least partially determined by the course of the latter [the nonreligious forces]." Berger (1999: 15) goes on to speak of religious movements "as a convenient legitimation for political agendas based on quite nonreligious interests." What Berger has in mind are conflicts, such as those in Bosnia or Northern Ireland, where national and ethnic interests in political power are clearly intertwined with conflicts intensified by differences in religious identity. Thus speaking of traditional religious contexts and institutions, Berger is finding them secularized from within by their association with the agendas and concerns of the secular world outside these institutions.

However, Berger also finds ample evidence of "more or less traditional motifs of religious consciousness outside their previous institutional contexts." Take, for example, the Evangelical movements in Latin America, where Pentecostals employ orthodox belief and ecstatic religiosity to break the hold of traditional forms of obligation to the Catholic Church, landlords, and popular notions about masculine identity that have subjected women to male domination. Berger (1999: 13) argues that "the Evangelical resurgence is positively modernizing in most places where it occurs" not least because Evangelicals become more upwardly mobile as they become more literate. Not only, then, are traditional religious contexts becoming secularized; mundane and every-day contexts are being infused with religious meaning by Pentecostal and evangelical religious movements. At last there is creative tension between the sacred and the secular under the impact of these move-ments: new spaces opening up where gender roles can be redefined, the home transformed, and new, less demeaning, more fruitful ways explored of getting and spending.

As a way of getting into the topic of disenchantment at the level of the nation-state and of civil religion, and of considering the fate of the sacred outside the realm of traditional religious institutions, Berger (1990: 107) begins by defining secularization in terms of the process of differentiation. In that process religion ceases to provide a "sacred canopy" for the whole society and becomes a special interest and sphere of influence: "The process by which sectors of society and culture are removed from the domination of religious institutions and symbols." To the extent that religion had a monopoly on the sacred, then, the removal of these various "sectors of society" from the control of religion would further shrink the scope of the sacred. However, the churches seldom, if ever, have had a monopoly on the symbols and practices by which God may be approached or induced to be present. To free schools from the domination of the Church need not necessarily imply that God is being removed from the classroom. On the contrary, the sacred may come into play within the schools in the form of a civil religion, or the sacred may indeed appear in the form of sacralized processes and rou-tines by which students are inducted into the society's patterns of soli-darity, deference, and respect. Beyond these societal forms of the sacred that appear in the classroom, there are aspects of Western civilization itself that carry the sacred into secular spheres, such as work and the development of the self. Here, too, the sacred may thrive in the class-room or in other secular contexts even as the educational or other sub-systems are being withdrawn from the control or tutelage of major religious institutions.

Berger (1990: 107–08) extends his argument about secularization by suggesting that it is not only social structures and institutions that undergo this process of separation or differentiation; the entire culture may be affected in such a way that science, art, philosophy, and litera- ture all become autonomous disciplines; they will ask their own ques- tions, provide their own methods, discipline their own practitioners, and come to their own conclusions without depending on religious institu- tions for guidance or religious perspectives. Furthermore, as religion becomes separate from various aspects of social and cultural life, it is also possible for individuals to "look upon the world and their own lives without the benefit of religious interpretations." One might think, in reading these passages in Berger, that religion and secularity were antithetical, except for the fact that we already know that for Berger, Western religion sowed the seeds of secularization by creating a world that was separate from the sacred and from the divine, and that religious institutions may become secularized from within.

In *The Sacred Canopy*, Berger works largely within the distinction that he has just made between the church and "the world." "The world" is initially a theological category, but it takes on sociological meaning as any area of institutionalized belief or practice outside the realm or con- trol of the church. In the process of differentiation, "the world" expands its sphere of ownership and control over work and politics, industry and the family, science and education, over the socialization of the young and the well-being and authority of the old. By theological definition, then, this is a process of secularization, and it is consistent with this theological framework that Berger himself sees modernity as a process of differentiation between religion and the other subsystems of the social order.

Let us return to this question of the inner secularization of religious institutions. Berger goes on to point out that in the United States of America, although religion and religious institutions seem to be more popular and widespread, and to have more influence, than in Europe, the religion contained in American institutions is itself highly secular- ized. As religion becomes increasingly a special interest, or caught up in utilitarian, practical or other "worldly" concerns, and to the extent that it serves personal rather than societal functions, it becomes secularized. Others have argued that religion in the churches also becomes secular to the extent that it loses any sense of mystery, and to the extent also

that the Bible provides information about the divine rather than embodying the presence of God or giving access to the divine. Given Berger's
thesis that secularizing tendencies are deeply embedded in Western
Christianity, it seems logical to state Berger's thesis in these rather simple
terms: Christianity tends to secularize the sacred and to sacralize the
secular.

Of course, at times the sacred may be in more direct opposition to
the secular: an opposition that allows for less creative interplay between
them and for more conflict, even violent opposition between the two.
Certainly, where religion has had a cultural and political monopoly of
the sacred in a nation-state, as in France prior to the revolution of 1789,
the formerly excluded secular aspects of the social order may become
militantly, even violently opposed to religion and may seek to move religion from the center to the periphery.

At other times, Berger notes, then, the Judeo-Christian tradition
becomes an influence conducive to the secularization of the larger
society by being in a creative, dynamic and dialectical tension with the
secular. As we have seen, he notes that the contemporary resurgence of
religion, in this case Protestantism, not only amounts to a desecularization of the world; its very resurgence also suggests that the secularization it opposes was not only relatively dominant but alive and well within
religious institutions themselves. Thus the resurgence of Protestantism
may be conducive not only to a desecularization but to a reseculariza-
tion of the world, especially as the forms of the religious movements
that are resurgent are themselves highly secularized.

Furthermore, in the process of secularization, the opposition between
the sacred and the secular may not only be reduced to creative tension
between them; it is further attenuated into a process of elaborating and
transposing sacred meanings into secular contexts, and of elaborating
and transposing secular meanings into sacred contexts. In this process,
creative tension is replaced by the mere interplay of interpretation. In
this latter process much may be lost in translation, and these lost meanings may indeed return to "haunt" the context from which they were
initially excluded. God may be returned to the Pledge of Allegiance or
to honorable mention in the public schools with or without exerting
any transformative effects on a nation or its educational institutions.
Similarly, the language of the liturgy in Protestant churches may be
modernized to exclude any references to theological terms that embody

elements of mystery, only to find that the laity hunger for something like "spirituality" without, at the same time, seeking radical personal transformation. This is the type of secularization that Berger (1969: 55) has in mind when he writes modernity "leads to a situation in which most plausibility structures are partial and therefore tenuous. They organize only a part of the individual's world and lack the compelling character of structures taken to be 'natural,' inevitable, self-evident. Most individuals in primitive or archaic societies lived in social institutions (such as tribe, clan, or even polis) that embraced just about all the significant relationships they had with other people. The modern individual exists in a plurality of worlds, migrating back and forth between competing and often contradictory plausibility structures, each of which is weakened by the simple fact of its involuntary coexistence with other plausibility structures." Secularization also proceeds through the process of differentiation by depriving any institutional set of beliefs of its taken-for-granted authority.

As a sociologist of religion working within the sociology of knowledge, Berger thus places a radical question-mark not only over the supposed truths of authoritative religious revelation but also over the taken-for-granted assumptions of sociologists about what constitutes modernity or even knowledge itself. It is one thing for sociologists of religion to debunk religion as a set of beliefs and practices that have lost their ability to help modern individuals to understand, explain, or navigate their many and complex social worlds. It is quite another for Berger as a sociologist of religion to question the ways in which sociologists imagine the past in terms of the present or limit authoritative knowledge to what can be established empirically within the assumptions of their own practice and enterprise. Berger (1969: 53) would debunk the debunkers of religion.

With Peter Berger we thus have a sociologist of religion who claims to have presented theologians with a starting point that is fundamentally anthropological, in a European, philosophical sense, as well as radically sociological. As Berger (1969: 59) puts it, "if the religious projections of man correspond to a reality that is superhuman and supernatural, then it seems logical to look for traces of this reality in the projector himself. This is not to suggest an empirical theology – that would be logically impossible – but rather a theology of very high empirical sensitivity that seeks to correlate its propositions with what can be empirically known. To the extent that its starting point is anthropological, such a theology will return to some of the fundamental concerns of Protestant liberalism – without, it is to be hoped, the latter's deference to the 'cultured despisers of religion' and their assorted utopianism."

It is not entirely clear who these despisers of religion are, but it may well be that they are like the theologians whom Berger criticizes earlier in the same chapter. Their tendency is to reduce Christian revelation to a set of existential or psychoanalytical questions, concerns, and propositions that are inherently modern because they fit a world riddled with uncertainty. They are modern also because these questions can be asked and answered within a framework that is nontheological and lacks the trappings of revelation, the supernatural, or mystery itself. Berger questions whether theologians can rescue the mysterious in Christianity by assigning it to the world of the sacred as opposed to ordinary history or to the world of faith as opposed to religion. For Berger, these distinctions fail to protect religion from the acids of sociological inquiry. He (1969: 49) argues that "The reason why this sort of reasoning won't do is twofold: First, the differentiation is meaningless to the empirical investigator – 'Christian faith' is simply another variant of the phenomenon 'religion,' 'salvation history' of the historical phenomenon, and so forth." From Berger's viewpoint, what passes for faith or sacred history is no less a make-believe form of understanding than any other. To posit something as faith or to interpret history as sacred requires a "plausibility structure" that allows individuals to suspend their disbelief, assume that they know what each other is talking about, and to avoid asking the fundamental questions about whether their beliefs and interpretations are true. Berger (1969: 49–50) therefore insists that "The differentiation [between faith and religion, salvation history and history] presupposes a prior exit from the empirical sphere, and therefore it cannot be used to solve a problem arising within that sphere." Berger thus not only debunks the debunkers but questions those who think they have injected enough existential uncertainty into religion to immunize it from the most virulent of modern viruses.

However, Berger permits religion ample ontological space within which to make its claims. Indeed, he produces what used to be called a natural theology that allows humans to understand the world in which they live because of an ontological correspondence between their mind and its projections, on the one hand, and on the other, the world itself.

Berger (1969: 58–59) asserts that "there is a fundamental affinity between the structures of his [man's] consciousness and the structures of the empirical world. Projection and reflection are movements within the same encompassing reality." Berger (1969: 58) asserts that "the mathematics that man projects out of his own consciousness somehow corresponds to a mathematical reality that is external to him, and which indeed his consciousness appears to reflect." Of course, as Berger (1969: 59) goes on to say, "Nothing is immune to the relativization of socio-historical analysis." It is just that someone in the first century is no more disqualified from knowing the truth by living in the first century than someone living in the twenty first century has an advantage in that regard.

In the end, Berger (1969: 59) concludes, "The theological decision will have to be that, 'in, with, and under' the immense array of human projections, there are indicators of a reality that is truly 'other' and that the religious imagination of man ultimately reflects." The phrase, "In, with, and under" comes from the theology of the sacraments; Berger is borrowing here a churchly formula for describing the way reality is constructed simultaneously to admit of several ambiguous or even contradictory levels of being and of interpretation. How else could it be, if consciousness offers clues as to the structure of reality itself?

As it turns out, there are several other ways in which consciousness might intersect with reality. Not only is transcendence perceived by the active consciousness to be "in, with, and under" the reality offered to ordinary sense. Some forms of transcendence virtually hit one in the face. Berger (1969: 82) writes that "There are certain deeds that cry out to heaven. These deeds are not only an outrage to our moral sense, they seem to violate a fundamental awareness of the constitution of our humanity. In this way, these deeds are not only evil, but *monstrously evil.*" That is, one finds it impossible to remain neutral or detached in observing and responding to them, and they cannot easily be under-stood or explained as relative to a particular situation or culture. There is something about such deeds that transcends the ordinary and defies being included with such a formula as "in, with, and under" the appear-ances of every life. As Berger (1969: 83) puts it, "Not only are we con-strained to condemn, and to condemn absolutely, but, if we should be in a position to do so, we would feel constrained to take action on the basis of this certainty." The word "absolutely" indicates that for Berger the grounds for condemning evil and for rejecting the evil aspects of the world are somehow other-worldly; they come from outside rather than from within and under the appearances of everyday life. As Berger (1969: 84) puts it, "the condemnation does not seem to exhaust its intrinsic intention in terms of this world alone."

As a starting point for sociological reasoning and inquiry then, Berger offers confidence in an immanent form of transcendence while remaining wholly skeptical of what passes for reality. On the one hand Berger sees congruity between the human consciousness and the world that consciousness seeks to describe, interpret, or explain. He has confidence in a consciousness that perceives the transcendent by looking beyond the world of appearance toward another reality that remains slightly hidden within the world of appearances and available only to the discerning consciousness. On the other hand, Berger sees consciousness as perceiving transcendence in the course not of understanding or explaining the world but of rejecting the world as it is. It is not hard to see in these two approaches echoes of a Weberian distinction between nonascetic and ascetic, the world-accepting and the world-rejecting forms of religious consciousness.

The underlying cause of any religious attitude that rejects the world is, for Berger, death itself. For some the fear of death and its inevitability may be hidden in, with, and under such ordinary situations as concern for one's work or for one's marriage. Love and work are, after all, areas in which one achieves a measure of transcendence precisely in one's refusal to let death interfere with completion and fulfillment. Because death is the implicit enemy, one worries that one might not live long enough to complete one's work or to fulfill the potential of one's marriage. For Berger (1969: 787–89), the fear and rejection of death emerge most explicitly when conditions become extreme, that is, when one's work and marriage may be threatened by illness or war. Religion conspires with this "denial of death implicit in hope" (Berger 1969: 78–79) by reinforcing childish hopes for protection and rescue or by colluding with various kinds of psychological denial. Although Berger accepts the psychoanalytic dismissal of religion as merely an echo of childhood's anxieties and magical thinking, he ascribes to such rejections of death an ontological reality. Berger (1969: 80) knows that "Man's 'no!' to death – be it in the frantic fear of his own annihilation, in moral outrage at the death of a loved other, or in death-defying acts of courage and self-sacrifice – appears to be an intrinsic constituent of his being. There seems to be a death-refusing hope at the very core of our *humanitas*. While empirical reason indicates that this hope is an illusion, there is something in us that, however shamefacedly in an age of triumphant rationality, goes on saying 'no!' and even says 'no!' to the ever so plausible explanations of empirical reason."

However, Berger seems to approve, on moral grounds, of a stoic acceptance of death as inevitable and final. He (1969: 79) asserts that "this kind of stoicism merits the deepest respect and, in fact, constitutes one of the most impressive attitudes of which man is capable." Clearly Berger has shifted here from an ontological to a moral argument which allows humans at their best not only to fight against or to deny death but to accept it as a "final reality." As for religion, it may reinforce either a stoic acceptance or resignation on the one hand, or an outraged defiance of death on the other: "religion vindicates the gestures in which hope and courage are embodied in human action – including, given certain conditions, the gestures of revolutionary hope and, in the ultimate irony of redemption, the courage of stoic resignation" (Berger 1969: 81).

Earlier in his discussion, Berger (1969: 77) noted other ways in which individuals deny or depreciate the finality of death, other "signals of transcendence, pointers toward a religious interpretation of the human situation." Some of them offer a less heroic defiance of death and rather ignore or side-step the realities of everyday life that lead inexorably over time to extinction. That is, they are nonascetic, and some of these evoke a world quite other than the one that offers so little hope for the future. Take, for example, Berger's (1969: 73) comments on play: "in joyful play it appears as if one were stepping not only from one chronology into another, but from time into eternity [hence the other-worldly aspect of this nonascetic form of transcendence]. Even as one remains conscious of the poignant reality of that other, 'serious' time in which one is moving toward death, one apprehends joy as being, in some barely conceivable way, a joy forever."

Note that this break between this-worldly and other-worldly transcendence involves the dimension of time. It is in times-out during play that one enters the other world in which time either stands still, as it does when one is transported to another world, or when time is at least ticking by a clock that has nothing to do with ordinary time. Games have their own clocks, and what matters is how many minutes there are left in the game, not what time it is in the outside world. Some of this extraordinary other-worldly time is created by sharp breaks with the past; other forms of transcendent, other-worldly time come when the future breaks into the present. In either case, the present is superseded either by the past or the future. Another world has imploded into this one.

There is, for Berger, still another way that everyday life offers hints of transcendence: a this-worldly, nonascetic form of consciousness. Berger (1969: 69) notes that there is at least one "experience that is absolutely essential to the process of becoming a human person." It is the experience of the infant who is reassured by a parent that "*Everything* is in order, *everything* is all right" (Berger 1969: 69). This is not a parental form of make-believe: not a carefully conjured appearance of order to mask the underlying chaos of everyday life. It is the discernment by the parent of an order that lies in, with, and under the appearances of disorder that may so upset a child that he or she becomes disoriented or even panicked, especially in the middle of the night. Berger (1969: 70) is making the claim that "human order in some way corresponds to an order that transcends it . . . that this transcendent order is of such a character that man can trust himself and his destiny to it." This world is continuous with another world that can be known within the experiences of everyday life. That transcendent order is reflected in the ways in which parents, for instance, calm a child's fears by stating, not as a wishful fantasy but a basic fact, that order prevails. As Berger (1969: 67) puts it, "every ordering gesture is a signal of transcendence" not an illusion but the real thing.

Central to Berger's notion of social life as pointing to an order beyond itself, that guarantees an ultimate reality underlying and transcending the social order, is the notion of the role, and especially the parental role. As Berger (1969: 70) puts it, "There is a variety of human roles that represent this conception of order, but the most fundamental is the parental role. Every parent (or, at any rate, every parent who loves his child) takes upon himself the representation of a universe that is ultimately in order and ultimately trustworthy." Berger is at some pains to assert that the role of the parent, in assuring the child that there is an order on which the child can depend, is not one of promoting make-believe. The parent's role is to convince the child that the social order itself is part of a cosmic order to which the child can trust his or her life, Berger (1969: 71) puts it simply: "The parental role is not based on a loving lie. On the contrary, it is a witness to the ultimate truth of man's situation in reality." This is a sociological truth with theological implications, and it is based on an anthropological approach to the problem of being itself.

In another context, however, Berger raises questions about the way individuals take their roles as a way of avoiding the truth about their own human condition. That truth is simply that they are free to say "No" not simply to death, as Berger was suggesting in his discussion above, but "No" to the roles offered to the individual by the larger society. To carry forward the illustration from the preceding paragraphs, no one has to take on the parental role of assuring the child that there is an order that is ultimately trustworthy. That reassurance may be necessary to still an anxious child's unquiet mind and to reinforce confidence that order will prevail over chaos. However, the role itself is a make-believe way of protecting the individual from the terror of facing death and ultimate extinction. According to Berger's (1963: 147) other viewpoint, "Society provides us with taken-for-granted structures (we could also speak here of the 'okay world') within which, as long as we follow the rules, we are shielded from the naked terrors of our condition. The 'okay world' provides routines and rituals through which these terrors are organized in such a way that we can face them with a measure of calm."

Occasionally social changes take place which make the social order itself no longer effective as a screen against despair or the fear of death. Somehow the social order becomes transparent to the possibility of death and no longer offers protection, reassurance, or guarantees that the individual, by taking part in social life, is part of a larger, cosmic order. If religion in the 1950s seemed to Berger (1977: 156) to "maintain this sense of the world being 'okay,' " by the end of the 1960s there had been a fundamental sea-change both in American society and in the role of religion. Berger (1977: 156) writes, "The change since then can be conveniently summed up by saying that more and more people have come to the conclusion that the world is *not* 'okay,' and religion has lost much of its ability to persuade them that it is" (emphasis in the original).

When in *Rumour of Angels* Berger discussed the anthropological starting point for a sociology of transcendence, he was quite clear that he did not think parents were engaged in a deception as they assured their children that not chaos, but order was the underlying and ultimate social and existential reality. However in *The Social Construction of Reality* Berger (1963: 145) takes a quite different approach: "Since society exists as a network of social roles, each one of which can become a chronic or a momentary alibi from taking responsibility for its bearer, we can say that deception and self-deception are at the very heart of social reality." It is a sign of "bad faith" when an individual invokes his role as a way of defending or explaining his or her actions. To hide behind a social role, even when assuring a child that order trumps chaos, would thus seem to be a form of "bad faith," no matter how much one loves one's child. Of course, simply knowing that one does not have to take a role or follow its prescriptions is potentially liberating. Berger (1963: 145) is quite clear that one does not have to hide behind a role or conform to its social expectations. One does not have to follow public opinion or obey convention but can live authentically "in full awareness of the unique, irreplaceable and incomparable quality of one's own individuality" (Berger 1963: 146).

Berger (1963: 130) goes on to discuss the fragility of any social order, no matter how deeply it is supported by tradition or how widely it is reinforced by commonsense and social expectations. He thus entertains the possibility of what has been called the Great Refusal. In one passage Berger (1963: 129) actually imagines a scene in which "The master expects a bow from his slave and instead gets a fist in his face." The master could be a distinguished professor meeting resistance or refusal from a student, a business executive being countermanded by an employee, a doctor being ignored, laughed at, or rebuked by a patient: the context could vary widely. The point in every context is simple enough: that individuals may discover their own individuality and refuse to have a self-understanding or self-image constituted by the expectations of others, even by those in positions of genuine authority. Crime and revolution alike, he argues, reveal the possibility of "the wholesale dis- and re-organization of an entire social system," and both of them show "the possibility of resistance to the external and (of necessity) also the internal controls. In fact, when we look at revolutions, we find that the outward acts against the old order are invariably preceded by the disintegration of inward allegiance and loyalties" (Berger 1963: 130).

If there is a specter haunting Western, or for that matter any other civilization, it is the ghost of the underived self. As we shall see, Berger is very clear that most people most of the time are all too happy to fill the prescriptions that are written for them: to become the sort of people that the society needs to fill its roles and perform its functions. The great weight of the social order leans heavily on and normally can suffocate whatever signs of individuality might pose a threat to its definitions of what is good or right, necessary or inevitable, required and obligatory. Berger, as I will point out, fully appreciates not only the fragility but the taken-for-grantedness of the social order and the lengths to which people will go to gain a place or acquire approval, even if that means playing their roles in a subversive or tongue-in-cheek manner and disguising their inner subversion or disbelief. Nonetheless, he (1963: 125) identifies himself as writing in the tradition of Max Weber's interest in the "voluntaristic" aspects of social life. Berger (1963: 125) distinguishes himself from Durkheim who stresses "the externality, objectivity, 'thing'-like character of social reality," and he aligns himself with Weber's emphasis on the "subjective meanings, intentions and interpretations brought into any social situation by the actors participating in it."

However, more is at stake than merely the question of how solid social life is, compared with the solidity of the individual. Of course, there are ontological questions at stake here; one underlying issue is whether social life is truly as *sui generis* as Durkheim thought or the net and unintended effect of individual actions and intentions, of individual words and deeds. If the individual is not merely derived from the social order, however, but has some ontological ground of his or her own on which to stand, then there is a basis for a Great Refusal. If Berger (and earlier, Weber) is right, then it is possible for an individual with charisma to say "No" to every form of authority other than that of the individual's own unaided inspiration and insight. In so doing, as Berger (1963: 127) points out, the individual may be like Jesus in asserting that "you have heard it said . . . but I say to you." As an irreducible social fact in its own right, but one that discerns in the individual a being who can stand up to every form of social life and stand over against every social authority, "charisma constitutes a tremendously passionate challenge to the power of predefinition. It substitutes new meanings for old and radically redefines the assumptions of human existence" (Berger 1963: 127).

There is something potentially elitist about Berger's formulation of charisma. Whereas Martin finds charisma widespread among those who are often overlooked by sociologists, i.e. the millions who gain spiritual authority from a Pentecostal experience of the spirit, Berger finds that relatively few bear the grace of pure charisma. Even if it is at all widespread at any time, charisma requires special social conditions in which to flourish. Some of those conditions are those enjoyed by intellectuals who are somewhat removed from the demands of everyday life and from the more routine or menial aspects of making a living; Berger refers to Mannheim's "free floating intellectuals" as a case in point. Although professors are involved in routine and in details in the course of making a living, they approximate more than most this category of the "free-floating intellectual." Even professors, however, have doubts about their own authority and authenticity. Earlier in *The Social Construction of Reality*, Berger (1963: 134–45) mentions professors and academics generally as people who know better than most that their performances have an element of charade or make-believe about them; one has to be something of a confidence trickster to make the claims that academics make for their own viewpoints. Even those who, like academics, are rewarded for their claims to extraordinary perception and authority, have their doubts and are not entirely taken in by their own performances.

Berger argues, then, that if charisma is relatively rare, it is because it is difficult to take seriously not only the social order but one's own counterclaims to authority. As a compromise, individuals engage in a wide range of tongue-in-cheek performances. Not having the courage of their convictions that the social order itself is a sham, they pay external obeisance to its demands, say their lines, perform their duties, show up on time, and do go through the motions of their roles while withholding their loyalty and allegiance. It is this inner withholding, as we have seen, that Berger finds to be indicative of a revolutionary potential. As Berger (1963: 130) points out, "long before social systems are brought down in violence, they are deprived of their ideological sustenance by contempt." Like the canary in the mine, disbelief, cynicism, and covert withholding of loyalty are early signs of a fundamental weakness in the social order.

Far more likely and more widespread are those who are indeed taken in by their own performances. As Berger (1963: 109) puts it, "Most people are sincere, because this is the easiest course to take psychologically. That is, they believe in their own act, conveniently forget the act that preceded it, and happily go through life in the conviction of being responsible in all its demands." These are individuals who may have been cynical as students in the university or as enlisted men in the army, but who, once they are given positions of authority find that they are now taking themselves far more seriously and in good faith as they defend their own rights to be taken seriously by their subordinates. They are not consciously engaging in a charade in order to con others into taking them seriously. "The moral effort to lie deliberately is beyond most people" (Berger 1963: 112). If the social order is based on make-believe, the taking of a role is the mechanism by which that belief is made. Those who have taken a role that presumes a certain authority usually find themselves quite serious in defending their own prerogatives in that role. It is as if the social order itself required such a defense, and they are its guardians.

Berger seems to find a "paradox" in the difference between Weber and Durkheim on whether the social order is fragilely based on the consent of the governed or is itself an ontological fact that defines and shapes everything else, including individuality itself: "The Durkheimian and Weberian ways of looking at society . . . are only antithetical since they focus on different aspects of social reality" (Berger 1963: 128). As Berger (1963: 129) puts this paradox, "We need the recognition of society to be human, to have an image of ourselves, to have an identity. But society needs the recognition of many like us in order to exist at all." Berger is clear that charisma does bring change, even if those changes are hardly as radical as the ones originally proclaimed or envisaged. He is also clear that the vast majority of individuals are capable at best of a tongue-in-cheek refusal to take the social order seriously, while giving external assent to its demands. Most people, he argues, are chips off the old social block and incapable of more than the slightest inner refusal. Individuality, especially the radical individuality that is based on a claim to charismatic authority, is found to be temporary at best, to lead usually to less than revolutionary consequences, and be thinly distributed at the top of the social order among those whose authority inspires the least questions and the most radical assent.

There is indeed a paradox that fascinates Berger. It is that "the institutions of society, while they do in fact constrain and coerce us, appear at the same time as dramatic conventions, even fictions. They have been invented by past impresarios, and future ones may cast them back into the nothingness whence they emerged." Social life is based on a fundamental "misrecognition" of the extent to which the society is imposing itself while appearing to give individuals all the latitude they need for self-discovery and self-satisfaction. Even rituals work only because individuals bring to them their own meanings and interests. However rituals also succeed in imposing the social order on the individual psyche in the subtlest of fashions. Individuals who engage in them may indeed know what they are doing, but they do not know how they are being affected by the social order.

References

(1963) *Invitation to Sociology. A Humanistic Perspective*. Anchor Books. New York: Random House, Inc.

(1969) *A Rumor of Angels. Modern Society and the Rediscovery of the Supernatural*. Garden City, NY: Doubleday and Co., Inc.

(1977) *Facing up to Modernity. Excursions in Society, Politics, and Religion*. New York: Basic Books Inc., Publishers.

(1990) [1967] *The Sacred Canopy. Elements of a Sociological Theory of Religion*. Anchor Books. New York: Random House, Inc.

(1999) *The Desecularization of the World. Resurgent Religion and World Politics*. Edited by Peter L. Berger. Ethics and Public Policy Center. Washington, DC; Grand Rapids, Michigan: William B. Eerdmans Publishing Company.

Niklas Luhmann

There is a direct connection between the work of Talcott Parsons and that of Niklas Luhmann, who, after studying with Parsons, left civil service and the law in Germany to become an academic sociologist and eventually Professor of Sociology at the University of Bielefeld in 1968. Luhmann compared modern societies to cybernetic systems linked not by individuals in roles acting out their goals and values but by singular acts of communication, each depending on and anticipating other acts of communication from a wide range of contexts both in the society itself and in its environment. Indeed, Luhmann made it clear that modern societies lack a clear definition of what is inside and outside the social order: the environment is everywhere and everything interacts with everything else. This thesis has clear implications for a study of the sacred, which under these conditions is difficult to define and localize, let alone institutionalize or contain within a stable or continuous cultural pattern or within religion itself.

One way to understand Niklas Luhmann's ideas about how societies relate to their environments is to think less about time than about space. Imagine yourself walking into the Metropolitan Museum in New York City from a very busy and noisy stretch of sidewalk along Fifth Avenue. There is a lot for sale on the sidewalk from food to art work, and people are there from many places not only from the United States, but from around the world. Many of the people on the sidewalk speak languages other than English, and virtually anyone at anytime might be on a cellphone or other device, whether they are talking with another human being, monitoring news from around the world, investing in stocks, or watching a movie or a sports event in real-time. They are also communicating, whether face to face or over the internet, whether they are using words, or money, or threatening gestures to communicate their wishes and intents. How could you possibly describe the vast range of possibilities that are visible in that one place at any one time?

Walking into the museum, however, you find a vast collection of objects culled from around the world, and they represent cultural possibilities from at least several millennia. You might be impressed by the variety and complexity of the museum's displays, which are only a small subset of its holdings, but you would now be in a world whose complexity and variety are exceedingly difficult to comprehend. How are they related to each other? That is, what is their meaning? As Luhmann would put it, what was their "principle of selection?" How were they selected? That is, what has been left out that might otherwise well have been included? Luhmann would call this a question about "contingency." What vast possibilities have been excluded simply in order to create a time and place for objects and symbols that purportedly span the globe and vast stretches of time? For Luhmann (1984: xx), this is a question about the "relation between the range of possibilities and the reductive strategies that structure the access to these possibilities." Luhmann (1984: xviii), according to one of his foremost interpreters, assumed that all "systems realize and reduce complexity." Because they realize complexity, we are able to compare the complexity within the system to the complexity outside, in the environment, and we will find, Luhmann (1984: xxv) argues, in every case, that the system's notion of complexity never corresponds exactly with the complexity in the environment.

A lot of information in the environment gets lost in any system, no matter how complex that system is. For Luhmann (1984: xviii), therefore, every system reduces the complexity in the environment by functioning like an abstraction. That is, the system takes the environment out of its original context, makes sense of it, and relates the pieces of the environment together in a new way. That is why social systems are "self-referential" (Luhmann, 1984: xxvi): their picture of the environment tells you more about themselves than it does about the environment. If you could put all the pieces together, inside the system and the environment, you would have a "world" (Luhmann, 1984: xxiii). If you knew why some pieces are included and others excluded, you would have a framework like the one religion used to supply for whole societies: an assignment of meaning to what lies inside the society, and of praise and blame for the aspects of the environment that are found worthy, respectively, of inclusion or exclusion.

Religion, in other words, used to be a way of reading how a society defined itself over and against the environment and understood the world. Indeed, the world is the sum total of all possibilities, those included and those excluded (Luhmann 1984: xvii). Religion, too, had a place for everything, even if everything was not always in its place. That is, religion used to be able to tell you where certain possibilities belonged: whether in the foreground or in the background; inside the system or outside; at the center or in the margins (Luhmann 1984: xviii).

No longer does religion perform this function of defining and shaping the system in relation to "the world." Religion in modern societies simply cannot function the way it used to, by defining the identity and meaning of a social system, shaping and policing its boundaries, offering a principle of selection for what is included and excluded, and a means of reincorporating what at any given time was held at a distance from the society and kept outside its boundaries (Luhmann 1984: xxxiv–xxxv). Religious and political rhetoric may define the nation as godly in order to contrast it with a godless nation with whom a godly nation should have little or nothing to do, but what was unthinkable becomes thinkable; the impossible becomes possible, and the possible becomes actual. A similar process may make previously unheard of relationships thinkable and possible *within* the society. As the churches become differentiated from the state, there are correspondingly more possible relationships between the religious and the political. Religion may enter politics and become politicized in new ways, just as politics may become a vehicle for the sacred. That is, the boundary between the godly and the godless becomes internal to the system, as the system realizes possibilities that had been relegated to some indefinite but very distant future; the godless are no longer external to the social system but have become internal. National godliness may become a possibility relegated, therefore, to the past as well as to a distant future.

New meanings are therefore assigned to the terms connoting godlessness. On the one hand, some of the meanings may be as negative as in the past; the godless are those whose religious beliefs and practices are unorthodox, insincere, liberal, or merely utilitarian or metaphoric. On the other hand, godlessness may be resurrected as a source of sane and humane secularity, with self-proclaimed godliness becoming the root of political evil. The political system becomes burdened with the task of assigning and sorting out meanings, selecting from an expanding horizon of possibilities, turning the possible into the actual, defining the boundaries of the society as a whole, and determining the risks associated with possible threats and opportunities. Under these conditions apocalyptic metaphors become plausible staples of political rhetoric. As the complexity within the social order becomes commensurate with the complexity outside the society, it becomes increasingly difficult to assign meaning, limit risk, and exclude danger from a wide range of possibilities. Under these conditions the meaning of the moment is often politicized into a crisis or Kairos.

To understand the role of religion in modern social systems, Luhmann argues, it is necessary first of all to understand the experience and social construction of time. Those are two different things, of course. Societies have ways of constructing time that depart significantly from the ways that individuals may actually experience time. For instance, societies may store up the past, offer continuity from one generation to the next, and make promises for the future, while individuals may feel caught up either in one crisis after another or in the relentless succession of more or less insignificant moments that lack either a past or a future. That is, as Luhmann suggests, societies may offer compensations for the meaning, the possibilities, and the security that individuals lack in everyday life and over their lifetimes, especially when the present time becomes more or less limited, uncertain and empty.

A society is, after all, a way that individuals have of being present to each other, even when they are separated by space and time. Future generations require savings and investment in the present. Those living in the present must therefore clear land and build roads, find water and store it, if their own generation is not to be the last to survive, and the society come to an end when that generation dies out. Similarly, no generation can entirely make life up from scratch; it is important to know the language and the time when to plant certain crops; and crucial to know how to make decisions that will be binding even on those who disagree, from one generation to the next. Thus every society provides a way for past generations to be present among the living, to offer help and advice in good times, and in times of crisis to offer extraordinary assistance in the face of enemies and death.

Every society, then, consists of a two-dimensional present: the present set of contingencies that need to be prepared for and taken into consideration; the presence of risks and opportunities; and the presence of prior generations that also foreshadow the future. Let us first consider the present that is full of the possibilities offered by any environment. Some of these are possibilities for life: access to mates from another village, to seeds for more viable or enduring crops, to weapons to ward off enemies, to water in the hills that might nourish the valleys if properly channeled, to knowledge that may help to build canoes or roads, ward off diseases or reconcile conflicts. Other possibilities are potentially lethal, like the demons that live in the forests, the ill intent hidden in certain characters and temperaments, enmities stemming from long memories or recent insults both within the community and among neighboring societies, a scarcity of water that will put neighbors into conflict over the channeling of rivers and the building of reservoirs, strange teachings that entice women from their families and set children against their parents, and blights that cause seeds to remain infertile or people to die suddenly or young. Luhmann is clear that every society has to become a store house of possibilities, like a granary that is filled with enough grain to withstand several years of bad crops and famine. However, a society cannot store as many threats and opportunities as there are in the environment. There will be no one-to-one correspondence between the possibilities for response and preparation stored up in a society and what is available or possible in the environment. Traditionally religion has had the function of choosing what possibilities are to be deferred, actualized, and abandoned, and of explaining these choices to people in a way that makes them appear so inevitable and legitimate that any choices made by individuals or groups will seem to them obligatory or rational. That is, societies generate their own complexity out of their manufactured sense of the possible.

Since they defend themselves against every possible eventuality or seize every opportunity, they must choose, and to choose they have to have principles that guide their choices: principles of selection. These principles make it possible for societies to develop a reduced set of adaptations against various possibilities for good or for ill. This reduced set is therefore always a matter of choice; it depends on what people thought possible at the time. It is a result of the way people were living in a present that was more or less open to the past and the future. The society is thus a set of preparations for contingencies that were understood to depend on a wide range of factors, both known and unknown, remembered and forgotten, foreseen and beyond imagination.

Religion used to be the way that a society made selections, imagined risks and opportunities, justified its choices as being either necessary and foreordained or simply chosen. Thus religion had to make it clear why some risks were taken and others avoided. Why indeed did Moses lead the Israelites out into the wilderness when there were plenty of graves in Egypt? Every choice thus raises the question of necessity and points to the possibility that one could have taken a different path or could have lead a different kind of life. According to Luhmann, the primary function of religion has been to find a basis for the principles by which choices and selections are made: an underlying reason for things being the way they are. That is why religion distinguishes between what is "determined" and what is "undetermined": part of a providential order, perhaps, or due to the exercise of free will. Religion helps a society to explain how some possibilities are realities and others left waiting for fulfillment or are relegated to the past.

That is why sociologists, at least since the time of Durkheim, have seen that social systems are the basis for time. If there were no society separating itself from the continuously flowing passage of time, there would be no need for calendars or schedules, sacred histories or apocalypses. Time like that proverbially ever flowing stream, would wash everything away leaving behind no traces or monuments. Nothing would stand the test of time. However, religion is the institution that represents the ways in which societies in the past have constituted time by creating the present, imagining horizons nearby or in the distance, and deciding what is relevant in the meantime. It is religion, then, that decides what is in the meantime and defines what constitutes the present. Societies have used religion to tell you what time it is, i.e. the present, and in so doing they define what is behind you, and what lies ahead. Religion is the subsystem that enables a social order to pluck you out from the passage of time, to call for your presence, and in so doing both to define the times and to constitute the present.

In Luhmann's view as well as in Durkheim's, societies constitute time by creating the present. Societies create the present in two ways. First, they reduce the wide range of possibilities that inhere in any moment to a subset of possibility that is manageable at any given time. Secondly, societies seek to harmonize the various time-perspectives of individuals who must have common memories and hopes if they are to understand and trust each other. That is, those who are present must live in the same present, with a common understanding that some possibilities are relegated to the future and others still to the past.

For Luhmann, religion is the way traditionally employed by social systems to define and create the present. It takes on the societal task of performing the present, and it does so by linking the present with the past and the future: thus a creation or an exodus may lead to an era of partial fulfillment that will be completed only on the last day, when all scores will be settled and all desires finally satisfied. With these "temporal horizons" in place religion then can tell you what is lasting or merely temporary. Further, religion announces what is "temporally relevant": seed time or harvest, grieving or rejoicing, giving thanks or repenting. Thus, in monuments and rituals, practices and markings, shrines and sacrifices, religion enables societies to be what Luhmann (1982: 285) calls "*nontemporal extensions of time*" (emphasis added). Societies take the separate pasts and futures of their individual systems and transform them into a common history. In this way everyone may imagine that his or her own story is connected with the larger narrative of the society as a whole and that personal memories and dreams of the future are also collective. As Luhmann (1982: 291) puts it, "Social systems thus constitute time, temporal horizons, and specific interpretations of what is temporally relevant."

The way that religion aids societies in creating such a present is the core subject matter of the sociology of religion. The way that religion has been replaced by other institutions and processes as societies go about their business of constructing the present is one of the major concerns pursued under the topic of "secularization." Finally, the way that the understanding and experience of time itself changes as a result of secularization comes under the heading of "secularity."

Let us begin with outlining one way that societies use religion to relegate certain possibilities to a more or less distant and unimaginable future, in order to create a manageable set of possibilities called "the present."

Societies exclude some possibilities forever. To define what will forever be unthinkable, unimaginable, and so impossible as to remain beyond the pale of history has traditionally been the function of religion. Without mystery and religious apprehension, there would be no place to put possibilities for which there is no hope of fulfillment or no cure in any conceivable future-present.

Societies have traditionally used religion to relegate some possibilities to an indefinitely postponed present sometime in the distant future: to some hypothetical or imaginary future-present. Thus religion may relegate some possibilities to a longed-for day, and then evoke those same possibilities in prophetic calls for justice. In some cases, religion may relegate certain possibilities to a dreaded time in which the unthinkable becomes ordinary practice: to a day, for instance, when the graves are opened, the secrets of the heart are revealed, and when old scores are finally settled. Religion may also evoke a time in anticipation of a Day of Wrath or a final, apocalyptic encounter between good and evil, when unspeakable practices are performed in public, or the Antichrist appears, and women are no longer circumcised. In some forms of apocalyptic prophecy, for instance, the present is imagined to include people who will still be alive on the day when the long-promised and long-dreaded future actually begins. Such a day may bring a radical transformation: the beginning of a new order. On the other hand, that future may only bring a day of partial but genuine improvement in the relationships, for instance, between men and women, parents and children, or the rich and the poor. The possibilities excluded in the present may be developed and introduced slowly over time or reintroduced with a vengeance at a time in the future when every excluded possibility has its Day.

In whatever way societies may actually use religion to create the present, they do so by enabling religion to relegate a wide range of possibilities either to an immanent, or to an imminent, or to a more or less distant and unthinkable time in the future. It is then the task of religion to constitute the present in relation to a more or less ambiguous and uncertain and expansive set of "future" possibilities. Thus religion will explain the necessity of waiting, give the reasons for postponement, and help to create and school people in the postures of obligatory expectation. People with raised hands, like people kneeling, are demonstrating the way in which societies through religion create a set of more or less imminent possibilities. The creation of the future is thus a dynamic and often a highly politicized process, whether or not it is controlled by priests or by prophets, by politicians or by pollsters.

Some people often may act as if the time has come in the present for them to receive long-promised recompense or restitution for past wrongs and injuries; others may prematurely demand prohibited and postponed satisfactions. Preempting the future thus disrupts the present in various attempts to resolve certain conflicts, heal wounds, redress grievances, or recompense injuries. In order to restore trust in the present as a very much reduced subset of future possibilities, religion then needs either to relegate certain satisfactions to the reconstituted future or to relegate them once and for all to the past, thus excluding them forever from the present unless and until a Day comes when the graves are opened, the dead return, and the ancients finally reappear demanding long promised glory. To create the past, hatchets may be buried and sins forgiven. Promises for the future may also be renewed and vows taken to restore some possibilities to the time-zone of Never; some actions will be taken "Never again." Religion performs these services for the community by quite literally performing the present and creating both the future and the past.

When societies have to relegate some possibilities to the past, here again it is religion that has traditionally provided the necessary services. Like the possibilities relegated by religion to the future, the possibilities relegated to the past often refuse to stay put. The excluded possibilities, both past and future, have a way of insisting on their untimely return. That is because, in every attempt to relegate certain possibilities to the past, as in comparable attempts to relegate them to the future, religion always reopens the door to the inclusion of the excluded possibility. Thus in aiding societies in restoring a manageable present, by relegating certain possibilities to the past as well as to the future, religion also creates the conditions for further disruptions whenever long-postponed or dismissed possibilities break into the present.

Possibilities relegated by religion to the past may come back in various forms. Some may come back in the form of demands for the satisfaction of old grievances; others may reappear as the incarnation of ancient but long discarded virtues. Whenever the present holds out too little in the way of possibilities for goodness or satisfaction, the past is needed as a storehouse of unfulfilled possibilities. To redeem the times it may therefore become necessary for religion to draw upon ancient wisdom, to recover long forgotten revelation, to restore long neglected virtues, and to fulfill ancient prophesies. Scholars explore the past to recover and popularize texts excluded from the canon. Preachers seek to define the possibilities in the present as the fulfillment of ancient prophecies and promises. Politicians turn to ancient testimonies and records to legitimate their claims to authority and sovereignty.

For religion to create or re-create the present requires many to be present, to offer presents, and to make presentations. To see religion in the act of performing its services for the social system, then, one simply needs to observe religious services: rituals, ceremonies, and performances like exorcisms. Exorcisms are particularly fruitful sites at which to see the past in the process of being created through the driving-out of spirits or other emotionally laden senses of possibility from the psyche and the relegating of them to a place of spiritual no-return. People with attachments to individuals who have died, for instance, are encouraged through exorcisms to let their passions and longing for the deceased become part of the past with little if any anticipation of a reunion at some point in the imaginable future.

As religion loses the power or authority to create or restore the present, other institutions and prophecies take its place. As exorcisms become less effective means by which longings and passions are relegated to a place of no return and the past thus created, other somewhat less ritualized processes may take the place of the rituals. Professions with expertise in counseling and in inducing various kinds of emotional renunciation may take the place of the drums and exhortations of the exorcist. That is one aspect of the process of secularization: the replacement of religious rites by nonreligious practices, and the displacement of religious by nonreligious functionaries.

When it becomes impossible for religion to integrate and harmonize the wide range of personal time-perspectives, of individuals' pasts and futures, into some form of collective present, that too is a side-effect of the process of secularization. Such an irreconcilable diversity of time-perspectives might emerge when two ethnic groups share the same social space, each with its own distinct sacred history, its own memory of suffering and victimization in the past, and each with its own dreams of future glory. When religion loses its capacity to enable a society to constitute the meaning and experience of time, time itself disintegrates into a series of moments unconnected by a single, let alone a sacred, history. That is what we mean by secularity: the reduction of the passage of time to its original constitution as a succession of moments, each replacing the last in an endless series with no beginning or ending in sight.

However, Luhmann (1982: 280) also argues that "Under conditions of overwhelming complexity, time becomes scarce. Time must replace reality as the paramount dimension of social life while the future obtrudes itself as the predominant horizon." Overwhelming complexity could mean many things, but for Luhmann it means at the very least that there is a surplus of possibilities for things to go right or wrong, of opportunities and of dangers. Societies that are very complex constantly have to choose between futures that are highly risky but improbable and futures that are more probable but less risky. If they make a disastrous choice in preparing for the future, it will not matter what other choices they made that were "right."

If time replaces reality as "the paramount dimension of social life," it is because reality is more difficult to identify. As reality comes to depend on choices that are in the process of being made and on incomplete communications that are only partially understood, reality is always a work in progress. What matters is how much time there is in which to make choices before their consequences become apparent and irreversible. Complexity can thus be reduced to a question of time or at least of timing.

For Luhmann, time is always scarce in societies because there are more possibilities than can be made actual, and one must choose. In modern societies, there are vastly more opportunities than there were in highly traditional, less complex societies, and yet individuals have no more time than before. They still have only their lifetimes. As a result, there will be an increasing surplus of possibilities in modern societies, as the possible exceeds what can be made actual. To close this gap in traditional societies was the function of religion, Luhmann (1995: 343) argues. For instance, in ancient Greece, there were two kinds of time, Luhmann (1995: 311) argues: chronos and kairos. Kairos was the time filled with a sense of possibility, that required decisive and immediate action to seize the moment before it passed by. It was time that was always running out with exceptional swiftness, rather than merely passing by. Aeternitas, then was "time without past and future: an unending, pure present." *Tempus*, according to Luhmann (1995: 311,) is "the time in which every moment constitutes a difference between the past and future." Some of those moments belong to *chronos* and are uneventful; they simply pass away as the future slides inevitably into the past. Other moments are filled with possibility, require acute observation and decisive action that marks or even creates the difference between the future and the past. These moments are what Luhmann (1995: 311) calls "insecure situations," and their outcome is eventful.

In modern societies, I would argue, the distinction between *chronos* and *kairos* begins to collapse. As a result, it becomes increasingly difficult to distinguish moments that are merely dots on an infinite line of successive points in time, from moments that are filled with what Luhmann calls a "surplus of possibility." Newspapers have therefore developed a rhetoric of the moment, ranging from defining or momentous moments to mere, momentary moments. As moments may be increasingly novel it becomes difficult to assign them meaning, especially in the absence of obvious precedent. As moments become filled with possibility, however, it becomes more difficult to determine what is the right form of action. Eventually crises never pass but continue until the times themselves become critical. There is no eternity left that can soak up the excess possibility that is left over after decisive action has been taken, however questionable the choice of means or uncertain the ends.

Thus modern societies are continually in the process of being self-made, and their decisions are being made in terms of other decisions that have already been made or are in the process of being made. Everything is dependent on everything else, and the last word is never spoken. There is no final tribunal outside the system with whom to lodge a complaint, and the existing laws amount to a set of principles that can only be honored in the breach. Even constitutions might have to contain provisions for their own suspension under certain conditions that remain unspecified. Social life enters what Agamben has called "a state of exception." Under these conditions the sacred offers little guidance or hope for the future. Sacred laws are there to be ignored or taken exception to. Prophecies are constantly being nullified. Time will simply tell.

Let us return to Luhmann's (1982: 285) point that "Social systems are nontemporal extensions of time. They make the time horizons of other actors available within one contemporaneous present." Benedict Anderson made just this point when he said that the experience of being an American came from the lives of Spanish colonial administrators who were born, raised, worked, and died in the New World, as compared with those other colonial administrators who were born and would return eventually to die in the Spain. A new society was emerging from the choices and the values of administrators whose time-horizons began and would end far from the Hispanic peninsula. Their own risks, the threats they faced and the opportunities they seized, would depend on the careers they pursued, their investments and business deals; that is why they treated the newspaper as a daily sacrament of their common life. It was the events of the times that mattered, and their future was beginning every day with the newspapers and the shipping news. Indeed the newspaper illustrates what Luhmann (1982: 291) means when he states that "social systems constitute time, temporal horizons and specific interpretations of what is temporally relevant."

Societies use religion to unite the separate time-horizons and temporal experiences of individuals into a common story about time. By analogy, individuals take the moments of their lives and link them with some sort of narrative into a past, a present, and a future. Thus societies also take the experiences of individuals with time, as if they were moments, and combine them in a sacred history, perhaps one that begins violently, proceeds with a flight to safety and freedom, and leads to the conquest of a new land that is secure and nourishing, and above all, given to them as their own. Such a history leads to an imaginary future that is partially realized whenever certain words are said or sung, gestures made, and food eaten: a liturgy in which the future momentarily becomes present. In the meantime all those present at the feast constitute the present. They re-present the society in the form of a gathering of all those whose presence counts and who can be held accountable.

As the present takes form in this representation, the past is brought forward into the present, and the future begins to be realized in the present through active anticipation. However, for the future to begin, some possibilities have to be denied as others are selected. That is because the future is an "overstocked storehouse of possibilities which we can choose only by means of negation" (Luhmann 1982: 272). Religion is precisely that system that relates the possibilities that are chosen to be made actual and those that, having been denied, are kept waiting in suspense for their day to come. That day may indeed be a day of wrath, as longstanding grievances and unsatisfied longings insist finally on having a time of their own.

To put it another way, the future begins the moment a society defines itself as being over and against a set of possibilities. For the time being a society must deny those excluded possibilities any kind of actualization except in the imagination as a sort of anticipated future-present that could reverse the present order of things: the first becoming last, for instance, or the last first. Just to select from the vast welter of possibilities a few that any society can tolerate is in itself a radical kind of reduction of mystery into actuality: a primitive sort of secularization. In that process secularization occurs in several ways. The unimaginable and unthinkable become knowable, and the possible becomes actual. A world that might become something is turned, by being denied an actuality for the time being, into a world that is passing away because it is running out of time. The only time that is now possible is the time that has been incorporated into the life of the social system: an imagined past and a future, as well as a realized present that constitutes the times, in which the society lives and moves and has its being. Thus societies reduce complexity by making the uncertain and possible into the realized and the actual. Societies constitute complexity by creating a social order that has a set of relationships between what is and what might be, and it is a set of relationships that can continually change as the possible becomes actual and the actual rendered blameworthy, unforgivable, or simply passé.

The same may be said about the way societies constitute time by reducing it to a set of possibilities that are either in the past or the future according to whether the society in question permits them in the present. The ones that are being negated are headed into the past, while the possibilities that are not yet permitted are relegated to the future. Both the past and the future, of course, may be imagined, and they become the past-present or the future present. So long as the past and the future alike may become present, it is possible for a day to come in which time itself is transformed and comes to an end: the past and the future imploding into the present and constituting an apocalyptic fulfillment. The end of time comes when the present absorbs into it all the unfulfilled longings of the past and anticipations of the future. The present thus passes away into nothing, as the passage of time comes to a halt. The world that was passing away, the secular world, becomes redeemed: no longer negated but actualized. The society that constituted the present by its own social order gives way to a social order that has long been relegated to memory or anticipation.

If Luhmann is right, however, there is no more room for this apocalyptic scenario in modern societies. It is a difficult argument to make, in the light of the resurgence of apocalyptic enthusiasm in Islamic, Jewish, and Christian societies, but the argument needs to be heard. In brief, Luhmann says that the present has lost a great deal of its meaning. In some passages he seems to argue that the present is a mere point in time. According to Luhmann (1982: 273) "the present becomes a turning point which switches the process of time from the past into the future." The present therefore has lost any organic or dynamic relation to the past or to the future. It is merely one point along the way, where the future becomes the past or the past switches over into the future. As Luhmann (1982: 272) puts it, "Time can no longer be depicted as approaching a turning point where it veers back into the past or where the order of this world (or time itself) is apocalyptically transformed. As a functional equivalent for the end of time, however, the future may itself contain emergent properties and yet unrealized possibilities. It has become an open future." *If Luhmann is right, the present can no longer be transformed by religious or political rhetoric into a Kairos: a critical, defining moment in which the past and the future hang in the very fragile and temporary balance of what one does in the present.*

The present, the, ignores all the possibilities contained in the future but a relatively few. Thus the present is a place that opens up into a future of possibilities, but in itself the present lacks any great value. Indeed, the present exists only to point beyond itself to a set of possibilities of which it is, in itself, a vast reduction. To refer to the "present time," then, suggests to Luhmann (1982: 273) a need to add "stress to the notion of the present, [to compensate for] an experienced loss of meaning and duration in the present moment itself." The present lacks any meaning of its own. You might think of it as a mere point on a succession of points whose only connection with each other is that one follows or precedes another. There is no story to be told, and no end in sight: no sacred history, and no End of Time for religion to provide or conjure so that individuals and groups, or the entire society, can place themselves in a context that transcends the passage of time itself.

The role of religion in modern societies is therefore inevitably very different from the one that prevailed in societies where the future was foreordained and hence closed around an End Time, and in which the past was carried forward through ritual and sacred history into the present and the future. With the onset of modernity and what Luhmann (1982: 273) calls "bourgeois society," "Nothing retained its old significance intact. A formal continuity in institutions and terminologies only superfi-cially concealed the fact that every facet of the social order achieved greater selectivity, that is, began to appear as contingent and changeable, or as merely one available option among many others" (Luhmann 1982: 273–74). That is the heart of the process of secularization, in which every moment could be other than it is.

Thus the present, as it used to be presented by religion through ritual, was simultaneously a vastly reduced subset of all the available possibilities, with the remainders being consigned either to the future or to the past, and it was also a place in which the past and futures of a wide range of individuals could be brought at least into a temporary harmony. As people came in touch with "the times" through the media rather than through religious ritual, however, they had a vastly increased range of choices as to what they could pay attention, and as to what they would respond. However, it would be a vast oversimplification to see the present in modern societies as simply a juncture, a connecting link, between the past and the future. The present may no longer be the place where unrealized or lost possibilities are resuscitated and actual-ized into a transfigured present. However, the present is still more than a mere point in time at which the future enters the present or the pres-ent becomes the past. Rather, the present is the place at which a society confronts the difference "between our (open) present future and our (eventual) future present" (Luhmann 1982: 282). *The present is no lon-ger a place constituted by the social order but a place of indeterminate possibility where the social order may be constituted.*

For Luhmann, an open future is one in which it is possible to imagine "several mutually incompatible future presents" (Luhmann 1982: 278). Some forms of religion will try to reduce these possibilities to one: an outcome already predetermined by the divine to arrive at a point in time and a place known only to the divine. That providential eschatology may be further reduced to an apocalyptic scenario, in which the one and only possible future could happen in the foreseeable future. That is, the future is a horizon that will not continually recede but can indeed be crossed. These are what Luhmann (1982: 280 ff.) would call utopian strategies for reducing the possibilities of the future, and they conflict with other strategies that he calls technological, but which can also take religious form. These other strategies imagine several possible futures, all of which are incompatible, but through the use of values create a present which can be "a possible past for future presents" (Luhmann 1982: 281). Imagine, for instance, a religious community that sees the present as a place of spiritual warfare among mutually incompatible demonic and spiritual forces, and the believer is urged to make a choice of one among many of these forces in order to exorcise the others. In this way the present is transformed into a staging area for a future present that would otherwise only be imaginary and utopian, and the present becomes a place in which to live as if that future had already begun.

These contrasting and competing forms of religion create presents that are antidotes to the experience of the present as simply a way station into the future; they are full of possibilities and offer many choices under a wide range of conditions. However, precisely for that reason, such a present may well be profoundly unsatisfying. That is, people do bring into social life their own longings for the future and their unsatisfied desires and grievances from the past. They want the present to be filled with promise and to experience the future as though it were present. Similarly they have their own ways of resuscitating the past and making it present, and some of these ways are creative, others filled with nostalgia or obsession, or grandiose visions of a return to some lost or imaginary greatness. Modern societies face a problem, then, in constructing times and places where these individual or collective expressions of the presence of the past and the future can be entertained. Sometimes modern societies reduce these personal and collective experiences of time to mere entertainment. The king returns; the lost kingdom recovers its ancient glory. The future arrives ahead of time. There is a vast entertainment industry catering to the temporal experiences of people who find no place in the office or the school, the campaign trail or the trading floor, for anything more than a rigorous accounting of the passage of time itself. For them the future is an extension of present trends. When they imagine the future-present, they are thought to be dreaming or utopian: anything but realistic.

It is this vastly disenchanted view of time that modern societies construct for themselves. They need to count how many days or hours or minutes lie between them and the realization of an investment or the advent of some danger. Their accounting procedures leave little to the imagination, although their accounting firms may never give a full accounting. Whatever mystery there is can be disclosed by a careful reading of the small print or by monitoring the flow of capital in thousands of transactions over time. Similarly, the future of the Social Security Trust Fund can be predicted by monitoring the inflow and out-flow of capital in the present and by predicting tax receipts for the future. The date at which the fund is predicted to run out of money therefore keeps changing according to changes in the economy in the meantime. The future is reduced to an extrapolation of ever-changing present trends.

That is, modern societies themselves become increasingly a matter of schedules and predictions, promises and disappointments. Those who rely on some ideal version of the society to be found in its constitutions or laws, its sacred history or sense of destiny, are destined to repeated disappointment. There will be no day of recovery and restitution for past losses. There will be no day when the long-awaited future finally arrives. The future-present, that imagined participation in the future, is increas-ingly a fleeting form of mass entertainment. The past-present becomes reduced to a retelling of stories in order to justify or criticize or legiti-mate the present conditions of a particular constituency.

Secularization and secularity

Drawing a picture of a world in which things could be other than they are, religion explains why they are not. Because societies, in order to become social systems, have to exclude certain possibilities, they also have to account for why these possibilities have been excluded; the problem is always, Luhmann (1984:: xxxiv–xxxv) argues, one of "contin-gency." Even systems that seem to be based on the bedrock of tradition or necessity have to explain why things are as they are and not as they might be or could have been. Choices and even sacrifices have been made on the basis of some principle of selection. By allowing people themselves to feel select, a religion may provide an advance guarantee of their choices, as though the land they acquired by force had been given to them.

In modern societies, however, religion loses its monopoly on this function. Indeed, religion undergoes one aspect of secularization as it becomes one subsystem among others. Thus in modern societies it may well be the political subsystem that has to account for why some possi-bilities are excluded and others realized. To assess the risk to a society of doing something, or of doing nothing, is now the task of political leaders far more than it is of priests or prophets. It was politicians who assessed the risks of invading, or of not invading, Iraq and Afghanistan, and they did so on the basis of what they perceived to be a wide range of threats and opportunities for whole societies. This is precisely what Luhmann means by the problem of contingency, and it requires a resolution at a level far beyond the reach of retrospective foresight. Thus some religious leaders evoked the nation's providential mission and the biblical tradition; others declared that the risks posed by weapons of mass destruction were so great that they themselves had no choice but to invade Iraq.

Luhmann (1984: xxxvii) also notes that when religion becomes politicized, even in the fulfillment of its assumed obligations to the larger society, it undergoes another sort of secularization. To begin with, religion becomes secularized as it loses its monopoly on grounding the larger society in some world beyond contingency. It undergoes yet another when to exert or recover this function, religion engages in politics and so appears to become merely political. It is as if, when religion loses its monopoly on providing the ultimate *raison d'etre* for a society, it has to rely on successful performances to demonstrate and exert its influence, but in so doing, religion becomes more obviously a special interest: one among many instead of the one that provides the grounding for the many.

Thus every society reduces complexity by selecting some possibilities and excluding others, but it also constitutes a certain kind of complexity: its own rules and customs or ways of doing things. Some of these rules and much of this order constitute what might be called the backbone of the society; it is what gives the system order, meaning, and continuity. Of course, it is often not clear just what activities constitute the basis of social order, and people fight over whether certain actions have meaning because they are central to the way a system works and defines itself, or whether they are merely personal or useful ways of getting by or getting things done. When is terminating a pregnancy or removing life-supports from a patient simply a way to make the best of a bad situation according to the needs and interests of the persons involved, or, on the other, an act that has meaning because it represents a possibility excluded by some church's rules for preserving life? As these illustrations suggest, the line separating mundane activities from activities that have meaning to and for the society as a whole and reflect on its identity is often blurred and contested, but it may also be a line separating the sacred from the secular. It is a line that will be drawn and redrawn as any society seeks to define itself over and against its environment and sees meaning in an action because it defines that action "in its own terms" (Luhmann 1984: xxv).

As laws, for instance, come to be applied, discussed, obeyed or disobeyed, revised and reinterpreted, a society acquires the ability to adapt to new possibilities that may emerge or to include possibilities that previously were excluded. These laws and other principles for selecting some possibilities and excluding others inevitably develop and change over time in response to changes in the environment, but they also acquire over time a certain identity above and beyond the particular decisions that people make or the interests they pursue or fight over and reject. Thus every society has a set of values or rules that come to stand for the society itself, even though their actual meaning and the ways in which they are applied may change more or less radically over time. Thus, for Luhmann (1984: xxv), societies are "self-referential," in the sense that actions have meaning only in relation to other actions, and their meaning derives from their importance to the society itself.

On the other hand, every society also has a set of rules and procedures for making day-to-day decisions, for resolving conflicts informally, for permitting innovation, for satisfying interests, for giving license, and for getting by. It is this rather mundane side of a society, in which the society's own traditions and identity are *not* at stake, that constitutes yet another form of the secular. People engage in actions every day that do not raise questions about their meaning or whether or not the actions are legitimate. They are purely pragmatic, and they lack meaning, except perhaps to the individuals involved, because they do not draw their inspiration or authority from the values and rules of the larger society. There is no clear opposition between the rules that are sacred to the social order and those that govern the mundane world of getting along or getting by: no line separating the sacred from the secular.

Still another aspect or form of secularization emerges when religion becomes one subsystem among many others. It begins to produce many more possibilities than when it attempted to ground the existence and identity of the society as a whole. When it represented the whole society, the excluded possibilities could usefully be lumped together in whatever was different from or opposed to the society as a whole. There were Israelites and then there were non-Israelites: tribes that were in the covenant and those that were wandering in the wilderness, the circumcised and therefore also the uncircumcised, the American god-fearing nation and the un-American. However, once religion effectively is reduced to being one subsystem among others, its environment expands to include what previously it encompassed. Now its environment includes the worlds of business and politics, of education and the family, of leisure time activities and the media. That is, there are many more environments, internal to the society but now external to religion, and each of these represents a set of possibilities that can be addressed, adopted, adapted to, or excluded. Here the sacred is in creative tension with the secular, and they compete in areas where their domains appear to intersect and overlap with each other. In these areas the sacred is mixed with secular concerns, and the secular is in the process of becoming sacralized.

Thus still another kind of secularization emerges, as religious groups, like denominations in the United States, develop complex bureaucracies staffed with professionals who are supposed to know something about how the economy works and businesses function, or about politicians and parties, or about education and the schools, or about communication and the mass media. Just as businesses can lobby politicians, so can religion. Whether religious leaders describe themselves as witnessing or lobbying, however, they are agents of the process of secularization. Becoming more like the other organizations and institutions in the fields in which they seek to function and compete, religious organizations become indistinguishable from secular professionals and marketeers and bureaucrats.

The process of secularization, then, is inherent in the process by which any society forms itself out of the possibilities, both threatening and opportune, that inhere in any environment. In the process of becoming a social system, a society self-selects those possibilities that it will entertain and adopt, and it defines as "too late" or "not yet" a wide range of other possibilities that it consigns to the past and to the future. Thus as societies come to constitute what passes for the present, they reduce the cosmos of possibility to what is real for the time being or temporal. The social order is thus from the outset inevitably "contingent" (Luhmann) or already in the process of passing away. Even though a social order will then present its own set of possibilities as lasting or eternal, and portray all other possibilities as merely adaptive to a changing environment, by constituting the present every social order immediately creates an inherent contradiction with its own claims to perpetuity and inevitability. To abridge that contradiction has traditionally been the function of religion.

That is, to return once more to Luhmann's (1982: 285) basic thesis about time and the social order, "Societies are nontemporal extensions of time. They make the time horizons of other actors available with one contemporaneous present." However, when individuals come together, each brings his or her own time-zone: each individual's personal history, set of memories and anticipations, and sense of the moment. In the same way, when groups come together, as do African Americans and Caucasians in American society, each brings a different set of memories and resentments, outstanding grievances and longings, that make it impossible for them fully to share a common past or anticipate together the same future. The future becomes what Luhmann (1982: 272) calls "an overstocked storehouse of possibilities" for experiencing, understanding, and constructing the passage of time.

Under the process of secularization, what was once regarded as an apocalyptic turning point in the course of history simply becomes another in a series of progressions toward the actualization of an open set of possibilities (Luhmann 1982: 272). Once more: to Luhmann (1982: 273), the present tends to become "a turning point which switches the process of time from the past into the future." The more that the present itself becomes simply one point of time in an endless succession of such points, the present becomes empty of meaning. Thus, if Luhmann (1982: 273) is right, *the present time* becomes momentary: secular in the extreme. So also is the sacred, momentous but temporary.

References

(1982) *The Differentiation of Society*. Translated by Stephen Holmes and Charles Larmore. New York: Columbia University Press.
(1984) *Religious Dogmatics and the Evolution of Societies*. New York: E. Mellen Press.
(1995) [1984] *Social Systems*. Translated by John Bednarz, Jr. with Dirk Baecker. Foreword by Eva M. Knodt. Stanford, CA: Stanford University Press.

Clifford Geertz

Born in 1926, for the last 36 years of his life, Clifford James Geertz was a Fellow at the Institute for Advanced Studies in Princeton, New Jersey. Perhaps more than any other contemporary social scientist, Geertz was responsible for transforming social anthropology and sociology from a study of social structures and their functions to an analysis of the signs and symbols, the meanings and the codes that underlay social life. Rather than see culture as a template imposed with more or less consistency on a society he found in ritual the very practices that created, sustained, and embodied culture itself, and he focused on the complex, ambiguous, and often dynamic relationships between religion and the sacred.

The sacred is eventful and to that extent momentous, however momentary is the act itself in which the sacred emerges. The passage of time is intensified in such a way that the shift from what went before to what comes after represents a watershed, a transformation, or a crisis that has been faced and overcome. A person is no longer the same, now that he or she has been inducted into a new status, whether that of the adult or, for that matter, the ancestor. What formerly was the present has become the past; the passing moment turns out to have been a moment in which the past itself has changed and now encompasses what it excluded before. Adequately enacted or symbolized in ritual, the threat of dissidence or death, of disorder or even chaos is averted, and a new order, a new life, a new period of vitality or life is introduced. The crisis, enacted and passed, is now over, and a new future appears.

The sacred is thus an emergent phenomenon, and when it emerges, something eventful happens, a fundamental change in attitude, perception, orientation, or self-understanding, an alteration of a person's or a people's way of being in the world. The sacred changes the way people see themselves, experience time, and act their parts in the social order.

That is why ritual performs an essential function: transforming the person's sense of the sacred so that he or she is enabled and required to experience both time and the self in ways that foster a predictable and responsible enactment of obligatory social roles. Ritual does this by mimicking and reenacting the critical moment or event that initially gave rise to the sacred.

If ritual alters the way people see and feel about themselves, it is because it is moderately successful in reenacting the emergence of the sacred in a crisis that transformed the way people experienced themselves in relation to the world around them. Ritual thus provides the first link that ties the sacred to religion by immersing the sacred in the framework of another world. That world may consist of the honors to be given to those who represent and maintain the social system, or that world may be a more imposing and universal cosmos; that other world may be Nature and its representations, or some supernatural universe of beings and of meanings that shapes and contain "this world." However transcendence is conceived, ritual begins the process by which the sacred is reframed within a more inclusive, more abstract and general, and, for the people in question, more authoritative worldview.

What is being transcended, of course, is the sacred itself and its deep roots not only in the mundane and in everyday life but in the personal needs and experiences of individuals or a community in a particular time and place. If the sacred accepts this offer of transcendence through ritual, the sacred loses an element of immediacy and particularity, of direct relevance to personal experience, and to the life of a people in a particular time and place. The momentary nature of the sacred becomes reframed as part of a world that transcends the passage of time, and the momentousness of the event in which the sacred emerged is set within a larger sacred history in which the momentous is reduced to the meaningful. Ritual thus reduces the extent to which the sacred enables people to get what they want, to pursue their own interests, and to satisfy their own desires, because ritual places the sacred within a tradition and reinterprets it in a context more abstract and universal than the conditions or the demands of everyday life.

In this chapter we consider Clifford Geertz, of whom Bloch was very critical on precisely the points raised in the preceding paragraph. Geertz notes that among the Javanese there is a conscious and consistent sense of obligation to make even everyday life conform to their religious worldview. That is, even shopkeepers are required to exhibit the kind of demeanor that would be appropriate for one who is centered in the religious tradition. Thus personhood is assimilated to some transcendent sphere; tranquility of the soul trumps making a profit, and economic exchanges are intended to be so ritualized that there is no room for greedy or aggressive behavior but only for the smooth flow of interpersonal interaction that one would expect to find in a well-performed rite. That is, for Geertz there is little to distinguish the mundane from the sacred, the everyday from the highly ritualized, but the sacred itself is conformed to a set of highly transcendental religious beliefs. It is worth remembering Bloch's complaint that Geertz overgeneralized from his observations of everyday life in such a way that, for Geertz, the entire society was so pervaded by the sacred that there could be no accounting for the rather hard-headed revolutionary strategizing of a political movement such as Sukarno's that sought to transform and modernize the society as a whole.

It is understandable, however, that Geertz did see that the person and his or her experience of time was embedded in a form of transcendence: a worldview that shapes what he later called "the moods and motivations" of everyday life. Individuals in their most mundane activities could thus conform their experience of time to a sacred calendar reflecting a cosmos in which personhood was largely sublimated or subsumed. Thus their demeanor and behavior were what one might expect of a person embedded in that cosmos. Even a spiritual quest might lead the individual to discover a god into whom the individual might enter, and through that god's eyes behold the cosmos. In so doing the individual would find that it was he or she who is divine; the individual is the god. Speaking of one cultural hero, Bima, known for his "courage, . . . purity, . . . [and] fixity of will," Geertz points out that the hero, "After slaying many monsters in his wanderings in search of . . . water which he has been told will make him invulnerable, . . . meets a god as big as his little finger who is an exact replica of himself. Entering through the mouth of this mirror-image midget, he sees inside the god's body the whole world, complete in every detail, and upon emerging he is told by the god that there is no 'clear water' as such, that the source of his own strength is within himself, after which he goes off to meditate" (Geertz 1973: 137). There is thus something highly psychoanalytic, even existentialist, about the religion of Java.

At first glance this myth would seem to restore to individuals owner-ship over their own personhood and control over their sense of time. If the moment is critical and the sacred is to emerge, it is because the individual is godlike. The individual sees "the whole world, complete in every detail" and knows that "the source of his own strength is within himself." Keep in mind, however, that this is a myth; it is like the libretto for an opera or the script for a play. In this dramatic reenactment of the sacred, individuals' experience of the moment is heightened by the meeting with a God who is a "replica" of themselves. The ritual under-lying the myth is indeed mimicking the individual at the moment of the individual's experience of the sacred. It is a moment at which individuals feel Godlike, seem to see through the eyes of God, and know them-selves to be invulnerable. However, what the individual is meeting is a facsimile of the self: a socially sponsored and authorized image of the self in the critical moment of encounter with the sacred.

In Java, as Geertz makes us see, religion authorizes a very strong sense of the sacredness of the inner self, but the sense of the self is mediated by religion and acquired only through a religious quest. It is not an unmediated, immediate experience of the sacred that makes the individual feel godlike, but only a sense of the self mediated and authorized by religion through ritual and religious drama. Ritual or myth expropriate the sacred and offer to the individual a sacralized replica of the self. Whether the religion in question offers words or images, doctrines or icons, intellectual completeness or sensory stimulation, it offers only a transcendent location for the sacred rather than a direct and unmediated experience of the sacred. Whether in the form of a sacred history or a worldview that contains a pantheon of sacred beings, religion itself is only a transcendent perspective within which the sacred can be described, understood, or explained. Javanese religion seeks to maintain an aura around certain moods and motivations by making them seem uniquely realistic in terms of a transcendental, religious worldview that employs "mystical techniques (meditation, staring at candles, repeating set words or phrases) and highly involved speculative theories of the emotions and their relations to sickness, natural objects, social institutions, and so on. On the ethos side, there is a moral stress on subdued dress, speech, and gesture, on refined sensitivity to small changes in the emotional state both of oneself and of others, and on a stable, highly regularized predictability of behavior" (Geertz 1973: 136).

As Geertz (1973: 136) puts it, "Both religion and ethics, both mysticism and politesse, thus point to the same end: a detached tranquility which is proof against disturbance from either within or without."

Remember Bloch's criticisms of Geertz for having been so absorbed in the highly regular, patterned, and sacred aspects of the social order that he could not imagine that order being upset or transformed through revolutionary social changes. To be sure, Geertz does seem to find an element of agreement here between the Javanese spirit and Durkheim's own insistence that the individual is a social product or phenomenon, even though society itself resides, if it resides anywhere, only in the psyche of the individuals. But the individual psyche is only a replica of its former self: a divinized surrogate that compensates the individual for his own, unmediated access to the sacred. Thus the individual understood through myth and ritual as divine, then, is not the product of the individual's own soul and experience of the sacred but the product of a highly religious worldview and of an ethos that offers a mystical superstructure transcending the psyche.

Such a society may harbor an extraordinary individual with his or her own direct access to the sacred or tolerate an extraordinary person with his or her own sense of the self and a wholly personal experience of time. Consider what Geertz (1973: 86–87), actually said about the charismatic and revolutionary leader, General Sukarno: "The point, so far as we are concerned, is that after 1960 the doctrine that the welfare of a country proceeds from the excellence of its capital, the excellence of the capital from the brilliance of the elite, the brilliance of its elite from the spirituality of its ruler reemerged in full force in Indonesia. . . . In his expansive, world-embracing manner he once told Louis Fisher that he was simultaneously a Christian, a Muslim, and a Hindu. But it was the shadow-play stories from the Ramayana and the Mahabharata that he knew by heart, not the Bible or the Koran; and it was in self-communion, not in churches or mosques, that he looked for divine guidance. In any case, the hero leaders are gone now."

Clearly Sukarno emerged as a spiritual leader precisely because his sense of his own personhood was radically transformed in these acts of "self-communion" in which he received "divine guidance." His personhood was not broken by the symbolic violence of rituals of initiation, or subsumed into an ancestral identity, or possessed by some supernatural figure, or simulated through a ritualized process offering a divinized replica of the self in exchange for self-abnegation and submission. On the contrary, Geertz argues that Sukarno's sense of himself as divinely inspired was at the heart of his vocation to lead Indonesia into a new era. Thus even his sense of the time, or of the times, was transformed in keeping with his radical awareness of his own personhood. That is why, as Geertz (1973: 87–88) put it, Sukarno was therefore able to communicate to his people "such an overwhelming sense of promise." The charismatic figure can indeed create a sense of the future hanging in the balance of the present moment, with the forces of chaos ranged against those of order, of evil against the good. Just such a dramatization of the play of opposites would suit Indonesian religious culture very well.

Geertz's emphasis on the power of the charismatic leader to engage a society in processes of transformation also suits very well Durkheim's notion that not only is the psyche a social phenomenon, but the larger society is a psychic phenomenon. The question is, what are the conditions under which individuals' experience of time and their sense of their own personhood will lead, on the one hand, to states of radical submission and self-sacrifice, in which the self is profoundly conformed to the requirements of the social order, and the conditions under which the transformed psyche creates persons whose sense of their own personhood is capable of radically altering their experience of time and placing their own dispositions in conflict with the patterns and requirements of the social order?

When Geertz discusses the relation between persons and their sense of time, it is difficult to see how, excluding a charismatic figure as inwardly transformed in his self-understanding as Sukarno, it would be possible for an individual to see himself or others outside of a socially given and constrained view of the passage of time. Geertz speaks at length of the ways in which persons sort each other into such categories as consociates or contemporaries, depending on how immediately they are engaged with each other. Consociates are actually present to each other, whereas contemporaries are virtual strangers to one another and share only a rather abstract sense of the present as a time they have in common. Similarly, individuals sort each other into predecessors and successors, and it is only in relation to predecessors that individuals feel themselves in any way engaged. It is not, as Bloch suggested, that Geertz exaggerates the scope of the sacred because Geertz somehow ignores everyday life. He is deeply engaged in the study of what he calls "the world of daily life as men confront it, act in it, and live through it" (Bloch 1973: 65).

However, Geertz does seem to assume that individuals are largely constructed according to preconceived social categories. They fit into and are shaped by social moulds, far more than they shape these moulds. Whereas Bloch found a dynamic interaction between culture and the way individuals actually lived and imagined their social life, Geertz is sure that, apart from exceptional cases, individuals are largely moving along well-worn social tracks. A case in point is his discussion of how individuals are fitted into preconceived social categories according to whether they are immediately or only indirectly present, and according to whether they have gone before, into the past, or are still ahead in the future. As Geertz (1973: 366) puts it, "There are, at least beyond infancy, no neat social experiences of any importance in human life. Everything is tinged with imposed significance, and fellowmen, like social groups, moral obligations, political institutions, or ecological conditions are apprehended only through a screen of significant symbols which are the vehicles of their objectification, a screen that is therefore very far from being neutral with respect to their 'real' nature. Consociates, contemporaries, predecessors, and successors are as much made as born."

To understand Geertz as he would like to be understood, I would suggest, it is necessary here to appear to disagree with him. Geertz is saying that individuals are construed in terms of preconceived temporal categories such as contemporary, predecessor, or successor. Their identity is temporal; who they are depends on how they are socially construed in terms of time. Do they live in a time shared with others in the present, or did they come before or will they follow after? It is as if the individual exists only to the extent that he or she can be construed in terms of socially constructed ideas about time. However, I would suggest that Geertz would also agree that it takes individuals to give place to time.

What I mean by this is fairly simple. Ideas about the passage of time, the past, the present, and the future exist in some limbo until and unless they are attached to individuals who give them an embodiment. Individuals thus provide a social space in which time can become real. They are embodiments of the passage of time. Geertz is very much aware of the role of theater in Javanese social life, and indeed tends to see social life in terms of drama. In this way, it is understandable that he would also conceive of individuals as actors assigned the part of playing roles in a play about the passage of time. In this sense, individuals give place to time: not only do they surrender their identities to time, but they give time a place in social life. Social life extends the experience of time.

In short, the relation between the ways individuals experience themselves in everyday life and the way in which the experience of everyday life is itself already socially constructed is for Geertz, as it was for Bloch, in the end a dynamic two-way relationship; it is dialectical. As Geertz (1968: 95) himself puts it, "There is a dialectic between religion and common sense – as there is between art, science, and so on and common sense – which necessitates their being seen in terms of one another. Religion must be viewed against the background of the insufficiency, or anyway the felt insufficiency, of common sense as a total orientation toward life; and it must also be viewed in terms of its formative impact upon the common sense, the way in which, by questioning the unquestionable, it shapes our apprehension of the quotidian world of 'what there is' in which, whatever different drum-mers we may or may not hear, we are all obliged to live." The world of everyday life is thus not merely mundane or self-explanatory; it is full of questions and on its own insufficient to give full play to the people who find their roles already given them. On the other hand, by offering indi-viduals a large sense of the play in which they are engaged, religion also brings them back to everyday life, back to their senses, with a sense of possibility that everyday life itself may not be able to fulfill. Clearly, for Geertz it is religion that offers a way of transcending, gives the limits of everyday life its sense of possibility; if everyday life is full of questions, it is because, as he said, there is "beyond infancy, no neat social experi-ences of any importance in human life." This is a precise description of everyday life when the sacred is wholly subsumed within the sphere of religion; otherwise the sacred would itself be the source of the unprece-dented, the novel, and the surprising, in the midst of the mundane. There are times, however, in which everyday life puts to religion questions that religion alone cannot answer: questions to which only a passionate engagement with the moment itself can supply at least a preliminary, if unsatisfying response.

Of the many variables that will inevitably have to be considered in investigating this question, one of the most important is the degree to which religion succeeds in creating a monopoly of the sacred. To the extent that the sacred itself is highly differentiated from religion, it is therefore to that extent autonomous. Whether or not the sacred is capable of exercising a transformative or disruptive effect on the social order, or is simply dispersed through the social system without exercising any systemic effects, varies in any one society over time, and of course varies at any time from one society to another. For sociologists to investigate the sacred without assuming that they will therefore inevitably be studying religion requires an exercise of the sociological imagination that seems to be unnatural or unwarranted, at least for those who, like Clifford Geertz, shift smoothly from discussions of religion to the sacred without a moment's hesitation. Geertz (1968: 100) notes, for instance, that "For the overwhelming majority of the religious in any population, however, engagement in some form of ritualized traffic with sacred symbols is the major mechanism by means of which they come not only to encounter a world view but actually to adopt it, to internalize it as part of their personality." Geertz is clearly assuming that the sacred is already highly ritualized; it is incorporated in a set of beliefs and practices that leaves little room for the sacred to be intense but momentary, local and very specific to a particular person and context. For Geertz, the sacred has already been caught up in a pattern of belief and practice that transcends the purely personal and the mundane. Stated here in Geertz's customarily succinct fashion is virtually his entire theory, that religious worldviews, and the ethical orientations that they create and sustain, and which give them some sort of legitimacy, create a way of experiencing oneself in the world that makes sense of that experience and give the individual a sense of direction.

If Geertz tends to describe religion as though it inevitably has access to or even shapes and contains the sacred, it is not because he misses the very real possibility that, as Max Weber put it, some people are guarding a shrine from which the god has long ago escaped. On the contrary, one can read his descriptions of religion in Indonesia as a critique of the ways in which Christianity in the West is becoming emptied of the sacred. Take, for example, his comment that "In the United States, where church attendance reaches new highs while the ability to internalize the Christian world view continues, apparently, to decline," the process of emptying religion of its sacred contents "has gone much further." Even in Indonesia or Morocco, however, although less dramatically than in the West, sacred symbols "are still generally regarded as housing imperishable spiritual truths. But now people find it harder and harder, so to speak, to make them work, more and more difficult to draw out of them the settled sense of moving with the deepest grain of reality that defines the religious mind" (Geertz 1968: 102). Geertz's assumptions could hardly be clearer. Without the protection of a religious framework, the sacred lacks transcendence over the everyday and the merely personal. Only religion can enable the sacred to house "imperishable spiritual truths" rather than those that emanate in but then disappear after a moment of intense personal experience. Formerly "the deepest grain of reality that defines the religious mind" the sacred is merely superficial, local, caught up in the play of personal interest and within the limits of a particular context. Clearly Geertz fears that Indonesia shares the fate of a Western Christianity emptied of its monopoly of the sacred and he shows that religion in Indonesia is moving in the same direction. Except for his analysis of Sukarno, there is little evidence in his writing that he believes that the sacred may thrive on its own terms in the midst of the practical interests and highly personal experiences of everyday life.

Such a secularization of religion makes religion itself no longer natural. Geertz (1968: 97) writes: "The heart of this way of looking at the world, that is, of the religious perspective, is, so I would like to argue, not the theory that behind the visible world there lies an invisible one . . . not the doctrine that a divine presence broods over the world . . . not even the more difficult opinion that there are things in heaven and earth undreamt of in our philosophies. Rather, it is the conviction that the values one holds are grounded in the inherent structure of reality, that between the way one ought to live and the way things really are there is an unbreakable inner connection. What sacred symbols do for those to whom they are sacred is to formulate an image of the world's construction and a program for human conduct that are mere reflexes of one another." Note the effortless, smooth way that Geertz proceeds from talking about what religion is and does to speaking of the sacred, as if the sacred is inevitably present wherever one finds religion and missing when religion loses its transcendence over everyday life.

Geertz's notions about secularization tend to affiliate the sacred with religion or even to assimilate the sacred to religion; it appears, at least to

Geertz, as if the sacred has some sort of need for religion. Where would the sacred be without a religion to protect it, to bind together the various and often quite different manifestations of the sacred, and to make up for the often rather imposing and problematic aspects of life that lie outside the scope of the sacred? Geertz (1968: 101) is very aware that "life continually overflows the categories of practical reason" and that events "are forever outrunning the power of our ordinary, everyday moral, emotional, and intellectual concepts to construe them." For Geertz, it is the world of the ordinary, the mundane, and the practical that is limited and lacking in transcendence, whereas the sacred, outside the sanctuaries imposed by religion and the ritualized practices provided by religion, is always and everywhere precisely that: intensely local and deeply embedded in the mundane precisely because it is both personal and practical as a healing, a spiritual gift, or a revelation. Geertz appears to believe that without the transcendence offered by ritualized practices and by religious beliefs, the sacred may be overwhelmed by the world that is outside the shrine; there life may indeed be precarious, exchanges vicious, and the meaning of life itself exceedingly elusive. Thus Geertz finds that a religion like Islam comes to the rescue of the sacred by making "the strange familiar, the paradoxical logical, the anomalous . . . natural" (Geertz 1968: 101).

If Geertz is right, not only does religion need the sacred, but the sacred needs religion. That is in part because the sacred itself is relatively fragile, ephemeral, and lacking in any grounding beyond the circumstance and the moment in which it appears. However, it is this intensification of the moment that constitutes some of the potency of the sacred. The sacred takes a particular moment and lifts it permanently out of the mundane, even though the moment itself is fleeting. It is not that the sacred makes the moment last so much that the moment itself becomes perennially available to those who seek to participate in it through ecstasy or devotion. Religion, however, seeks to make the moment available under religious auspices so that those who subscribe to the religious tradition may participate in it by faith time and time again as the moment becomes enshrined in a sacred calendar and reenacted on prescribed occasions through various rites. This sort of religious protection for the sacred moment, of course, dilutes the capacity of the sacred by making it part of a sacred history. With friends like religion, one might almost say, the sacred does not need enemies. However, without the sacred, religion itself would be seeking to provide a uniformity of belief and practice that lacks the substance of devotion or the experience of a moment so compelling that it creates a turning point within itself between the past and the future.

If under the auspices of religion the sacred is continually recycled from one season or year to the next, things remain largely the same without the disruption of the sacred moment into history. The momentous, ie the sacred, becomes part of a story about other events, some of which prefigured the sacred moment in question, others of which followed. The story becomes filled with references to other times and places, like the narrative of the transfiguration of Jesus on the mountain top, which places him in the company of Moses and Elijah. Even though the text includes a warning against erecting a shrine at the spot, the story itself enshrines the moment in sacred memory, and it makes of the events surrounding the life of Jesus something prefigured by earlier moments. Whether one is speaking of incarnations or avatars, the moment itself becomes not only prefigured but perhaps predicted or even providentially arranged. Its sequels, too, will be part of the sacred moment, so that the event itself, apparently a tipping point in history after which things were never the same again, becomes instead a prelude to later transformations and transfigurations.

As Geertz reminds us, religion makes the strangeness of the sacred, its uncanny quality, less unfamiliar and unsettling. The sacred sacrament may be reserved, its place marked by a lamp, but one can approach with proper care, and one can have access to it at the right times and places if the right people follow the right procedures. Religion can take what is ominous or even dangerous about the sacred and make it safe, if the proper precautions are taken and the proper procedures are followed. Religion is in the business of being calculating and prudential, when it comes to granting access to the sacred. Without the sacred, religion becomes mere procedure: the empty tabernacle becomes an iron cage from which the spirit has gone, leaving in its place only people who stand on ceremony. Geertz's comment that the churches are being filled by people who do not internalize the religious tradition applies Weber's notions about formal organizations in general, and to bureaucracies in particular, to some aspects of institutionalized religion, wherever the life has gone out of the practices, leaving only a shell of procedure and routine.

The disenchantment of religion, as it loses its grip on the sacred, also illuminates some of the inconclusive and at times polemical arguments about what has been called "civil religion" in the United States. Some investigators have argued that either there is such a religion in the United States, or else that there is a religious dimension to American political life that warrants the label of religion; Robert Bellah, whose 1967 article stimulated some of the discussion on this topic, was himself not clear on this point. Others have argued that there is little evidence for a fully differentiated civil religion, although some aspects of the American nation-state such as the Constitution could well be regarded as sacred. Always unclear has been the level at which the discussion of civil religion was taking place: what might be called principles or values deeply embedded in American civilization, or the ideology and composition of the nation-state, or more populist notions of the American people, or views on the relationship of the church to the state. Following Geertz, it would be profitable, if the discussion of religion were to be renewed at this point, to focus on what he called worldview and ethos rather than on aspects of the nation-state as specific as the Constitution, or on some aspects of nationalism.

Finally, the notion that religion tends to soften the episodic and uncanny aspects of the sacred by incorporating the sacred into a system of belief and practice does not seem adequately to describe aspects of American society that at times do appear sacred, and do so episodically and with surprising power, but with only a tangential relationship to religious tradition. In the aftermath of the bombing of the Pentagon and the World Trade Center on September 11, 2001, many observers remarked on the fervent and devoted expressions of national loyalty and devotion, whether on solemn occasions, concerts, or sports events, or in more commercialized form on storefronts and in advertisements. The fact that these forms of national piety and pride had not been evident in the period prior to the bombings raised again the question of the episodic nature of civil religion, but if it is the sacred, and not religion, that was being manifest at this time, there is nothing surprising, however potent or uncanny, about its expression in so many ways and on so many occasions. The spontaneous eruption of the sacred is due to the increasing separation of the sacred from religion. Whether the sacred, once it is separated from religion and relatively autonomous, loses its capacity to impact the larger society, and whether it loses an element of its own vitality once it lacks the support of a religious worldview that would make the sacred seem to be natural or inevitable, is quite another matter.

Clearly for Geertz the sacred emerges in the moments of everyday life, and yet these only become momentous, and somewhat less fleeting, to the extent that they are enshrined or embedded in the society's self-understanding and thus made part of the story that the society tells itself about its own origin and history: about its own continuing progression from the past through the present and into the future, and about its own deep anchorage in the nature of things. For Geertz, in the absence of religion and ritual the sacred simply falls apart, and individuals are left to their own devices to declare themselves, to utter their own anguish, to seek their own direction, and to resolve their own most intractable dilemmas and grief. It is one thing for Queen Elizabeth to progress through the City of London in various rituals, repeated over the years, in which she is reminded that she personifies a wide range of virtues that are in themselves part of the ultimate nature of things and the end toward which history and humanity converge. In this rite, Geertz (1983: 125 ff.) argued, we witness "the sacredness of sovereignty." That sovereignty is sacred because it is embedded in a history that gives it transcendence and ultimate authority and does not depend therefore on the person of the Queen. It is quite another for a man to watch his dead son's body begin to putrefy in the sun on a hot day as it awaits a burial long delayed because the usual officiant is of the wrong religion, and religion no longer knits together a single moral community of people who know each other, live and work together, worship and grieve together. That is where, for Geertz, rituals fail, and the sacred itself therefore fails to emerge.

References

(1968) *Islam Observed*. The Terry Lectures. New Haven and London: Yale University Press.
(1973) *The Interpretation of Cultures: Selected Essays*. New York: Basic Books.
(1983) *Local Knowledge: Further Essays in Interpretive Anthropology*. New York: Basic Books.

Maurice Bloch

Maurice Bloch of the London School of Economics has trained at least two generations of social anthropologists over the last 50 years. Working primarily with African studies, Bloch has generalized his findings to make possible an historical and comparative science of the ways cultures develop themselves through the interaction between generations, through autobiographical "takes" on collective memory, and on the assimilation of the psyche to sacred texts. Marxist in orientation, he provides an antidote to the sociological tendency to overlook the secularity of everyday life and the extent to which individuals cooperate in creating the very social systems by which they are duped into making sacrifices.

In the world according to Maurice Bloch, the sacred emerges when there are fundamental changes in an individual's experience of himself or herself as a person, and equally fundamental changes in his or her experience of time. These experiences are typical of critical moments or events; they are the basis of any crisis. The intensification of the experience of time, and the unsettling or dissolution of the person's experience of the self, are fundamental to the emergence of the sacred. However ephemeral, idiosyncratic, and episodic are an individual's experience of the sacred, that experience is mimicked, repeated, reenacted and reinforced under the auspices of ritual in ways that virtually guarantee that an individual's experience of the self and of time, even at critical moments, will stay within the boundaries that a particular society considers normative and essential for its own continuity and survival.

For instance, in Bloch's (1992) excellent study of sacrifice and rites of initiation in an African context, *Prey Into Hunter*, he demonstrates how ritual takes the highly particular, local, momentary, and deeply personal aspects of the sacred and transforms them into a more general, societally based form of transcendence that makes the sacred work for the revitalization of the community and the larger society far more than for the person. In this process, Bloch notes, an animal that was rendered sacred by its close identification with a person who was killing it, the "sacrificer," becomes a mere animal suitable for consumption and feasting; the sacred animal becomes secularized. The vitality that was once part of the human being, his animal vitality or spirits, is now owned and controlled by the society and turned to the use of restoring order and vitality to the society as a whole. Part of that reordered vitality goes to, and comes from, consuming not only meat but, in effect, other communities; these sacrifices are preparations, in many cases, for war. The violence directed against the animal as a symbol of the self's own vitality becomes redirected toward the external world of animals and alien peoples. As Bloch (1992) puts it, regarding his notion of "rebounding violence," "The eating of the meat of the cattle restores vitality which had been analogically lost in the first part of the ritual [as the animal, standing for the individual sacrificing it, was weakened and eventually slaughtered]. Those who had allowed their native vitality to be symbolically vanquished by following the advice of the diviner and performing the sacrifice are now rewarded with the actual vitality of an external being." That world, made fit for consumption, is thus secularized, deprived of any aspect of the sacred, by the same rituals of sacrifice that reduce the person, in the form of the sacrificial animal, to a mere object of the transcendent power of the community.

In Bloch's description of these rituals there is simply no doubt that transcendence trumps the personal vitality of the individual. Transcendence, the ongoing vitality of the community as a whole, feeds on and supersedes the strength and life-force of the individual. The continuity of the society subsumes and incorporates in itself the moment in which the individual as the sacrificer is restored to vitality in the sacrificial feast. The particular scene of the ritual, which was performed for the purpose of ridding the society of a specific ill or illness, is now transformed into the general well-being of the whole society. "What has happened in the sacrifice is that the specific problem, which was the original cause of the ritual, has been dealt with in a way which is not specifically addressed to it but is, rather, an action which generally reactivates the strength and activity of the social group and which, it is hoped, will overcome the particular difficulty with its general force" (Bloch 1992: 37). The general order of the society trumps the specific and the particular, transcends the most intense and personal of the needs, hungers, and sufferings of the individual, by imposing fresh and indeed sacrificial deprivations and by rewarding the mortified individual with a license to consume and if need be to kill those outside the precincts of the community itself.

It is fair to ask, of course, whether Bloch himself is not keenly aware of the criticisms of Christian religion which have found in it sacrificial tendencies as exclusive and primitive as those of traditional African religious communities. Certainly the cost of this transformation of the moment into the ongoing life of the society, of the particular into the general, and of the personal into the societal, is paid by the individual who henceforth enjoys only a socially authorized and derived form of vitality. Transcendence overcomes the last shreds of purely personal vitality as the priest wields a spear over the ritual and the entire community, surrounding the sacrificed animal, utters the words of Divinity. It is not their own words but speech that emanates from the Divine that now animates the community. The triumph here is of the word over the flesh, of speech over animal spirits, and of language over the transitory: clearly forms of transcendence which, as Bloch notes, resonate with the background of Western anthropologists from largely Christian cultures. Bloch includes in this description of rites of initiation, sacrifice, and exorcism comments on the way in which social anthropology has been biased in favor of interpretations and explanations that derive from Christian theological assumptions, e.g. the assumption that Christianity itself completes and corrects the sacrificial tendencies in native or "natural" religions.

In a more highly secularized society, therefore, ritual would no longer be able to perform this transforming function of turning the sacred, imbued with the highly personal and particular, the practical and the intensely momentary, into a more general, even universalized source of authority and vitality placed at the disposal of the society as a whole. The sacred might well continue to have a life of its own embodied in particular moments, at very specific times and places, in settings far less ritualized than the spear ceremony. The attack on the individual, who endures a symbolic loss of life itself in the sacrifice, would be mitigated, perhaps even eliminated. The self no longer would deeply internalize the demands of the larger society, and individuals would manage not to have their own animal spirits exorcised. Self-possession would become more permissible as individuals are freed from the accusation that, if they exhibit too freely their own animal spirits, they will somehow be possessed by a demon or an alien spirit. The larger society in turn could enjoy elements of transcendence and lay claim to a more generalized form of authority and to continuity over time but would do so without fresh infusions of personal sacrifice. For instance, when speaking of a popular revolt among the Merina of Madagascar in the nineteenth century, when their own leaders had failed to protect them and their ways of life from foreign intrusion, Bloch notes a refusal of the usual rites of submission to traditional authority and of symbolic self-mortification such as circumcision, as the people themselves assumed sovereignty, rejected the rule of their leaders, refused to participate in rites that would foster life and legitimate the consumption of earthly forms of vitality. Speaking also of Pauline Christianity in the first century, Bloch (1992: 94) notes that Paul was therefore opposed to the following of Jewish law on circumcision and on other matters, not principally because he was a universalist, but because these laws were a matter of continuing earthly life informed by the God-inflicted wound and he wanted to end earthly life. He wanted the Christians to join in Christ's death to the extent that life "as we know it" would end. "In both cases [the early Christians and the Merina] however, having given up hope of a mundane solution to their ills, they refused the re-entry implied by a second conquest of alien and conquered vitality."

However, as Bloch (1992: 94) goes on to say, Paul also considered the possibility of a long-term alliance between the Christian community and a state, whether Jewish or Roman, that would succeed in organizing the territory, keeping order, and legitimate not only rulers but a return to earthly consumption and vitality. Similarly, speaking at length of Japanese Shintoism, Bloch (1992: 63) makes it clear that when a nation-state is involved, the rebounding violence associated with the ritual of a tribal community can have far more devastating consequences: "rebounding violence, which in certain contexts may simply be a matter of assuring the image of the continuation of permanent institutional structures by a special image of reproduction, can, under certain circumstances, develop into a profound and convincing legitimation of actual political and military expansionism."

The purpose of ritualizing the sacred is so to transform the individual's sense of his or her own self that the person, if not obliterated in rites of initiation, is at least subsumed with a social category of some sort.

Within the sphere of the sacred identity thus conferred, either in a rite of initiation or over a lifetime of maturing and effort, the individual is divorced from his or her own immediate sense of vitality and significance. Perhaps only after death does one acquire a solid self. Not only does the sacred, thus ritualized, transform the individual's experience of the self, but of time. Once engaged with the sacred, one may experience one's own time as being contemporaneous with that of one's ancestors. In some societies, the effect of rituals in transforming both the person and time is achieved informally in the action of story-telling, in which the young imagine themselves as having lived in the midst of the events being recounted: so much so that they feel as if they were there at the time these events occurred, and it becomes possible to speak of the history of that earlier generation in terms of "We" rather than "They." For Bloch, however, these ways of transforming the person and the experience of time are limited to the times and places, events and ceremonies in which the sacred is more or less separated from the tasks of everyday life and transferred to a world that is far less natural than it is socially constructed.

When the sacred first emerges, the experience of the sacred may be in the midst of the most mundane and practical activities of everyday life. As the names of ancient demons suggest, the sacred may be manifested in such ordinary experiences as a nagging headache or spouse, an aggravating friend or a pain in the neck, chronic illness or losses in one's business. On the other hand, individuals may be caught in a storm, famished with hunger, overwhelmed by fear, lost in unfamiliar territory, or beset by visions. These all constitute crises or critical moments in the life of a person or a community; they intensify the experience of time and threaten the person's experience of his or her own being. One cannot go on, precisely because these moments are as intense as they are momentary. It is one of the functions of ritual so to mimic and reenact such events that individuals find their own most critical moments within the context of a society's own dramatic self-representations. The transformation of the individual's experience of the self and of time thus takes place within the authority of the society itself. In experiencing these critical moments the individual is required to transcend his or her own experience by setting it within the context of the authority of a society's leaders or elders, and by finding meaning in such critical moments that is far more collective than it is personal, far more enduring than momentary.

The society's offer of transcendence, however, comes at a price. The experience of the sacred is separated from its most immediate and direct contact with personal needs and everyday contexts. The world of the sacred, reframed through ritual to fit within a society's collective sense of its own authority and history, removes the experience of the sacred both from the ownership of the individual and from the context of everyday life. That is why Maurice Bloch is skeptical of scholars who generalize from observations about sacred rituals to the whole of a society, as did Durkheim. Such students of religion and the sacred miss the extent to which a society is open to entirely secularized experience and activities; they fail to see how individuals do not imagine that they are participating in a time that transcends the moment or the everyday. Such scholars, he argues, tend to mystify social experience, introduce unnecessarily ontological assumptions into their descriptions of a social order, imagine that there is such a thing as social structure that transcends the generations and shapes everyday life, and so miss the infrastructure in which there may be far more equality and less hierarchy, far more clarity and less mystification, than otherwise would appear to be the case when sociologists infer from the sacred to the life of the society as a whole.

Bloch is therefore the strongest alternative to the vulgar Durkheimian assumptions that social thought and communication, the ways people think and talk, and the patterned ways in which they act, are determined by social structure. The problem, as Bloch (1989: 5) succinctly puts it, is "to see why some of the actors at a certain point in the social process cannot say: this social system is no good at all, let us take a fresh look at the situation and build up a new system. The reason why they cannot, within the theoretical framework discussed, lies in the unanalyzed notion of the social determination of thought. Simply if all concepts and categories are determined by the social system a fresh look is impossible since all cognition is already moulded to fit what is criticized."

It is no way out of this trap to imagine people fitting into social positions that place them at odds with the larger society, because they still have to communicate, and to do so involves them in the use of language. Language by its very nature encodes meanings, assumptions, and an implicit social theory, all of which are deeply indebted to the past. In a society where communication and thought are so deeply influenced by a culture that has transformed the work of religious ritual into the customary and taken-for-granted assumptions of everyday life, there is no way out of the dominant social theory or "imagination." Indeed, it is difficult to understand how social change can emerge from within a system that is itself the source of cognition, action, and communication itself. Thus even the Reform tradition, itself an attempt to break with the influence of ritual and to disenchant the social universe, becomes repressive in the absence of any source of a dialectical opposition to the dominant way of thinking and speaking.

Bloch is seeking to overcome a failure of the anthropologists' social imagination, but the same failure also resides in the mind of the theorist or philosopher, the sociologist or the historian. These academics are like "the historians who so well explained the logic of the feudal system that they also explained why peasants' revolts could not occur" (Bloch 1989: 6). Not even rituals of protest, like Carnival and Mardi Gras, really offer a dialectic because their meanings are enshrined within the taken-for-granted language, and within patterns of communication that ensure that everyday life will resume with business as usual.

For Bloch any society is likely to have its own internal sources of tension and social change if only because persons have different ways of understanding themselves, of acting, and of experiencing time. Taking aim at Clifford Geertz's views of how Balinesians interact socially and experience or imagine time, Bloch comes up with his own definitive formulation of why and how it is that even among Balinesians, and in other societies more generally, large numbers of people have at least two ways of engaging in social interaction and, correspondingly, two ways of imagining and experiencing time. Geertz, we are reminded, saw Balinesians as interacting smoothly, without friction, in a social life that was designed and imagined to be uneventful, since it took place in a time that was itself smoothly constructed to follow the natural, and hence cyclical alteration of times and seasons. There could be little in the way of eventfulness, novelty, or disruption in a social order in which such a natural calendar was embedded and embodied. Bloch goes on to remind us that Balinesians experienced social revolutions under Sukarno, and that they were intensely engaged in political and practical actions not only at the level of the nation but of the village. Whereas Geertz focused on the ritualized aspects of social life, "By contrast the contexts in which notions of durational time are used are practical activities, especially agriculture and uninstitutionalized power" (Bloch 1989: 11).

It is in these mundane contexts that individuals are likely to innovate or to subvert tradition if only for the sake of getting by or getting on.

Why are sociologists as likely to be mystified or misled by a society as are the people who live in it? Many sociologists seem to take as inevitable, as a part of "social structure," elements of hierarchy that persist from one generation to the next. The more that sociologists assume that there is something mysterious about social structure, or that it transcends the passage of time, the more likely they are to participate in the same sort of mystification that affects the members of that society. Similarly, to the extent that persons seem to be embedded in structures of more or less extreme inequality, a society seems to have a life of its own quite apart from the work that people do in everyday life or what they say in everyday language.

In fact, sociologists are more likely than the average member of a particular society to be mystified by its structure to the extent that they focus their studies primarily on the ritualized aspects of social life, whether these be highly formal rites of passage or more simply such ritualized aspects of everyday social life as greetings and partings. As Bloch pointed out in his essay on "Women, Death, and Power," if one only studied the roles of women in the context of various rituals, one would have to conclude that women are required to pollute themselves with physical contact even with corpses. Women thus do the dirty work of the social order, and have the most dangerous and self-demeaning part to play in the ceremonies by which a society seeks to overcome the power of death itself. However, if you look instead at the role of women in bearing and raising children, you would have to conclude that women enjoy fairly equal terms with men in perpetuating the society and are amply rewarded for their services. These practical activities and economic exchanges are the infrastructure of the social order, and without it, a society would collapse. What sociologists might therefore mistake for social structure is really a superstructure overlaid on the infrastructure of everyday life, of work and politics, in which individuals, especially those who perform essential tasks or have a command of the language have a large say in the way the society actually works.

More is at stake here than Bloch's criticisms of the way in which sociologists and anthropologists have continued to mystify social life. Underlying Bloch's critiques of the field is a theory that focuses only on the moments when persons and time are constructed, experienced, and imagined (Bloch 1989:14-15). Rites uproot persons from their everyday life activities and stripped of their personal identity, and in these extreme circumstances they acquire a personhood that does transcend the passage of time; they may even become the bearers of ancestral spirits. In rites of passage among the Orokaiva, for instance, Bloch found young boys being chased from the village by crowds apparently intent on killing them; torn away from the company of women and children, exhausted through rigorous and frightening observances, and turned into shadows of their former selves, like ghosts, the boys were finally infused with the spirit of an ancestor. In this process, violence is indeed done to the psyche of the young boy; the proceedings are clearly traumatic. In return, if the boy survives induction into the social order as an adult, he is equipped with a spear and a shield and permitted to prey upon the members of other communities (Bloch).

At other moments, however, individuals are quite free to engage in very practical activities without any attempt being made to mystify their psyches or to divest them of their personal identity. Especially in societies where there is a high degree of equality between the genders, there is little need for such traumatic or dramatic rites. In some societies, as Bloch has reminded us, men and women are very likely to be found together working in the fields, and even there they do very much the same sorts of labor. In these communities there is little in the way of ritual precisely because there is little in the way of hierarchy to impose on the person. In societies where individuals seek to impose their wills on each other, whatever oppression exists is ritualized and all the more likely therefore to be mandatory. As Bloch observed in his work on *Political Oratory in Traditional Societies*, it is command of the language, of the powers of persuasive speech, that enables young men in particular to challenge their elders and, if successful, to displace them from positions of authority (Bloch 1984: 23 ff.)

By focusing on the categories of the person and time, Bloch has given us key terms for understanding not only the manufacture of the sacred but the sources of social change. On the one hand, ritualized forms of the sacred emerge as individuals are deprived of their own personal identity and invested with a socially derived or imposed form of personhood. Bloch is clearly not speaking of those aspects of the sacred that are intensely personal and local but only of those that are in fact part of the authorized social order that determines the relationships between men and women, the young and the old, the living and the dead, insiders and outsiders. In this process, furthermore, individuals and what they personally hold sacred are separated from everyday life and forced for the time being to participate in a socially conceived and structured time that transcends the momentary and the mundane. For Bloch, the more individuals are engaged in mundane or everyday activities, and the more their sense of time reflects their personal experience of natural conditions, the more likely they will be to resist mystification and to exist in a world that is relatively open and profane. Their sense of their own personal identity is more likely to reflect the real conditions under which they work, and those conditions in turn are less likely to be sacralized, and less likely to be conditioned by socially imposed hierarchies based originally upon differences in gender. Bloch's own critical theory does not allow room for him to find the sacred in the mundane apart from the language and social structure that order a society's self-reproduction over time.

For Bloch there are various ways in which a society may constrain and transform both the individual's sense of himself or herself and his or her own experience of time. Some of these are highly ritualized, but others are more informally ritualized, as in the ways in which the elders tell stories to the young or encourage the young to imagine that they are participants in the events being recalled and retold. These processes are cultural because they are widely shared ways of understanding and talking about social life and personal experience. They are processes, because they keep changing as individuals experience their social and natural worlds in different ways, ways that are often highly particular or even peculiar to themselves, and yet they communicate this experience in ways that can be understood more generally by people who did not share them. One of Bloch's best examples, I believe, is the story of how natives in Madagascar passed on to a younger generation their experience during the Second World War in resisting French soldiers who invaded their hill country and slaughtered some of them. As the eye-witnesses told their story to a generation that at the time of the massacres had not yet been born, the younger generation responded as though they were personally participating in those same events. Thus the history became autobiographical, and individuals spoke of themselves as having been present at the time, even though they had not even been conceived when the events they were recounting as part of their personal experience were taking place. Bloch is making the point that culture is never something static or given, passed on from one generation to the next; rather, culture emerges in the telling of it and is shaped by its reception. He also wants to make the point that when even the very young interact with their environment, that environment has already been shaped for them by their culture. It is a dynamic process, and Bloch's point has been taken up by others like Catherine Bell who find in ritual and the ritualization of everyday life a very similar process of emergence, interaction, and the mutual shaping of tradition and the self.

In this story Bloch is describing the interaction of two kinds of time. There is the time of the elders of the community, filled with the memory of the French soldiers and their invasion of the community's land: memories of fear and destruction. There is also the time in which the young hearers are experiencing these stories: moments in which the immediate and mundane become filled with something that is beyond their experience and recall but not beyond their imagination. They can and literally do project themselves into the scenes being described as if they had been there at the time. There is a wedding here between the experience of the original eye-witnesses and the experience of those listening to their eyewitness stories, as if in the telling and receiving two different generations joined, along with those who had died in these massacres, in a single ongoing present. It is as if those present engaged in a larger present uniting the living and the dead. The young, although they imagine themselves as having been present in the original events, clearly are of a more recent generation, and their time of seniority is yet to come.

This form of ritualized story-telling unites the sequence of events with a time in which one generation unites with another. On the other hand, those doing the telling and those listening are caught up in the moment by moment account of an event; on the other hand they enter into a single time spanning generations and uniting the living with the dead; they are in this sense coeval with one another, and thus they are on the same temporal footing. The moment itself is caught up in a time that transcends sequence and succession.

Bloch is very clear that there are two kinds of cultural processes taking place. One has to do with the ways in which a society talks about itself, understands itself, justifies and perpetuates its own stories, reaffirms ways of life, and shores up basic institutions. The other has to do with the ways individual cope with their immediate experience, engage others around them, and perceive and understand their social and natural environments. These two processes are both cultural and psychological. They both involve ways of perceiving, understanding, and communicating the life of the community as a whole, but they both also are ways in which individuals themselves shape as well as accept the community's rendition of itself. Culture is an emergent phenomenon, like the psyche itself. But it is in the conjunction of these two kinds of time, one having to do with the individual's or community's adaptation to its circumstances and environment, the other having to do with its narrative about itself over time, that the sacred emerges in the form of ritual and of ritualized speaking and story-telling (Bloch 1984:87-88).

Sociologists and anthropologists tend to stress the ways in which culture patterns an individual's experience of his or her social and natural environments. Bloch reminds us that the emergence of the psyche is culturally patterned, but culture itself is shaped by the way in which the psyche learns and comes to terms with what was already known and told before. The moment always shapes the story and its telling. The story and its telling are always formed in the moment of repetition. Thus, as the sacred emerges, it holds the life of the community in its grasp, but that grasp is always a bit tenuous or slippery. Transcendence always is at the mercy of immanence. Much can be changed, lost or transformed in the telling, and yet in the telling the living are united with the dead in a world, however imagined, that links the past and the future with the present. The everyday and the momentary shape and construe the ongoing story that a society tells of itself. The momentary comes into contact once again with the momentous, and the past is never quite the same again, just as the present becomes part of the newly and differently told past. That is why Bloch, speaking of culture as it is received, and as it is learned in the more dynamic processes of everyday life, concludes that we must "try not to think of knowledge as a whole, either unitary or fragmented, but to see it as *the momentary crystallization* of different processes which interact on each other, to focus on the processes of formation and their interaction rather than on the finished product" (emphasis added).

That is also why, in thinking about the sacred, it is necessary to see it as a momentary phenomenon, even though it is also momentous. Any society's attempts to make the moment last or to embed that moment in the social or in a society's narrative about itself will never exempt the sacred from change and reinterpretation, from abuse or indifference, or from loss over the passage of time. On the other hand, a society will always find a way to take the moments of an individual's life and to intensify them in ways that seal the psyche with the mark of the social system. The way the moment is sealed may be more or less violent, psychologically and physically; and the imposition of that seal may expropriate from the individual his or her sense of his own initiative, priority, or "agency," transforming the individual's own experience by making it appear to have originated from the center of the society or from the top of its social hierarchy. Individuals may be encouraged or required by a society to understand the moments of their lives in terms of a cultural framework that places their individual stories in a collective narrative that the society and its representative alone can tell with authority. Individuals may be expected to see the moments of their lives as part of a development that only in their old age and in their death confers on them a soul, an identity that will stand the test of time.

In all these cases, it is the individual's own psyche, his or her way of perceiving the world, that is under attack. Following Durkheim, Bloch is quite clear that even in societies where the processes of becoming an adult, for instance, of getting married, or even of dying, seem to build on the natural, everyday experience of individuals, there is in fact a major assault on the psyche and its perceptions, on the individual and his or her own unaided and natural understanding. Furthermore, it is in ritual that this attack on the psyche occurs; in ritual the society substitutes its own ways of looking at life for the individual's own, everyday, practical and realistic self-understanding and view of the world.

Take, for example, Bloch's (1989: 126–29) description of a circumcision ceremony among the Merina. The ritual begins with an emphasis on the way things are: women are the ones who bear children, raise them, care for them. The first part of the ritual would therefore seem to be "based on the recognition of a state of affairs seen in terms of the psychologically built up cognition system" (Bloch 1989: 126). In fact, however, the individual's personal perceptions and experience of the world are only apparently being validated. What is being portrayed is in fact an exaggeration, since in the ritual men are excluded from producing, raising, and caring for children: "in the first stage of the Merina circumcision ceremony the world is represented as being a place where women and only women are responsible for the control of the production and nurturing of children." In the third stage of the ritual, however, the excluded possibility returns with a vengeance. The social and the natural world are owned and controlled by men, and those in power also hold a monopoly on authority. It is not merely that the natural is trumped by the supernatural, although men are portrayed as having transcended life and death, and they come, like the ancestors, |from beyond. It is also as if the supernatural is the only true nature. "It . . . turns out to be an apparition of the world where everything is in its place and where the power-holders are the source of everything" (Bloch 1989: 128).

To accomplish this substitution of social ideology for the actual commonsense perceptions of the role of women in the producing and raising of children, it is necessary for the middle stage of the ritual to do violence to such basic elements of experience as the person and time. The attacks on the person may take various forms, but they all open up narcissistic wounds that can only be healed by some external source of personal identity or of vital presence. The young initiate may be torn away from family and friends, terrified in the wild, kept in the dark, and told that he is as good as dead, in fact, only a ghost; he is thus very susceptible to the idea that he may live if and only if he acquires the identity of an ancestral sprit. A young male may be terrified by the removal of the foreskin of his penis, only to have water poured on him in a vicarious substitution of the capacity to reproduce: a capacity conferred on him by an elder who represents the community's sole ownership of and control over the rights and powers of reproduction.

The attack on the psyche of the individual comes in the various ways in which a ritual may intensify the moment, so that it seems unique, unprecedented, unrepeatable, and thus a source of existential terror. Suspended over an abyss of time, the individual no longer finds the past accessible, and the future, if there is to be one, is murky at best if it is not wholly terrifying. In the meantime, life becomes a series of moments without continuity or development: pure sequence, over which the individual has little foreknowledge and no control. It is therefore with some relief, we are led to assume, that the individual finds life returning in the form of a gift from someone in power, whose authority is ancestral.

Participation in time is restored as the individual receives an ancestral gift of identity and the chance to live in communal memory. The terrors are so primordial that the ritualized restoration of life, of personhood and time, are of critical significance to the person. Such a ritual is able to give the appearance of inevitable authority to whomever is the officiant, whether that be a king or an elder, or in a society undergoing rapid modernization, a professional capitalist, or state bureaucrat (Bloch 1989: 132–33). Thus through ritual transcendence trumps the moment and the mundane and subordinates the psyche to the collective identity and authority of the society as a whole.

References

(1989) *Ritual, History, and Power: Selected Papers in Anthropology*, London: Athlone Press.
(1992) *Prey Into Hunter: The Politics of Religious Experience*. Cambridge: Cambridge University Press.

Catherine Bell

Catherine Bell, trained as an historian specializing in Chinese religion and culture, has written two extraordinarily learned, accessible, and critical works on ritual. Simply to study them is to become immersed in the self-reflective discipline of the sociological study of religion. On the faculty of the University of Santa Clara in California, she remains, in my opinion, the outstanding contemporary American historian and sociologist of religion.

For Catherine Bell, ritual is the way in which the sacred is manifested and shaped. In many ways, however, Bell is unlike those sociologists who identify the sacred with the transcendent. Sociologists focused on and concerned with the transcendent find in ritual not a surrogate experience of the sacred but a way in which the individual may come together for an experience of the sacred that rises above the temporary and the ephemeral, the ordinary, and the purely personal or particular manifestation of the sacred. Sociologists who study ritual examine the ways in which rituals authorize a heightened sense of the self and a transformed experience of time. Without such ways of transcending the immediate and the everyday, the obvious and the practical, individuals could hardly understand or apprehend the sacred. From their own sociological viewpoint, ritual enshrines the ephemeral moment in a story or play, a drama or symbolic conflict. Indeed, enacting the sacred moment in a cockfight or in a drama about the conflict between personified good and evil, ritual not only offers a sanctuary for the sacred but places it in an authorized and ongoing social context which transcends the momentary and the mundane, the local and the particular, the self-interested and the merely practical utilitarian. On their view, transcendence may begin in the sacred moment, but it would not endure without being suspended in a web of meaning that transcends the individual and the particular time and place of the sacred's initial manifestation.

Ritual articulates the values people pursue and makes sense of those values in the larger order of things; ritual also unites what goes on more or less intentionally or consciously or implicitly in everyday life with what can be revealed about underlying motives. Ritual intensifies, and yet also offers a remedy and a resolution for, the fundamental divisions in social life. Thus, as Bell (1992: 125) puts it, "The internal organization of . . . a ritual system is usually a complex orchestration of standard binary oppositions that generate flexible sets of relationships both differentiating and integrating activities, gods, sacred places, and communities vis a vis each other. . . . That is, the orchestration of rituals in time, some reproducing local communities, others later integrating them or parts of them into larger communities, enables each unit in the system to experience both its own autonomy and its dependent place within a network of relationships with other groups." It is this larger network that provides the initial experience of transcendence over the merely personal, immediate, particular, and local.

From a sociological viewpoint that conflates the sacred with a notion of transcendence, the sacred needs to find sanctuary in the enduring structures of a society and in a natural, moral, or cosmic scheme of things. Conversely, by embedding the sacred in the ways of life of a particular community, ritual reinforces and sacralizes the ordinary patterns of what people do and of the statuses they occupy; ritual is not about change or transformation but about setting the sacred in a larger, more universal, enduring, and inevitable context. Bell (1997) notes a number of such rituals: those, like potlatches, in which "the guests are formally witnessing and acceding to the host's claims to possess the rights to particular prestigious titles, dances, and masks" (Bell: 121); "rites of affliction" which not only are "particularly effective in maintaining the status quo of the traditional social order in a community," but also "open up opportunities for redefining the cosmological order in response to new challenges and new formulations of human needs" (Bell 1997: 120); and "rituals of sacrifice" which not only reestablish a proper form of social order at the expense of life, and often of human life, but they also allow the boundaries between the living and the dead, humans and the gods to be relaxed and even crossed (Bell 1997: 114). Thus Bell is always aware that transcendence, especially in rituals that require human sacrifice, or the driving out of all-too-human spirits, or gestures of subservience by the relatively poor to the relatively well-to-do and powerful, may well contain, that is, both suppress and embody, elements of revolt, dissent, or self-interest. Thus when Bell is reporting these elements of potential dissidence or subversion in various rituals, she is pointing to the alchemy by which rituals are capable of expropriating and mimicking the sacred while turning it into an authorized performance that serves traditional authority.

Therefore there is always something subversive about the sacred. The sacred can be purely local and particular to a place, entirely personal and self-enhancing, caught up in a particular moment that trumps the importance of any traditional or well authorized social occasion. The sacred can even be subversive when it is transforming a person from a child to an adult, a lonely and discouraged woman to a powerful shaman with a vision, from a follower to a leader, from a devotee of the gods to a messenger or even a divine embodiment. To counteract the subversive potential of the sacred, ritual enlarges the temporal and physical horizons of sacred moments and transfers the sacred from the ownership of the person to that of the community. In this way ritual makes the original source of the sacred more apparently mundane and momentary. In return, ritual gives to the sacred a place in a community's calendar of festivals, where it becomes part of the story that the people tell of themselves. Thus made part of the social order, the sacred loses in uniqueness and potency what it gains in currency and longevity, while the beliefs, traditions, and practices of the community or society gain from the sacred elements of much needed immediacy and power.

In a society in which rituals are capable of transforming momentary, personal and local forms of the sacred into observances that celebrate a society's traditions, established authority, and conventional practices, the sacred is relatively undifferentiated from religion. Even though some purely personal and particular, even anomalous aspects of the sacred may remain as sources of self-definition and discontent, the sacred is largely subsumed within the religious authority of the society as a whole. In societies where some rituals are largely devoted to particular places and moments in the lives of individuals or the family, without being turned to the benefit of the society's traditional authority, such rituals may be systematically linked to other observances in which the social order itself is more effectively sacralized by precisely such a linkage with the most personal and local forms of the sacred. It is in the absence of such linkages, and in a society where the sacred has a life of its open apart from a society's religious traditions, that it is possible to speak of the sacred as free from religious control and as having a life of its own.

Some societies are quite hospitable to a wide range of forms and experiences of the sacred, because they lack the capacity to contain and control the sacred within established forms, whether those forms are rituals, myths, or a systematic set of religious beliefs about the people, nature, or the cosmos. Under these conditions, as with the Mau of Kenya, rituals of protest and liberation may break free from all the constraints of traditional authority. As Bell (1997: 134) puts it, "the Mau-May tended to focus on two main themes: first, destroying their old way of life by demolishing what they owned and transgressing the traditional taboos that defined the old social and cosmic order; second, bringing on the new by performing ritual activities thought capable of producing the apocalyptic age they envisioned."

Social life thus may be read by the sociologists or anthropologist as if it were a text. There social life, along with the moods and motivations that comprise it, the values and beliefs that orient and make sense of social life, are on display. This display not only reveals but also creates and shapes the order, which is reproducing or transforming itself in the act of dramatic self-representation. In that sense the moment is even more momentous than the witnesses to the drama or the cockfight can realize.

Bell (1997: 74–75), speaking of theorists who see rituals as a performance, argues that "ritual is an event, a set of activities that does not simply express cultural values or enact symbolic scripts but actually effects changes in people's perceptions and interpretations. . . . Although there is not much agreement in this area, most performance theorists imply that an effective or successful ritual performance is one in which a type of transformation is achieved . . . this event is seen to have brought about certain shifts and changes, constructing a new situation and a new reality: a boy is now recognized as a man, prestige has accrued to some but not others, certain social relationships or alliances have been strengthened and others undermined." Such moments are indeed momentous. A person is not the same again. Old possibilities have been foreclosed, and new ones opened up. There may even have been some violence done to the psyche, as Durkheim and later Bloch have noted, in order to achieve these transformations and to make sure that the proceedings are indeed eventful.

For Bell, however, the sacred is not merely a way of talking about the beliefs and values, the ethos and worldview, of a society as these are revealed, reinforced, and recreated through ritual. The sacred is performed through ritualized moments in which the lives of a people become eventful and transformative. As Bell (1992: 130) puts it, "expedient systems of ritualized relations are not primarily concerned with 'social integration' alone, in the Durkheimian sense. Insofar as they establish hierarchical social relations, they are also concerned with distinguishing local identities, ordering social differences, and controlling the contention and negotiation involved in the appropriation of symbols."

In the absence of adequate ritualization, the sacred may emerge in the form of a crisis, in which the past and the future, chaos and order, are hanging in the balance of the moment. The crisis may be due to the sheer novelty of a situation, in which it is not clear whether or how to act. As Bell points out, some anthropologists and sociologists have theorized that ritualizing an activity allows a culture to update itself by becoming useful in novel situations, and enables one to act in novel ways while claiming to be following established precedent or traditional values. Discussing the work of the anthropologist Marshall Sahlins, Bell (1997: 77) notes that "ritual enables enduring patterns of social organization and cultural symbolic systems to be brought to bear on real events; in the course of this process, real situations are assessed and negotiated in ways that can transform these traditional patterns or structures in turn." Ritualized activity, whether formal or informal, in practices that are carefully scripted or left up to local improvisation, makes history itself.

The inability to act in a ritualized fashion creates "a cosmological crisis," simply because not only the continuity of social life and of the people, but the nature of things itself is at stake. Under these conditions genuine violence rather than symbolic killing may reestablish the ritualized order (Bell 1997: 77). Bell's work takes us to the point at which we understand that not only do ritualized practices help to avoid or forestall a crisis, but that their failure constitutes a situation that may therefore be experienced as a crisis. In an extreme crisis chaos may threaten order, and the connection of the present with the past may suddenly seem to be vulnerable or even broken by the sheer novelty of the situation. In a society with apocalyptic imagery in its cultural repertoire, prophets may foresee or announce the impending end of history itself. In a more secularized society, the rhetoric of crisis may become highly political or be disseminated through other media such as newspapers and television. That is, the failure of ritual may lead to a situation in which the sense of crisis becomes more pervasive and even endemic to the society as a whole.

A sense of crisis which calls for ritualized activity may emerge when the pressure of everyday events, of personal or corporate interests, forces individuals to take actions which are viewed negatively or even forbidden by various values and beliefs. When everyday life collides with traditional standards, ritualized acts permit the transgression of old boundaries for the sake of allowing new life to emerge. Such an insight is not foreign to anyone brought up in a tradition which allows symbolic deaths, such as drowning, to be ritualized in the form of baptism, for instance, to permit a child to acquire a new status as a member of the community. Similarly, the Christian Eucharist requires participants to engage in a symbolic act of violence for the sake of letting new life begin. As Durkheim pointed out, worship involves acts of sacrilege. In discussing the work of the French sociologist Pierre Bourdieu, Bell (1997: 78) takes up the sacrilegious aspects of ritualized activity: "When that which nature has divided or united, according to the culture's taxonomy of categories of the natural, must be changed or reversed, it is ritual that can neutralize the dangers associated with such sacrilege. . . . Echoing Van Gennep, Bourdieu finds that ritual licenses these violations even as it reinforces the underlying sense of order that the violation transgresses. It affirms the differences and boundaries between the sacred and the profane, the divine and the human; but it is in ritual that these differences and boundaries are allowed, for a few careful minutes, to break down."

Whenever a novel situation requires people to violate traditional standards, or whenever the sheer, practical necessities of social life require that conventional or even sacred boundaries be transgressed, at least symbolically, ritual enables the new or the transgressive to be expressed, contained and justified within a framework that may be relatively modern or traditional. The point, as Catherine Bell so well points out, is that the sacred survives many processes of change in religion.

Indeed, religion may lose its monopoly or even control over the sacred, without the sacred being in any way diminished. On the contrary, the more that religion is unable to control the sacred, the more the sacred may thrive in a wide range of ritualized forms and activities. Bell (1997: 201) is very clear that ritualized forms of the sacred may flourish in a society that is secular, in the sense that the sacred is no longer dominated, defined, or integrated by any particular set of religious beliefs or practices: "The more widely shared rituals will be only vaguely religious, giving rise to a vast body of 'civic' rituals that include pledging allegiance to the flag, swearing in political leaders, jurors and witnesses in courts of law, costumes on Halloween, and turkey on Thanksgiving. As the typological theories suggest, this type of secular society is also likely to emphasize moral-ethical commands over religious duties, even within the different religious subgroups, in part because moral-ethical injunctions are sufficiently abstract, universal, and embracive to enable religious people to have a sense of how to address, and live in, a nonreligious society."

In a complex, rapidly changing society, the sacred may take a ritualized form in many ways that depart from the precedents with which we are familiar in more traditional societies. The sacred may have far less to do with the heightened sense of the presence of the past and focus more on the needs and demands of everyday life. Rather than sacralize traditional forms of authority, rituals in a complex society may authorize the voices and demands of people, apart from any roles they may have in the larger society or in religious institutions. The needs of the moment may take precedence over any perennial or ongoing concerns of the larger society or of the community as a whole, and thus the momentary as well as the mundane, the ordinary as well as the self-interested, may take precedence over the requirements of membership in the institution or the larger society. The search for a self that is viable, authoritative and fulfilling may take precedence over a self that fits within a normative framework prescribed by religious tradition or precedent. Bell (1997: 202) puts it succinctly: "If, in some fundamental way, we continue to see 'modernity' as antithetical to religion and ritual, it may be due in part to how we have been defining religion. For example, Gallup polls on declining church attendance have not asked about people's attendance at weddings and funerals or the civic or occupational rituals – such as weekly attendance at Alcoholics Anonymous, Labor Day cookouts, ethnic festival activities, and Earth Day demonstrations – that have become important to the lives of many people and communities." Those who look for the sacred in the traditional sanctuaries of organized religion may miss the sacred's appearances in a wide range of contexts ignored by sociologists whose thinking has been shaped by theological premises or their own religious preferences.

Bell's work is an antidote to a wide range of biases that are still quite apparent not only in theological but in sociological treatments of religion, especially in the West. One of those biases, clearly, favors notions of transcendence over immanence when imagining the way religion is related to social life. Transcendence can take many forms: a high god in relation to whose being everything and everyone else is secular; or lesser forms of transcendence such as traditional authority embodied in ancestors, historic precedent, communal beliefs and practices passed on from one generation to the next, or simply hierarchical beliefs and values, as well as the practices associated with them, as compared with the interests and demands of ordinary people engaged in the more mundane dilemmas and transactions of everyday life. Other biases are more clearly associated with the Reformed tradition in Western Christianity: a tendency to favor revelation embodied in the Word or in words as opposed to sacraments or more conventional circumstances; in texts and traditions as opposed to nature or the supernatural; in beliefs or values as compared with practices and customs, especially those associated with the local community and the laity.

Catherine Bell also provides us with ways of viewing the sacred that are far more varied and descriptive than those which are indebted to particular religious beliefs and traditions. For instance, a religious tradition that emphasizes orthodoxy and entertains a rather high view of the deity is likely to regard the sacred as ineffable, numinous, and wholly other to the natural, conventional, or mundane interests, views, and experience of ordinary people. Only the religious elite, the virtuoso or the charismatic, the mystical or the recipients of extraordinary revelation are likely to be credited with the sacred. Similarly, the sacred will exist in a wholly transcendent, dialectical or at the very least oppositional relation to every day life. A view of the sacred that credits the experiences and views, the practices and preferences of people who lack any specific religious status or authority is likely to credit personal or communal notions regarding the nature of the sacred as well as the times and places in which the sacred is located and accessible. From this latter viewpoint the sacred may be widely accessible, varied in its occasions, relatively devoid of mystery, highly temporary in its manifestations, momentous, if only for the time being, and lacking in any religious authority beyond its own traditions and authenticity. The sacred, on this view, is likely to reside in a wide range of objects, from playing fields to places where sudden and often violent death occurred, in found objects or in objects of extraordinary artistic significance, in texts derived not only from higher authorities but from the words of the not-ordinarily inspired. The semantic range of sacred words is likely to be relatively broad, rather than subjected to the narrower constrictions of religious specialists or authorized interpreters.

To understand the sacred in a complex, modern society, it may therefore be necessary to suspend belief in several sociological assumptions. The first assumption to be laid aside, at least for a while, is the notion that the sacred exists in some sort of tension either with the secular or the profane. The sacred may simply provide a sense of the momentous within the moment, like that supplied in a game between two opposing teams, in which the momentous is circumscribed by the significance of the game itself. Whether that significance is defined in terms of statistical precedents or a chance for the teams in question to enter into the playoffs or finals is a matter of circumstance and commentary. There is no tension between the time and place of the sacred, in such a case, and either the conduct of everyday life or the structure of the larger society.

A second notion to be laid aside, at least for the time being, is the notion that the sacred contains within itself highly potent charges, both positive and negative. You will remember from the study both of Freud and of Durkheim that the sacred must be kept at a safe distance from the unauthorized or impure, not only to protect the sacred from pollution but to protect the ordinary person from the powers, often lethal, of the sacred itself. It is not at all clear what dangers exist when the performance, say, of a concert is interrupted by late arrivals or when a major league ball game is interfered with by an overzealous spectator whose attempt to catch a ball deflects the ball in question from the glove of an outfielder. The audience of the concert, as well as the performers, are likely to disapprove heartily of the late arrivals, and a few of the fans of the ball game may issue a death threat against the unfortunate and interfering fan, but it is difficult to determine whether these passions are evidence that the occasion is in any way sacred.

In investigations of the sacred in modern societies it is no longer relatively easy to identify the sacred as distinct in some way from ordinary times and occasions. That is, people may speak lightly of the sacred who are rather insensitive to its existence, just as others may trump up as sacred a time or place that does not warrant the heightened attribution of significance. Those who talk most seriously about the sacred may not know what they are talking about, just as those who speak lightly of the sacred or ignore its presence may well be indifferent to their own ignorance. Whether or not there is a need, then, to acquire immunity from insults to the sacred is a moot point, when it may be extremely difficult to know when one is in the presence of, or even talking about, the sacred itself, and whether it is prudent to adopt a certain mode of speaking about it. This uncertainty is particularly acute when what may be sacred is the result of a performance intended to create the very conditions that it requires for its own success, whether those conditions are a measure of credulity, openness, suggestibility, or outright faith in the authority of the performer. That is, there is a broad similarity between rituals, revivals, concerts, and games that elicit the emotions and beliefs appropriate for the occasion, whether or not there is a religious framework deployed to authorize a sense of transcendence over the immediate and the mundane. As Bell (1997: 75) puts it, "Performance theory is apt to see a wide variety of activities – theater, sports, play, public spectacles – as similarly structured around cross-cultural qualities of performance . . . [Thus] overcoming the misleading boundaries too often drawn between rituals, festivals, healings, dance, music, drama, and so on."

The difference between religion and the sacred is the starting point for Catherine Bell's own recent reflection on how practitioners, religious leaders, and scholars in general seek to understand religion in terms of tradition. Scholars, Bell (2001: 5–6) notes, "define 'tradition' by looking for the facts of institutional and ideological continuity over time." That is, they are oriented toward transcendence. As Bell points out, however, what scholars take to be the essential facts of a tradition often says more about the scholars and their interests than it does about the so-called traditions. Some scholars have sought to posit an ideal form of Buddhism or Confucianism against corrupt local versions with a tendency toward magic and superstition in order to "trump" contemporary church practices which they oppose (Bell 2001: 4–5). Thus a purified Buddhism is opposed to more popular Tibetan religious practices by scholars who want to draw a contrast between "Reform Protestants and their view of the Roman Catholic Church – that is, rational, non-ritualistic moralism versus devotional, ritually elaborate authoritarianism" (Bell 2001: 5). The point is not only that scholars have their own religious axes to grind when trying to get at the essence of a religious tradition; it is that they seek to produce an account of religion that discerns its continuity, despite local diversities, over long periods of time. Religion is thus defined in terms of its capacity to transcend the novel and the diverse, the local and the episodic, in order to reveal continuity or even development over time. Local or temporary forms of the sacred may be mere distractions or anomalies when compared with the essence of the religious tradition itself. Local culture is just that: a variant, more or less anomalous or antiquated form of the sacred, with little if any place in the normative religious tradition.

According to Bell, religious leaders are far more likely than scholars to recognize or even affirm a wide range of local variations of a tradition. Unlike the scholars, who assimilate various local forms of the sacred to the religious tradition for the sake of identifying elements of continuity in that tradition, religious leaders are far more interested in claiming that there is an essential coherence within a tradition's diversity. On the one hand, religious leaders "present a body of doctrines and beliefs as a timeless and coherent whole. On the other hand, they take pains to show that this holism is tightly tied to the key sacred events of the past" (Bell 2001: 6). Thus Bell herself recognizes that there is an essential symbiosis, at the very least, between sacred events and a religious tradition. Without those events a tradition lacks a fundamental grounding in the temporal and the momentous, that is, in the sacred. It is sacred events that over time are the stuff of a religious tradition. Without leaders who could emphasize the coherence of that tradition, however, these events would simply be a series of happenings without an organic or necessary relation to each other. There would be no unfolding revelation. The law or the gospel, for instance, would simply be current teaching without the authority of sacred events. Thus it is not continuity that, for religious leaders, makes a tradition viable. It "is the self-conscious link between the here-and-now to the all-important-then-and-there. This is what makes a tradition vital, renewable, the past made in the present where it can shape the world" (Bell 2001: 6).

For Bell, however, the relation between religious traditions and the sacred goes even further. Sacred events would simply lie in their historical bed like so many fossils or deposits of essential ore if it were not for religious leaders who can unearth them and give them an active and conscious relation to the living present. "If there were no innovative interpretations, the events of the first century CE would be locked in time and irrelevant to later ages" Bell (2001: 6). Rather than speak of a symbiosis, then, it would be better to speak of a dialectical relation between the sacred and religious tradition. The tradition assures a certain timeless quality to sacred events that are as deeply immersed in a particular moment as they are in a particular place. Religion binds together the disparate forms of the sacred by redeeming them from their isolation in time and space. On the other hand, the sacred redeems religion from its empty timelessness, its dull coherence, by giving the tradition a vital link not merely to a moment in the past but to a moment that has its own form of transcendence, its own enduring and vital character.

Secularization, then, may well be a process in which this dialectical relationship between religious traditions and sacred events loses its creative tension. Sacred events remain events located in time and place. Access to them is made available not by religious leaders but by people who manage their own religious tourism into the past and who have available through the media a wide range of choices in texts or on tape or on digitalized recordings that enable them to listen, as it were, to the words of the Buddha, or to be moved by Gregorian chant. The past is made present by being presented through the media to an audience that needs no permission or mediation from religious leaders who in the past have stood between the seeker or devotee and the sacred events at the heart of the tradition. The sacred is regaining its immediacy to the person and the moment regardless of any mediation by a religious tradition offering or at least claiming to place the sacred in a transcendental context.

Whether it is religious leaders or simply scholars who seek to frame the sacred within their own notions of what constitutes transcendence, the sacred is always being modified in the process. Left to its own devices, the sacred is momentary as well as momentous: in a word, eventful. However much rituals may reenact the original moment through forms of speech that are in themselves eventful, the original moment becomes cloaked by the vestments of tradition. There is, in other words, an element of repetitiveness in the reenactment of the original, novel, and unrepeatable moment in which the sacred initially emerged. Novelty, then, is subsumed within a tradition whose leaders emphasize its coherence. The radical discontinuity posed by the sacred, its unprecedented eruption in the present, is masked by a tradition that claims to provide continuity over time to the unique and unrepeatable. In being shaped into an integral part of a tradition that is claimed to possess coherence and continuity, the moment of the sacred becomes less fleeting, more enduring, but less momentous. What began as a tipping or turning-point, a present whose very existence created a past and initiated a future, becomes an episode in a series or a chapter in a larger and continuing story. There is thus a limit to which the sacred can be subsumed within religious practices and traditions without losing its original sacredness and acquiring a sanitized form of sanctity that makes it less disruptive and eventful but also less momentous.

As we have seen, Catherine Bell is well aware of the opposition as well as the symbiosis between religion and the sacred, but she leaves us with a few questions that derive from her awareness of their dialectical relationship. The first question concerns whether the sacred ever becomes fully differentiated from religion. If it does, how does the autonomy of the sacred effect its creative tension with religion itself? Does the relationship between religious tradition and the sacred become either less dangerous or more beneficial to either or both parties? Is the sacred more vulnerable, although more immediately eventful and potent, without the "protection" of religious institutions, leaders, and traditions? Is religion able to manufacture and control its own forms of the sacred if indeed it loses its grip on the sacred events that originally constituted its traditions?

More interesting to a range of scholars whose concern is more with the sacred per se than with religion is the fate of the sacred in complex, modern societies. As we have seen in our discussion of Luhmann, tradition itself is less viable and of less functional significance in societies engaged in a continual process of self-production through acts of communication, and in these societies significance comes not from an appeal to transcendental sources of meaning or legitimacy, such as a "culture" or "tradition" but to symbols that in themselves refer back to the social system, like cases that are decided on the basis of legal precedent rather than on the basis of some appeal to an abstract notion of equity or justice. As Catherine Bell (2001: 12) puts it regarding the role of history in enabling one religious tradition to own up to its failings and depredations on other religious traditions, "religious definitions of tradition will find an historical consciousness increasingly helpful, if sometimes sobering, for the challenges of living in a multi-religion world . . . global diversity is the new context for being religious; it is not going to go away; no one religion is going to dominate it; and all will be changed by it, sooner or later." This is a world, as Luhmann put it, in which everyone has to take everyone and everything else into account everywhere and all the time. It is a world constituted by communication among black boxes, where every act of communication is predicated on how others will read and respond to it. Thus even when the Pope apologizes to Jews for centuries of oppression but finds fault only with the "sons and daughters of the Church," he must take into account that others will not excuse the Church fathers or the Church itself. As (Bell 2001: 12) puts it, this form of accountability to other traditions is not "easy or instinctive for any religious community."

In these societies does the sacred recover much of its initial novelty, its capacity to disrupt, and its eventfulness, like an Islamic headscarf in a secular school, or does it become lost in a series of moments in which one act of communication supersedes another, and the sacred is not only far less momentous but also only momentary, like an online ordination that allows one to perform one's own marriage?

In a social system which largely makes itself up as it goes along and which rewrites its own history as a way of communicating with other communities or societies in an evolving and indefinite present, the sacred may well be in the hands of people whom Bell calls the practitioners. They do not derive their sense of the sacred or their own identity from what scholars say about the history and continuity of a tradition, and though they may have personal admiration for certain religious leaders, they are not overly impressed by them and do not define what is central or significant about the sacred in the leaders' terms. On the contrary, their interests are profoundly and intensely local. Indeed, "In most religions practitioners are likely to downplay doctrinal matters and emphasize imagery that is personally compelling with little regard for coherence . . . you have practitioners exercising independence over how the sacred is to be experienced – claiming, in fact, that it can be experienced rather directly and immediately outside the ritual life of the church" (Bell 2001: 8).

We get a further clue to Bell's own thinking as she moves to a more complex discussion of ritual. For instance, Bell (1997: 70) points out that "Bloch demonstrated the 'poverty' of expression in ritual, how *what* can be said is greatly restricted by the *way* it must be said in order to be recognized as authoritative and legitimate ritual." In making this move toward Bloch, of course, Bell is moving beyond Geertz's discussion of the sacred as a complex world of meanings already available in a social order and made accessible and real to individuals through ritual; something more than meaning is at stake in ritual, and individuals' hearts and minds, instead of being expanded to allow the individual to experience even the momentary and the mundane in a more universal and enduring context, are being pressed into a narrow range of meaning and an impoverished sense of possibility. Transcendence restricts a sense of possibility to the already authorized.

Thus Bell (1997: 73) focuses on "what ritual actually does, rather than on what it is supposed to mean." That is why Bell (1997: 73) is interested in theories of ritual that tend "to see such activities less as expressions of an existing system and more as the very form in which culture as a system actually exists and is reproduced." In the study of ritual, then we can catch a society in the act of producing and reproducing itself, of shaping the individual psyche, even through more or less symbolic violence, into something that will carry the ideas and have the imagination that the society finds useful and suitable for its members. That psyche will at best be a very restricted form of what consciousness is inherently capable.

REFERENCES

(1992) *Ritual Theory.* Oxford and New York: Oxford University Press.
(1997) *Ritual. Perspectives and Dimensions.* Oxford and New York: Oxford University Press.
(2001) The Santa Clara Lectures. "Who Owns Tradition? Religion and the Messiness of History." Public Lecture. Santa Clara University. February 4.

Key Works

Emile Durkheim

The Division of Labor in Society. Glencoe, IL: Free Press, 1933.

Durkheim and the Law. Edited by Steven Lukes and Andrew Scull. New York: St. Martin's Press, 1983.

Durkheim on Politics and the State. Translated by W. D. Halls. Edited by Anthony Giddens. Cambridge: Polity Press, 1986.

Durkheim on Religion: A Selection of Readings. Edited by W. S. F. Pickering. Boston: Routledge & K. Paul, 1975.

Educational Sociology. Glencoe, IL: Free Press, 1956.

The Elementary Forms of Religious Life. Translated by Karen E. Fields. New York: The Free Press, 1995.

Emile Durkheim, 1858–1917: A Collection of Essays. By Emile Durkheim and Kurt H. Wolff. Columbus: Ohio State University Press, 1960.

Emile Durkheim on Institutional Analysis. By Emile Durkheim and Mark Traugott. Chicago: University of Chicago Press, 1978.

Emile Durkheim on Morality and Society. By Emile Durkheim and Robert N. Bellah. Oxford: Berghahn Books, 2002.

Incest: The Nature and Origin of Taboo. By Emile Durkheim and Albert Ellis. New Jersey: Lyle Stuart, Inc: 1963.

Moral Education: A Study in the Theory and Application of the Sociology of Education. New York: Free Press, 1973.

On Morality and Society: Selected Writings. Chicago: University of Chicago Press, 1973.

Pragmatism and Sociology. By Emile Durkheim and John B. Allcock. New York: Cambridge University Press, 1983.

Primitive Classification. Boston: Needham Publishers, 1963.

Professional Ethics and Civic Morals. New York: Routledge, 1992.

Readings from Emile Durkheim. By Emile Durkheim and Kenneth Thompson. New York: Tavistock Publications, 1985.

The Rules of Sociological Method. Translated by Sarah A. Solovay and John Henry Mueller. Edited by George Edward Catlin. Chicago, IL: The University of Chicago Press, 1939.

Selected Writings. By Emile Durkheim and Anthony Giddens. Cambridge: Cambridge University Press, 1972.

Socialism and Saint-Simon. By Emile Durkheim and Alvin Ward Goulder. Yellow Springs, OH: Antioch Press, 1958.

Suicide: A Study of Sociology. Glencoe, IL: Free Press, 1951.

Sigmund Freud

The Basic Writings of Sigmund Freud. By Sigmund Freud and Abraham Arden Brill. New York: The Modern Library, 1938.

Beyond Freud: A Study of Modern Psychoanalytic Theorists. By Joseph Reppen and Sigmund Freud. Hillsdale, NJ: Analytic Press, 1985.

Beyond the Pleasure Principle. London: Hogarth Press, 1950.

Character and Culture. By Sigmund Freud and Philop Rieff. New York: Collier Books, 1963.

Civilization and its Discontents. New York: W. W. Horton, 1962.

Collected Papers. By Sigmund Freud et al. New York: The International Psycho-analytical Press, 1924–1950.

The Complete Correspondence of Sigmund Freud and Ernest Jones, 1908–1939. By Sigmund Freud, Ernest Jones and R. Andrew Paskauskas. Cambridge, MA: Belknap Press of Harvard University Press, 1993.

The Complete Correspondence of Sigmund Freud and Karl Abraham, 1907–1925. By Sigmund Freud and Ernst Falzeder. New York: Karnac, 2002.

The Complete Introductory Lectures on Psychoanalysis. By Sigmund Freud and James Strachey. New York: W. W. Norton, 1966.

The Complete Letters of Sigmund Freud to Wilhelm Fliess, 1877–1904. By Sigmund Freud, J. Moussaieff and Wilhelm Fliess. Cambridge, MA: Belknap Press of Harvard University Press, 1985.

Delusion and Dream, and Other Essays. Boston: Beacon Press, 1956.

Dora: An Analysis of a Case of Hysteria. By Sigmund Freud and Philip Rieff. New York: Collier, 1993.

The Ego and the Id. By Sigmund Freud and Richard F. Blackmur. London: L & Virginia Woolf at Hogarth Press and the Institute of Psycho-analysis, 1927.

Five Lectures on Psycho-analysis. New York: Norton, 1977.

Freud and Contemporary Culture. By New York Academy of Medicine, Sigmund Freud and Iago Galdston. Freeport, NY: Books for Libraries Press, 1971.

Freud and Judaism. By Sigmund Freud, David Meghnagi and Mark Solms. London: Karnac Books, 1993.

The Freud–Jung Letters. By Sigmund Freud et al. Princeton, NJ: Pan Books, 1979.

Freud on War, Sex and Neurosis. By Sigmund Freud et al. New York: Arts & Science Press, 1947.

Freud on Women: A Reader. By Sigmund Freud and Elisabeth Young-Bruehl. New York: W. W. Norton, 1990.

The Freud Reader. By Sigmund Freud and Peter Gay. New York: W. W. Norton, 1989.

Freud without Hindsight: Reviews on His Work, 1893–1939. By Sigmund Freud and Norman Kiell. Madison, CT: International Universities Press, 1988.

Freud's Moses: Judaism Terminable and Interminable. By Sigmund Freud, Yerushalmi and Yosef Hayim. New Haven: Yale University Press, 1991.

The Future of an Illusion. By Sigmund Freud and Philip Wylie. New York: Liveright Publishing Corporation, 1953.

Inhibitions, Symptoms and Anxiety. By Sigmund Freud et al. London: The Hogarth Press and The Institute of Psycho-analysis, 1961.

The Interpretation of Dreams. By Sigmund Freud and Abraham Arden Brill. London: G. Allen & Unwin Ltd. and New York: The Macmillan Company, 1915.

Jokes and Their Relationship to the Unconscious. By Sigmund Freud and James Strachey. New York: W. W. Norton, 1963.

Letters of Sigmund Freud. London: Hogarth Press, 1961.

The Living Thoughts on Freud. By Sigmund Freud and Robert Waelder. Philadelphia: D. McKay Company, 1941.

The Meaning of Illness. By Sigmund Freud and Georg Walther Groddock. New York: International Universities Press, 1977.

A Moment of Translation: Two Neuroscientific Articles. By Sigmund Freud, Mark Solms and Michael M. Saling. London: Institute of Psycho-Analysis, 1990.

Moses and Monotheism. By Sigmund Freud and Katherine Jones. New York: Random House, 1961.

On Aphasia: A Critical Study. New York: International Universities Press, 1953.

On Creativity and the Unconscious: Papers on the Psychology of Art, Literature, Love, Religion. New York: Harper, 1958.

On Dreams. London: Heinemann, 1914.

The Problem of Anxiety. By Sigmund Freud and Henry Alden Bunker. New York: The Psychoanalytic Quarterly Press, 1936.

Reflections on War and Death. By Sigmund Freud and Abraham Arden Brill. New York: Moffat, Yard and Company, 1918.

Sex as a Sublimation for Tennis: From the Secret Writings of Sigmund Freud. By Sigmund Freud and Theodor Saretsky. New York: Workman Publishing, 1985.

Therapy and Technique. By Sigmund Freud and Philip Rieff. New York: Collier Books, 1963.

Three Contributions to the Theory of Sex. By Sigmund Freud, Abraham Arden Brill and James Jackson Putnam. New York and Washington: Nervous and Mental Disease Publishing Company, 1918.

Totem and Taboo: Resemblances Between the Psychic Lives of Savages and Neurotics. By Sigmund Freud, Abraham Arden Brill and Robert Mitchell Lindner. New York: New Republic, 1927.

The Unconscious. London: Penguin, 2002.

Wit and Its Relationship to the Unconscious. By Sigmund Freud and Abraham Arden Brill. New York: Moffat, Yard and Company, 1916.

Writings on Art and Literature. Stanford, CA: Stanford University Press, 1997.

Max Weber

The Agrarian Sociology of Ancient Civilisations. London, Atlantic Highlands: Humanities Press, 1976.

Ancient Judaism. Glencoe, IL: Free Press, 1952.

Basic Concepts in Sociology. By Max Weber and H. P. Secher. Secaucus, NJ: Citadel Press, 1962.

The City. Glencoe, IL: Free Press, 1958.

Confucianism & Taoism. By Max Weber and Michio Morishima. London: London School of Economics and Political Science, 1984.

Critique of Stammler. New York: Free Press, 1977.

Economy and Society: An Interpretive Sociology. New York: Bedminster Press, 1968.

Essays in Economic Society. By Max Weber and Richard Swedberg. Princeton, NJ: Princeton University Press, 1999.

The Essential Weber: A Reader. By Max Weber and Sam Whimster. New York: Routledge, 2004.

From Max Weber: Essays in Sociology. By Max Weber, Charles Wright Mills and Hans Heinrich Gerth. New York: Oxford University Press, 1958.

General Economic History. By Max Weber and Frank H. Knight. Glencoe, IL: Free Press, 1950.

Max Weber on Capitalism, Bureaucracy, and Religion: A Selection of Texts. Boston: Allen & Unwin, 1983.

Max Weber on Charisma and Institution Building: Selected Papers. Chicago: University of Chicago Press, 1968.

Max Weber on Law in Economy and Society. Cambridge: Harvard University Press, 1954.

Max Weber on the Methodology of the Social Sciences. By Max Weber and Edward Shils. New York: Free Press, 1969.

Max Weber: Selections in Translation. By Max Weber and Walter Garrison Runciman. Cambridge: Cambridge University Press, 1978.

Max Weber: The Theory of Social and Economic Organization. By Max Weber, Alexander Morell Henderson and Talcott Parsons. New York: Free Press, 1964.

The Protestant Ethic and the Spirit of Capitalism. Los Angeles, CA: Roxbury Publishing Company, 2001.

The Rational and Social Foundations of Music. Carbondale: Southern Illinois University Press, 1958.

Religion in India: The Sociology of Hinduism and Buddhism. Glencoe, IL: Free Press, 1958.

The Russian Revolutions. Edited by Max Weber, Gordon C. Wells and Peter R. Baehr. Cambridge, UK: Polity Press, 1995.

Talcott Parsons

Action Theory and the Human Condition. New York: Free Press, 1978.

American Society: A Theory of the Societal Community. By Talcott Parsons and Giuseppe Sciortino. Boulder, CO: Paradigm Publishers, 2007.

American Sociology: Perspectives, Problems, Methods. Edited by Talcott Parsons and Voice of America (organization). New York: Basic Books, 1968.

The American University. By Talcott Parsons and Gerald M. Platt. Cambridge: Harvard University Press, 1973.

The Early Essays. Edited by Talcott Parsons. Chicago: University of Chicago, 1991.

Economy and Society: A Study in the Integration of Economic and Social Theory. By Talcott Parsons and Neil J. Smelser. Glencoe, IL: Free Press, 1956.

Essays in Sociological Theory. Glencoe, IL: Free Press, 1954.

Essays in Sociological Theory: Pure and Applied. Glencoe, IL: Free Press, 1949.

Essays on the Sociology of Parsons: A Felicitation Volume in Honor of Professor Talcott Parsons. By Talcott Parsons and Indian Journal of Social Research. Meerut: Indian Journal of Social Research, 1976.

The Evolution of Societies. Englewood Cliffs, NJ: Prentice-Hall, 1977.

Explorations in General Theory in Social Science: Essays in Honor of Talcott Parsons. Edited by Talcott Parsons and Jan J. Loubser. New York: Free Press, 1976.

Family, Socialization and Interaction Process. By Talcott Parsons and Robert Freed Bales. Glencoe, IL: Free Press, 1955.

The Negro American. Edited by Talcott Parsons and Kenneth Bancroft. Boston: Houghton, Mifflin, 1966.

Politics and Social Structure. New York: Free Press, 1969.

Readings from Talcott Parsons. Edited by Talcott Parsons and Peter Hamilton. New York: Tavistock Publications, 1985.

Social Structure and Personality. New York: Free Press of Glencoe, 1964.

The Social System. Glencoe, IL: Free Press 1951.

Social Systems and the Evolution of Action. New York: Free Press, 1977.

Societies: Evolutionary and Comparative Perspectives. Englewood Cliffs, NJ: Prentice-Hall, 1966.

Sociological Theory and Modern Society. New York: Free Press, 1967.

Structure and Process in Modern Societies. Glencoe, IL: Free Press, 1960.

The Structure of Social Action: A Study in Social Theory. Glencoe, IL: Free Press, 1949.

The System of Modern Societies. Englewood Cliffs, NJ: Prentice-Hall, 1971.

Talcott Parsons on Institutions and Social Evolution: Selected Writings. By Talcott Parsons and Leon H. Mayhew. Chicago: University of Chicago Press, 1982.

The Talcott Parsons Reader. By Talcott Parsons and Bryan S. Turner. Malden, MA: Blackwell, 1999.

Theories of Society: Foundations of Modern Sociological Theory. Edited by Talcott Parsons. New York: Free Press, 1965.

Toward a General Theory of Action. By Talcott Parsons and Edward Shils. Cambridge: Harvard University Press, 1951.

David Martin

Anarchy and Culture: The Problem of the Contemporary University. Edited by David Martin. London: Routledge & K. Paul, 1969.

The Breaking of the Image: A Sociology of Christian Theory and Practice. New York: St. Martin's Press, 1980.

Christian Language and Its Mutations: Essays in Sociological Understanding. Burlington, VT: Ashgate Publishing, 2002.

The Dilemmas of Contemporary Religion. New York: St. Martin's Press, 1978.

Does Christianity Cause War? Oxford: Clarendon Press, 1997.

Forbidden Revolutions: Pentecostalism in Latin America and Catholicism in Eastern Europe. London: SPCK, 1996.

A General Theory of Secularization. Oxford: Blackwell Publishers, 1978.

Pentecostalism: The World Their Parish. Oxford: Blackwell Publishers, 2002.

Peter Berger and the Study of Religion. By David Martin et al. Edited by Woodhead, Linda and Paul Heelas. London: Routledge, 2001.

Reflections on Sociology and Theology. Oxford: Clarendon Press, 1997.

The Religious and the Secular: Studies in Secularization. New York: Schocken Books, 1969.

Restoring the Image: Essays on Religion and Society in Honor of David Martin. By David Martin et al. Sheffield: Sheffield Academic Press, 2001.

Rights and Duties of Dual Nationals Evolution and Prospects. By David Martin and Kay Hallbronner. New York: Kluwer Law International, 2003.

Sociology and Theology: Alliance and Conflict. By David Martin et al. New York: St. Martin's Press, 1980.

Tongues of Fire: The Explosion of Protestantism in Latin America. Oxford: Blackwell Publishing, 1990.

Tracts against the Times. Guildford: Lutterworth Press, 1973.

Bryan Wilson

Contemporary Transformations of Religion. London: Oxford University Press, 1976.

Human Values in a Changing World: A Dialogue on the Social Role of Religion. By Bryan Wilson and Daisaku Ikeda. New York: Macmillan, 2008.

Magic and Millennium: A Sociological Study of Religious Movement of Protest among Tribal and Third World Peoples. Edited by Bryan Wilson. New York: Harper & Row, 1973.

The Noble Savages: The Primitive Origins of Charisma and Its Contemporary Survival. Berkeley: University of California Press, 1975.

Rationality: Key Concepts in Social Sciences. Boston: Blackwell, 1977.

Religion in Secular Society. London: Watts & Company Publishing Group, 1966.

Religion in Sociological Perspective. Oxford: Oxford University Press, 1982.

Sects and Society: A Sociological Study of Three Religious Groups in Britain. Westport, CT: Greenwood Press, 1978.

The Social Dimensions of Sectarianism: Sects and New Religious Movements in Contemporary Society. Oxford: Clarendon Press, 1992.

Values: A Symposium. Edited by Bryan Wilson and Brenda Arnold. Atlantic Highlands, NJ: Humanities Press International, 1988.

Peter L. Berger

Against the World for the World: The Hartford Appeal and the Future of American Religion. By Peter L. Berger and Richard John Neuhaus. New York: Seabury Press, 1976.

Facing Up to Modernity: Excursions in Society, Politics, and Religion. New York: Basic Books, 1977.

A Far Glory: The Quest for Faith in the Age of Credulity. New York: Free Press, 1992.

The Homeless Mind: Modernization and Consciousness. By Peter L. Berger, Brigitte Berger and Hansfried Kellner. New York: Random House, 1973.

Invitation to Sociology: A Humanistic Perspective. Garden City, NY: Doubleday, 1963.

Marxism and Sociology: Views from Eastern Europe. Edited by Peter L. Berger. New York: Appleton-Century-Crofts, 1969.

The Other Side of God: A Polarity in World Religions. Edited by Peter L. Berger. Garden City, NY: Anchor Books, 1981.

Peter Berger and the Study of Religion. By Peter L. Berger et al. London, New York: Routledge, 2001.

The Precarious Vision: A Sociologist Looks at Social Fictions and Christian Faith. Garden City, NY: Doubleday, 1961.

Pyramids of Sacrifice: Political Ethics and Social Change. New York: Basic Books, 1975.

Redeeming Laughter: The Comic Dimension of Human Experience. New York: Walter de Gruyter, 1997.

Religion in a Revolutionary Society: Delivered at Christ Church, Alexandria, on Februay 4, 1974. Washington, DC: American Enterprise Institute for Public Policy Research, 1974.

A Rumor of Angels: Modern Society and the Rediscovery of the Supernatural. Garden City, NY: Doubleday, 1969.

The Sacred Canopy: Elements of a Sociological Theory of Religion. Garden City, NY: Doubleday, 1967.

The Social Construction of Reality: A Treatise in the Sociology of Knowledge. By Peter L. Berger and Thomas Luckmann. Garden City, NY: Doubleday, 1966.

Sociology: A Biographical Approach. By Peter L. Berger and Brigitte Berger. New York: Basic Books, 1972.

Speaking to the Third World: Essays on Democracy and Development. By Peter L. Berger and Michael Novak. Washington, DC: American Enterprise Institute for Public Policy Research, 1985.

The Structure of Freedom: Correlations, Causes, and Cautions. By Peter L. Berger et al. Grand Rapids, MI: W. B. Eerdman Publishing Company, 1991.

To Empower People: The Role of Mediating Structure in Public Policy. By Peter L. Berger and Richard John Neuhaus. Washington, DC: American Enterprise Institute for Public Policy, 1977.

The War Over the Family: Capturing the Middle Ground. Garden City, NY: Anchor Press/Doubleday, 1983.

Niklas Luhmann

Art as a Social System. Stanford, CA: Stanford University Press, 2000.

The Differentiation of Society. New York: Columbia University Press, 1982.

Ecological Communication. Chicago: University of Chicago Press, 1989.

Essays on Self-reference. New York: Columbia University Press, 1990.

Law as a Social System. By Niklas Luhmann and Fatima Kastner. Oxford: Oxford University Press, 2004.

Love as Passion: The Codification of Intimacy. Oxford: Polity Press, 1986.

Observations of Modernity. Stanford, CA: Stanford University Press, 1998.

The Reality of Mass Media. Cambridge, UK: Polity Press, 2000.

Religious Dogmatics and the Evolution of Societies. New York: E. Mellen Press, 1984.

Social Systems. Stanford, CA: Stanford University Press, 1995.

A Sociological Theory of Law. Boston: Routledge & Kegan Paul, 1985.

Theories of Distinction: Redescribing the Descriptions of Modernity. By Niklas Luhmann and William Rasch. Stanford, CA: Stanford University Press, 2002.

Trust and Power: Two Works. Chichester, NY: Wiley, 1979.

Clifford Geertz

After the Fact: Two Countries, Four Decades, One Anthropologist. Cambridge, MA: Harvard University Press, 1995.

Available Light: Anthropological Reflections on Philosophical Topics. Princeton, NJ: Princeton University Press, 2000.

The Development of the Javanese Economy: A Socio-cultural Approach. Cambridge, MA: Center for International Studies, Massachusetts Institute of Technology, 1956.

The Impact of Capital-intensive Agriculture on Peasant Social Structure: A Case Study. Cambridge, MA: Center for International Studies, Massachusetts Institute of Technology, 1956.

Islam Observed: Religious Development in Morocco and Indonesia. New Haven: Yale University Press, 1968.

Kinship in Bali. By Hildred Geertz and Clifford Geertz. Chicago: University of Chicago Press, 1975.

Local Knowledge: Further Essays in Interpretive Anthropology. 3rd edn. New York: Basic Books, 2000.

Meaning and Order in Moroccan Society: Three Essays in Cultural Analysis. By Clifford Geertz, Hildred Geertz and Lawrence Rosen; with a photographic essay by Paul Hyman, 1979.

Myth, Symbol, and Culture. Edited by Clifford Geertz. Essays by Clifford Geertz and others. New York: Norton, 1971; 1974.

Negara: The Theatre State in Nineteenth-century Bali. Princeton, NJ: Princeton University Press, 1980.

Person, Time, and Conduct in Bali: An Essay in Cultural Analysis. New Haven: Southeast Asia Studies, Yale University; [distributor: Cellar Book Shop, Detroit], 1966.

The Rotating Credit Association: An Instrument for Development. Cambridge, MA: Center for International Studies, Massachusetts Institute of Technology, 1956.

The Social History of an Indonesian Town. Cambridge, MA: MIT Press, 1965.

Works and Lives: The Anthropologist as Author. Stanford, CA: Stanford University Press, 1988.

Maurice Bloch

Death and the Regeneration of Life. Edited by Maurice Bloch and Jonathan Parry. Cambridge, Cambridgeshire; New York: Cambridge University Press, 1982.

Essays on Cultural Transmission. Oxford; New York: Berg, 2005.

From Blessing to Violence: History and Ideology in the Circumcision Ritual of the Merina of Madagascar. Cambridge, Cambridgeshire; New York: Cambridge University Press, 1986.

Gender and Kinship: Essays toward a Unified Analysis. Contributors: Maurice Bloch et al. Edited by Jane Fishburne Collier and Sylvia Junko Yanagisako; Stanford, CA: Stanford University Press, 1987.

How We Think They Think: Anthropological Approaches to Cognition, Memory, and Literacy. Boulder, CO: Westview Press, 1998.

Marxism and Anthropology: The History of a Relationship. Oxford, Oxfordshire:
    Clarendon Press; New York: Oxford University Press, 1983.
Marxist Analyses and Social Anthropology. Edited by Maurice Bloch. New York: Wiley;
    London: Malaby Press, 1975, London; New York: Tavistock Publications, 1984.
Money and the Morality of Exchange. Edited by M. Bloch and J. Parry. Cambridge,
    UK; New York: Cambridge University Press, 1989.
Placing the Dead: Tombs, Ancestral Villages and Kinship Organization in Madagascar.
    London: Berkeley Square House, Berkeley Sq., W1X 6BA; New York: Seminar
    Press Ltd., 1971.
Political Language and Oratory in Traditional Society. Edited by Maurice Bloch.
    London; New York: Academic Press, 1975.
Prey into Hunter: The Politics of Religious Experience. Cambridge; New York:
    Cambridge University Press, 1992.
Ritual, History and Power: Selected Papers in Anthropology. London; Atlantic
    Highlands, NJ: Athlone Press, 1989.

Catherine Bell

Ritual: Perspectives and Dimensions. New York: Oxford University Press, 1997.
Ritual Theory, Ritual Practice. New York: Oxford University Press, 1992.
Teaching Ritual. Oxford; New York: Oxford University Press, 2007.

Bibliography

Austin, J. L. *How to Do Things With Words*, 2nd edn. Cambridge, MA: Harvard University Press, 1975.

Bateson, Mary Catherine. "Ritualization: A Study in Texture and Texture Change." In Irving I. Zaretsky and Mark P. Leone, eds, *Religious Movements in Contemporary America*. Princeton University Press, Princeton, N.J., 1974, pp. 150–65.

—"Ritual, Change and Changing Rituals," *Worship* 63, no. 1 (1989): 31–41.

—"Ritualizations of Texts and Textualization of Ritual in the Codification of Taoist Liturgy," *History of Religions* 27, no. 4 (1988): 366–92.

Bellah, Robert N. "Civil Religion in America." In William G. McLoughlin and Robert N. Bellah, eds, *Religion in America*. Boston: Houghton Mifflin, 1968, pp. 3–23.

Bloch, Maurice, ed. *Political Language and Oratory in Traditional Society*. New York: Academic Press, 1975.

Bloch, Maurice. "Symbols, Song, Dance and Features of Articulation: Is Religion an Extreme Form of Traditional Authority?" *Archives Européenes de Sociology* 15 (1974): 55–81.

Bourdieu, Pierre. *Distinctions: A Social Critique of the Judgment of Taste*. Translated by Richard Nice. Cambridge: Cambridge University press, 1977.

—*Outline of a Theory of Practice*. Translated by Richard Nice. Cambridge: Cambridge University Press, 1977.

Bourdieu, Pierre and Jean-Claude Passeron. *Reproduction in Education, Society and Culture*. Translated by Richard Nice. Beverly Hills, CA: Sage Publications, 1977.

Brown, Peter. *The Body and Society: Men, Women, and Sexual Renunciation in Early Christianity*. New York: Columbia University Press, 1988.

Burkett, Walter. *Homo Necans: The Anthropology of Ancient Greek Sacrificial Ritual and Myth*. Translated by Peter Bing. Berkeley: University of California Press, 1983.

Douglas, Mary. *Natural Symbols*. New York: Random House, 1973.

—*Purity and Danger*. New York: Praeger, 1960.

Edleman, Murray. *Politics as Symbolic Action*. Chicago: Markham Publishing Company, 1971.

Erickson, Erik. *Toys and Reasons: Stages in the Ritualization of Experience*. New York: Norton, 1977.

Evans-Pritchard, E. E. *The Nuer*. Oxford: Oxford University Press, 1940.

—*Nuer Religion*. Oxford: Oxford University Press, 1956.

—*Theories of Primitive Religion*. Oxford: Clarendon Press, 1965.

—*Witchcraft, Oracles and Magic among the Azande*. Oxford: Clarendon Press, 1965. Originally published 1937.

Fabian, Johannes. *Time and the Other: How Anthropology Makes its Object*. New York: Columbia University Press, 1983.

Foucault, Michel. *The Archeology of Knowledge*. Translated by A. M. Sheridan. New York: Pantheon, 1972.

—"Body/Power." In *Power/Knowledge: Selected Interviews and Other Writings 1972–1977*. Edited by Colin Gordon. New York: Pantheon, 1980, pp. 55–62.

—*Discipline and Punish: The Birth of the Prison*. Translated by Alan Sheridan. New York: Vintage Books, 1979.

—*The History of Sexuality, Vol. I: An Introduction*. Translated by Robert Hurley. New York Vintage Books, 1980.

—*Language, Counter-Memory, Practice*. Translated by Donald F. Bouchard and Sherry Simon. Ithaca, NY: Cornell University Press, 1977.

—"Nietzsche, Genealogy, History." In Paul Rabinow, ed., *The Foucault Reader*. New York: Pantheon, 1984, pp. 76–100.

Geertz, Clifford. *The Interpretation of Cultures*. New York: Basic Books, 1973.

—*Islam Observed*. Chicago: University of Chicago Press, 1968.

—*Local Knowledge: Further Essays in Interpretive Anthropology*. New York: Basic Books, 1983.

—*Negara: The Theatre State in Nineteenth Century Bali*. Princeton: Princeton University Press, 1980.

Geertz, Clifford, ed. *Myth Symbol and Culture*. New York: Norton, 1971.

Girard, Rene. *Violence and the Sacred*. Translated by Patrick Gregory. Baltimore: Johns Hopkins University Press, 1979.

Gluckman, Max. *Essays on the Ritual of Social Relations*. Manchester: Manchester University Press, 1962.

—"On Drama, and Games and Athletic Contests." In Sally F. Moore and Barbara G. Myerhoff, eds, *Secular Ritual*. Amsterdam: Van Gorcum, 1977, pp. 227–43.

—*Order and Rebellion in Tribal Africa*. Glencoe, IL: Free Press, 1963.

—*Politics, Law and Ritual in Tribal Society*. Chicago: Aldine, 1965.

Goffman, Erving. *Asylum*. Chicago: Aldine, 1962.

—*Interaction Ritual*. Garden City, NY: Doubleday, 1967.

Goody, Jack. "Religion and Ritual: The Definitional Problem," *British Journal of Sociology* 12 (1961): 142–64.

Grimes, Ronald L. *Beginnings in Ritual Studies*. Washington, DC: University Press of America, 1982.

—*Research in Ritual Studies*. Metuchen, NJ: Scarecrow Press and the American Theological Library Association, 1985.

—"Ritual Studies." In Mircea Eliade et al., eds, *The Encyclopedia of Religion*, vol. 12. New York: Macmillan, 1987, pp. 422–25.

—"Sources for the Study of Ritual," *Religious Studies Review* 10, no. 2 (1984): 134–45.

Jameson, Frederic. *The Prison-House of Language*. Princeton: Princeton University Press, 1972.

Land, Crystal. *Rites of Rulers: Ritual in Industrial Society—The Soviet Case*. Cambridge: Cambridge University Press, 1987.

Leach, Edmund R. "Ritual." In David L. Sills, ed., *International Encyclopedia of the Social Sciences*, vol. 13. New York: Macmillan, 1968, pp. 520–26.

Lévi-Strauss, Claude. *The Savage Mind*. Translated by George Weidenfield and Nicholson Ltd. Chicago: University Press, 1966.

—*Tristes Tropiques*. Translated by John Weightman and Doreen Weightman. New York: Atheneum, 1975.

Lincoln, Bruce. *Discourse on the Construction of Society*. New York: Oxford University Press, 1989.

Lukes, Steven. "Political Ritual and Social Integration," *Sociology: Journal of the British Sociological Association* 9, no. 2 (1975): 289–308.

—*Power: A Radical View*. New York: Macmillan, 1974.

Moore, Sally F. and Barbara G. Myerhoff, eds. *Secular Ritual*. Amsterdam: Van Gorcum, 1977.

Searle, John R. *Speech Acts*. Cambridge: Cambridge University Press, 1969.

Shills, Edward. "Ritual and Crisis." In Donald R. Cutler, ed., *The Religious Situation 1968*. Boston: Beacon Press, 1968, pp. 733–49.

Shills, Edward and Michael Young. "The Meaning of the Coronation," *Sociological Review*, n. s. 1 (1953): 63–81.

Smith, Jonathan Z. "The Bare facts of Ritual." In *Imagining Religion: From Babylon to Jonestown*. Chicago: University of Chicago Press, 1982, pp. 53–65.

— "The Domestication of Sacrifice." In Robert G. Hamerton-Kelly, ed., *Violent Origins*. Stanford: Stanford University Press, 1987, pp. 191–205.

—*To Take Place: Toward Theory in Ritual*. Chicago: University of Chicago Press, 1987.

Turner, Victor. *Dramas, Fields and Metaphors*. Ithaca, NY: Cornell University Press, 1974.

—*Forest of Symbols: Aspects of Ndembu Ritual*. Ithaca, NY: Cornell University Press, 1967.

—*The Ritual Process: Structure and Anti-Structure*. Chicago: Aldine, 1966.

—-"Variations on a Theme of Liminality." In Moore, Sally F. and Barbara G. Myerhoff, eds, *Secular Ritual*. Amsterdam: Van Gorcum, 1977, pp. 36–52.

Index